MBA

Strategy

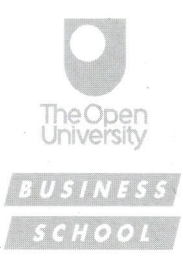

The Open University

BUSINESS SCHOOL

The Open University,
Walton Hall, Milton Keynes MK7 6AA

First published 2000. Reprinted 2001

Edited, designed and typeset by The Open University

Printed in the United Kingdom by Henry Ling Ltd., The Dorset Press, Dorchester,
Dorset DT1 1HD

ISBN 0 7492 9836 7

Further information on Open University Business School courses may be obtained from
the Course Sales Development Centre, The Open University, PO Box 222, Milton Keynes
MK7 6YY (Telephone: 01908 653449).

1.3

19243B/b820b5-8i1.2

BOOK 5

CHOOSING STRATEGIES

Prepared by the B820 Course Team

MBA

Strategy

Contributors to this book:

Eric Cassells
Geoff Mallory
Bob Marshall
Richard Mole
Paul Quintas
Lez Rayman-Bacchus
Susan Segal-Horn

CONTENTS

1 INTRODUCTION

This book is about how organisations choose strategies. It pays no regard to whether an organisation's strategy is planned in a deliberate way, or whether it emerges from a stream of decisions and actions by managers. These, and the issues of culture, power, and ethics which impact on a manager's choices, will be considered in Books 6 and 8 of the course. The purpose of this book is to explain the wide choice of strategies available and to identify criteria to aid the strategist's choice. These two things will help you think about the choice of strategy in your organisation, and how your organisation might pursue a successful strategy.

The first topic we will discuss is that of the sources of competitive advantage, in Section 2. This is a central concern of strategy, and any choice of strategy should be based on a grounded understanding of an organisation's advantages and how these may be best exploited. The exploitation of advantage through generic strategies is considered in Section 3, to identify the basic choices which face an organisation.

The identification of advantage and choice of generic strategy is not enough, however, to ensure a strategy is successful. For that, greater knowledge is needed about products and markets, for example, and we consider the significance of many of the strategic choices that must be made at this level of detail to implement strategy successfully in Section 4.

Finally, in Section 5, we identify a range of tests and selection criteria that can be used to evaluate possible strategies and which should help an organisation choose one with the best chance of success.

In this book we concentrate on the development of a strategy for a business unit. Other considerations often apply to the development of *corporate* strategy, that is strategies for multiple business units. These broader considerations were introduced briefly in Book 1 and will be dealt with in depth in Books 9 and 10. We will, however, make some reference to them in our discussion of competitive strategy and advantage.

To study this book you need:
    Set Book

1.1 LEARNING OBJECTIVES OF THIS BOOK

After studying this book you should be able to:

*   further your understanding of the concepts of competition and strategic advantage
*   critically evaluate several conceptual approaches to strategy formulation and strategic choice
*   identify criteria and tests against which strategic options can be evaluated
*   appreciate the inherent risk and uncertainty when choosing strategies.

2 STRATEGY FORMULATION AND SOURCES OF COMPETITIVE ADVANTAGE

2.1 COMPETITION, PERFORMANCE AND STRATEGIC FIT

Superior performance is often expressed in terms of profitability or market share, which are essentially comparative measures. Organisations can and do, however, use a variety of other performance criteria, financial and non-financial. They may measure success in terms of the value of their assets or returns on equity, sales, investment or capital employed. They may also 'benchmark' themselves against similar organisations on non-financial ratios such as output per employee, awareness/favourability ratings and so on.

In thinking about organisational performance and how competitive strategies achieve success, you should bear in mind the discussion from Book 2 about organisational objectives. Shareholders probably assume that management strive daily to build shareholder value, whereas management may have other goals to meet. A taxpayer may assume that hospital consultants strive only to make patients better, when they may also have personal research objectives. Such multiple objectives naturally impact on the choice of strategy.

Objectives and performance indicators may be financial and non-financial. Some of these can comprise a 'basket' of weighted individual measures. For example, university 'league tables' can comprise a basket of student accommodation availability, drop-out rates, completion rates, graduate employment rates and so on, aggregated to form a single index. Not-for-profit organisations may deploy resources to achieve high ratings on these indicators as a means of seeking sustainable competitive advantage in the competition for resources.

As discussed in Book 1, management may seek a strategic 'fit' between the opportunities available in the competitive environment and the organisation's internal resources and capabilities. This does not imply the pursuit of some kind of equilibrium or co-existence among competitors. Rather, 'fit' is about exploiting some perceived environmental opportunity, based on a clear understanding of the organisation's distinctiveness and competitive advantage. For this it must understand *how* its resources and capabilities give it a competitive advantage in relation to the capabilities of its competitors. An organisation's profit potential depends on whether its managers can use or develop its internal resources and capabilities to fit the emerging external opportunities.

2.2 AN INTRODUCTION TO STRATEGIC CHOICE

The question arises: 'If an organisation knows that its strategy will surely adapt with the passage of time, is there a sense in which it does not know where it is going?' Putting the question another way, is there any purpose in formulating strategy when strategies and plans will change? The answer is surely 'yes', if we allow that an 'intended' strategy will evolve during its implementation. Of course there are limits on what constitutes a feasible strategy. The degrees of strategic freedom open to an organisation can be summed up in the three test questions that you met in Books 1 and 2.

Where are we now?

The organisation can be viewed as a set of present 'states', perhaps measured by headcount, assets and liabilities, market positions and so on. In summary, 'Where are we now?' concerns the organisation's current resources and capabilities, irrespective of whether it is strong or weak. Importantly, the strategies by which the organisation arrived at its present state are implicit in this question.

Where do we want to go?

'Where do we want to go?' is about strategic intent. It subsumes organisational 'wishes' (such as to be number one in a market) as well as the resource-based considerations that you met in Book 4. As always, these considerations are moderated by the wishes of the more powerful stakeholders.

How do we get there?

This is the area of strategic choice and will be the subject of the rest of this book. Strategic choice involves, among other things, the management of the boundaries of all three questions.

In answering these three questions, it is instructive to note how, in the decades since the 1970s, a range of strategic approaches have come and gone almost like fashions. In the late 1970s to early 1980s, it was fashionable for large industrial concerns to diversify into related areas. For example, BOC Industrial Gases in the UK acquired a string of companies that *used* gas (a 'forward' vertical integration strategy) such as fish farms (that use oxygen) and pizza chains (pizzas are chilled under nitrogen). In this respect, BOC was interpreting 'Where do we want to go?' in a very wide sense. The mid–late 1980s saw a divestment of these acquisitions as the notion of 'sticking to the knitting' became fashionable. BOC divested itself of everything except its 'core businesses'.

2.2.1 Limits on the formulation of strategies

In public and private not-for-profit organisations, the answer to the question 'Where do we want to go?' may be given or assumed. For example, a country's tax collection agency has strict limits placed on its freedom. 'Where do we want to go?' is circumscribed. In the case of some organisations, therefore, freedom to make strategic changes may be limited by constitutional or legal arrangements.

In contrast, some charitable organisations may suffer from a lack of focus in their mission and be particularly susceptible to being side-tracked, as they do not have the straightforward measure of profit as a gauge of ultimate success. 'Where do we want to go?' may be interpreted broadly. For example, a newly-appointed Chief Executive to a child telephone helpline organisation could take up new causes such as the rights of the unborn child, or a natural parent-tracing service for foster children. The organisation will have to find or divert resources from its current mission to pursue these causes. It may also find itself competing with other voluntary organisations for the same philanthropic resources.

A useful pair of frameworks for understanding some of the limits on strategic choice is *mandate analysis* and *stakeholder analysis* (Smith, 1994).

Mandate analysis

Mandate analysis is used both by public and private not-for-profit organisations. The purpose of the analysis is to clarify and be consistent about the boundaries between:

1   what must be done

2   what could be done

3   what must not be done.

In not-for-profit organisations, the minimum that must be done is usually documented in legislation, health regulations, trust deeds and so on. Clarification of what is not ruled out is particularly important, however. For example, the UK Driving Test Agency is mandated to provide driving tests, but there is no explicit restriction about, say, holding tests on a Saturday (a convenience for a working public) and charging a higher price. Alerting organisational members to what they *might* do can lead to valuable discussions about the constraints on strategy formulation. A boundary also needs to be set between what could be done and what must not be done. Smith suggests that efforts should be made to identify activities that might be regarded as natural extensions of current ones.

Stakeholder analysis

You will remember the discussion of stakeholder analysis in Book 2. One of the main reasons for performing a stakeholder analysis is that any formulated strategy would, of necessity, have to take account of the main power-wielding stakeholders. The way in which the main stakeholders measure the performance of the organisation now and in the future needs to be understood by the management, if they are to formulate strategies that will, as far as possible, be accepted by the stakeholders.

Activity 2.1 _____

Carry out a mandate analysis for an organisation you are familiar with. Now compare this to the outcomes of the stakeholder analyses you carried out in Book 2. What are the main differences you see between stakeholder and mandate analysis?

Discussion _____

As suggested above, a mandate analysis will often turn to what is documented to identify what could, must and must not be done. The focus is on the legal and formal constraints, rights and duties that an organisation has. These documents, laws and regulations may be external or internal in nature.

For example, a UK public limited company quoted on the London Stock Exchange is defined as a legal 'person', bound by all UK Parliamentary and statutory law – not just company law. Thus, ferry-operating companies can be, and have been, charged with criminal manslaughter when their ferries sink due to recklessness or negligence. These companies are also subject to the devolved legal powers of regulatory agencies such as utility regulators, the Stock Exchange, financial services regulators and environmental protection agencies. They are subject to European legislation and regulation, other international law to which the UK government has subscribed, and to the laws of other countries in which they operate.

As a legal 'person', a UK company is also subject to the vast body of Common Law (such as the law of contract) and Equity (such as the law of trust) which is recorded in the findings of the judiciary over many centuries. Thus, the law of contract, if enforceable, will bind companies to perform contracts they have agreed to, with few exceptions. In the construction industry, for example, unfavourable major contracts can end up bankrupting companies. The law of trust is more open, but nevertheless creates a duty of (implied) trust on, for example, directors towards shareholders, creditors, employees, government and the company itself. Thus, directors can be personally liable to creditors if they continue to trade, concealing the company's position, after they know it is technically insolvent – essentially fraudulent trading.

Under company law, UK companies are required to write up their own constitution (their 'memorandum and articles of association') which further defines the company's mandate. Finally, the law provides that it is the directors' duty to create a system to manage the company effectively. Therefore, all the decisions made by the board of directors, policy set under this framework, regulation and procedure for implementation, become part of the mandate of the company, which should govern its behaviour and that of its employees.

Overall, mandate analysis offers a framework to analyse what an organisation should do. It implicitly considers the power and influence of various stakeholders as they are enshrined in formal and legal relationships.

When we review stakeholder analysis and some of the associated concepts in Book 2, however, we find an emphasis on the resources provided by stakeholders, the rewards they expect in return and the effective balance of power and influence between them. In Book 2 we identified many other sources of power that stakeholders bring to an organisation other than simply formal (or legal) sources of authority. There is, therefore, an important emphasis on unwritten rules and implied norms of behaviour in an organisation. Finally, the contract theory that we studied in Book 2 may help us to recognise situations where the documented mandate of a company is important ('classical' long-term contracting) and where expectations from repeated interaction and co-operation ('relational' long-term contracting) is more relevant.

2.3   COMPETITIVE ADVANTAGE AND CORPORATE SUCCESS

Kay (1993) asserts that *corporate success* derives from a *competitive advantage* – which may vary from one market or industry to another. Competitive advantage is based on *distinctive capabilities and strategic assets*. These assets and capabilities are most often derived from and matched with the *relationships* that the organisation has with its customers, suppliers, employees, the government and so on. This approach is summarised in Figure 2.1, below.

Figure 2.1   Sources of corporate success (adapted from Kay, 1993)

Why is competitive advantage necessary for success? To some extent, this depends on how we think about and measure 'success'. In economic terms, a useful measure of success is superior added value or 'rent' (Kay, 1993). 'Rent' can, by definition, only be achieved when the organisation is performing better compared with others in the same industry. If an organisation's capabilities and strategic assets are not distinctive, there is unlikely to be sustained advantage. On the other hand, distinctiveness is just a necessary, but certainly not sufficient, condition for competitive advantage, as we will see later.

Kay suggests that there are three types of distinctive capabilities:

• architecture

• reputation

• innovation.

Architecture is the term used to describe relationships, both formal and informal, between internal staff, with customers and suppliers, and inter-firm collaborative arrangements (networks). Architecture provides an effective conduit for organisational knowledge and routines, which are often the key source of sustainable competitive advantage (as we discussed in Book 4).

Reputation is built on relationships with an organisation's suppliers and customers. A particular reputation, perhaps for reliability or speed of service, is a source of advantage where a buyer values this reputation over a competitor's at the moment when a contract is placed. Reputations are, however, a wasting source of advantage if they are not maintained.

Innovation is Kay's third type of distinctive capability. Innovation can be a source of competitive advantage when it provides means for an organisation to compete more efficiently, offering a product which is more valuable to a customer; or when it allows the organisation to compete in new ways (for example, using new distribution channels). Innovation is only sustainable as an advantage, however, when it cannot be easily imitated or superseded by alternative innovations. Think back to the case of Apple computer's GUI discussed in the mini-case in Book 4.

Competitive advantage can also derive from the organisation's ownership of strategic assets. *Strategic assets* can be classified as:

- *natural monopolies* such as scale economies, or closed systems compatibility standards such as the PC operating system from Microsoft, or proximity to high-value or low-cost inputs (rare minerals, a labour pool with particular skills, research laboratories or low-labour cost regions)

- *sunk costs*, such as prior investment in capital equipment (such as plant for oil and gas refining), knowledge, or established skills (for example, in managing large and complex projects)

- *exclusivity*, such as exclusive importation or distribution agreements, licences to use a particular technology, or legislative protection.

MINI-CASE: GLAXO AND ZANTAC

You will remember the introductory mini-case on Zantac in Book 1. If not, refresh your memory by re-reading it now. Glaxo was one of the cases studied by Kay as the basis for his ideas on the sources of advantage. Using Kay's terminology the following sources of advantage can be identified in the strategies adopted by Glaxo.

Innovation

Although Zantac was not a highly innovative product, Glaxo managed to convince doctors that it was innovative and worth paying a premium for. Perhaps more importantly, Glaxo pioneered a number of innovations in the way that the product was developed (reducing the development time through parallel engineering), produced (building a factory before regulatory approval was won) and launched (achieving near-simultaneous product launches internationally).

Architecture

Some of the innovations in product development, production and launching depended on a reconfiguration of the relationships between departments charged with R&D, obtaining regulatory approval and planning the marketing of Zantac. In addition, Glaxo were able to achieve rapid market penetration internationally by arranging a network of marketing and sales joint ventures and agencies to complement their own sales forces.

Strategic asset-exclusivity

Having achieved such a strong market position for Zantac, Glaxo are, of course, protected by patent and licence legislation from any other company exploiting the same chemical compound as a pharmaceutical drug for a period of twenty years.

If these are the main sources of advantage that Glaxo exploited in developing Zantac, what of their future when the strategic asset of exclusive exploitation expires? Glaxo will be faced with a host of licensed 'generic' competitors who will undercut their prices. Will Glaxo have new or further sources of advantage it can exploit?

- First, Glaxo has re-invested a higher percentage of its revenues (largely from Zantac) in researching a portfolio of new drugs. It must hope that the scale of its effort produces a new 'blockbuster' drug to replace Zantac although clearly this cannot be guaranteed.

- Secondly, Glaxo has continued to excel in the rapid worldwide approval and launch of the new drugs it has developed. The unique arrangements and routines it has built up have continued to deliver advantage to it. This is clearly a distinctive capability.

- Finally, Glaxo has gained a *reputation* as a very reliable, safe, effective and innovative brand with those doctors using Zantac. Glaxo must hope that this loyalty will transfer to new ethical drugs it launches.

Glaxo's future after Zantac's patents expire remains uncertain, but Glaxo must hope it can continue to derive advantage from its *innovation*, *architecture* and *reputation*.

As the example of Glaxo and Zantac shows, the more successful companies often combine architecture, reputation, innovation and strategic assets to deliver competitive advantage. Much of Sony's success, for example, is attributed to the rotation of staff between different functions, its involvement of suppliers in manufacturing process design, its technical creativity in product innovations (such as merging electronic and mechanical technologies) and its established skills in miniaturising electronic products.

Note that competitive advantage involves organisations in finding some way of disturbing the bases of 'perfect' competition in an industry or sector. All organisations must compete in some way or other for scarce resources (indeed, the working capital provided by customers in commercial organisations is no more than a scarce financial resource with which to pay suppliers, wages and salaries, dividends, etc.). Monopoly providers such as UK universities are now forced to compete for students and research grants as universities in the USA have always done, and many charitable organisations are being driven to adopt strategies based on competition as the struggle for scarce funds intensifies.

Activity 2.2

 At this point, you should read and make notes on Chapter 7 in the Set Book. While reading, list the key assumptions that Grant makes on the nature of competition. What does he have to say about competing in service-based industries? Pay particular attention to the section on sources of competitive advantage which we will discuss in the next section.

3   GENERIC STRATEGIES FOR PURSUING COMPETITIVE ADVANTAGE

3.1   INTRODUCTION

As discussed in Book 3, organisations can achieve above-average profits, relative to *all* organisations, by locating in an attractive industry. Some industries with above-average profits, such as the drug abuse industry, tend, however, to operate outside socially acceptable and formally recognised legal frameworks! Others, despite attractive features, may be very difficult to enter. More commonly, the opportunity to earn supernormal profits within an industry depends on exploiting some competitive advantage *within that industry*. By casual observation, sources of competitive advantage seem infinitely variable. Competitors continually jostle for customer attention by adding more features or extra service at no charge, by cutting prices or supplying extra product at the same price. We regularly see airline advertisements claiming to service more destinations with more comfortable seating than competitors; business information providers claim more up-to-date statistics and business trends than other providers; courier services claim faster parcel delivery to more destinations than their competitors.

We have argued in this course that seeking competitive advantage is a key component of strategy. In the Set Book, Grant refers to the work of Michael Porter (1985) and his generic strategies of cost leadership, differentiation and focus. These are a useful way of identifying some generic approaches to exploiting competitive advantage, and are reviewed below.

3.2   PORTER'S GENERIC STRATEGIES

Porter's summary is shown in Figure 3.1 (overleaf).

We can summarise the features and scope of Porter's generic strategies in the following manner.

Cost leadership

Here the organisation sets out to be *the* low-cost producer in its industry, using any or all of the various sources of cost advantage. If an organisation can achieve and sustain cost leadership, then it will be an above-average performer in its industry, provided it can command prices at the industry average or increase overall sales volumes from lower prices. The organisation may price its offerings at a level that is comparable with, or lower than, its competitors but yet achieve higher gross margins. Note that superior profits and advantage derive from lower *cost*, not price. Low costs do, however, give an organisation increased flexibility on the pricing strategies it can pursue. Further, being the lowest-cost producer does not mean that the value package offered to customers is unimportant. The low-cost producer must offer a level of functionality and quality that is acceptable to its market sector.

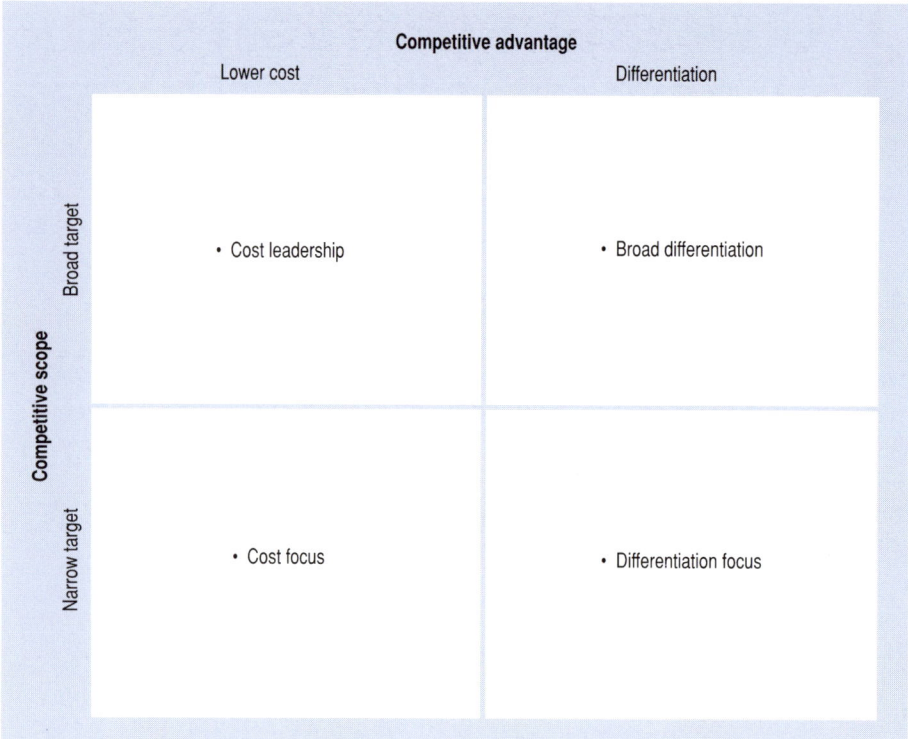

Figure 3.1   Porter's generic strategies

Differentiation

Here an organisation seeks to be unique in its industry along some dimensions that are valued by buyers. It selects one or more attributes that buyers in an industry perceive as important and uniquely positions itself to meet those needs. The means for differentiation are peculiar to each industry and each organisation. It is rewarded for its uniqueness with a premium price. A firm that can achieve and sustain differentiation will be an above-average performer in its industry provided its price premium exceeds the extra costs incurred in being unique. The product or service must continue to be valued by the customer if the price premium is to hold up. Of course, the differentiator cannot ignore cost, since a poor cost position will erode any gains that result from a price premium.

Focus

A firm may pursue advantage from cost leadership or differentiation, either in the broad market, or by pursuing a strategy of *focus*. Segments, or a group of segments, in an industry are selected for either a cost or a differentiation strategy, to the exclusion of other segments. By optimising strategy for the target segments, the focuser seeks to achieve a competitive advantage in its target segments. It aims to use its cost or differentiation strategy to out-focus its broadly-targeted competitors. This requires a clear appreciation of (a) where its focus is and (b) how narrow or broad a market segment or sector to compete in. A segment may be broadly defined by geographic coverage, product application, distribution channel, or particular customer characteristic (such as age, gender, ethnicity or income group).

Taking differentiation, cost advantage and focus together gives the four generic strategies shown in Figure 3.1: cost leadership, cost focus, broad differentiation and differentiation focus.

1   A cost leadership strategy involves being the lowest-cost producer across the broad sector or industry.

2   A cost focus strategy aims for cost advantage within a specific segment.

3   A broad differentiation strategy involves offering a differentiated product or service across a broad sector or industry.

4   A differentiation focus strategy aims for differentiation within a specific segment.

We now look in more depth at these generic strategies.

3.3 COST-BASED STRATEGIES

In the set book, Grant suggests that there are eight drivers of cost advantage:

- economies of scale
- economies of learning
- process technology
- product design
- process design
- capacity utilisation
- input costs
- residual differences in operating efficiency.

A broadly targeted *cost leadership strategy* is appropriate where significant economies of scale or scope are possible and where it is difficult to differentiate the product. Take oil refining and petrol distribution, for example. Here the industry structure has led to established practices for managing large capital investments and distribution channels are often shared. The competitive arena cuts across many markets and so the competitive scope is broad. This is also true for many cosmetics, such as soaps, deodorants, shampoos and after-shave lotions. These are promoted for everyday use by all sections of the population, at very competitive prices. Most of these products are likely to be mature in terms of their product life-cycles.

On the other hand a *cost focused strategy* is appropriate where a product or service is clearly defined and offered in a budget-conscious market segment. This strategy depends on the existence of segments whose needs are for products or services with fewer functional features than those aimed at the broad market. The YMCA and YWCA provide examples of 'cost focus' strategies that aim to provide minimum-cost accommodation to young people. Although they attract travellers with different motivations – the temporarily homeless, tourists, low-pay trades people – their common denominator is an overriding concern for the basics of decent accommodation at minimum cost. Then again, car manufacturers such as Lada and Hyundai have established themselves in Western markets by targeting a segment of the population whose needs for personal transport are relatively modest, with extremely low prices. The manufacturers of these cars rely on older-generation technologies and low input costs, such as low labour rates and unsophisticated manufacturing processes.

The Lada Samara hatchback – a strategy of using older technology to produce low-price cars for a specific segment of the market

Cost control is clearly central to competitive strategy, whether the organisation is pursuing a strategy of cost advantage or differentiation. A sensible programme for cost reduction is not the same as pursuing a strategy for cost advantage, however. Competitors may also be seeking a cost advantage, and there may be a jointly shared interest in making an assessment of their own cost position in relation to others.

While most managers would agree that the control of cost is critical to their organisation's health, there is often wide disagreement within the organisation about what those costs are. Furthermore, the cost behaviour of a product or service tends to be poorly understood in terms of knowing how the real costs affect profitability. In some instances, a firm's allocation of costs to its various activities may remain unchanged for a decade or more despite obvious changes in the activities themselves. In addition, firms often have very little understanding of their competitors' cost position, which is essential for understanding their own *relative* cost position. What is needed is a systematic analysis of cost to determine an organisation's cost position *relative* to its competitors and to identify ways that an organisation may gain sustainable cost advantage. Existing accounting systems have a limited role here.

Activity 3.1

Think of several examples of organisations pursuing cost-based strategies.

 Now read and make notes on Chapter 8 in the Set Book. Do the organisations that you have identified in the previous part of this activity derive their cost advantages from the sources identified in this chapter?

How could you analyse the costs of a competitor in your industry? In the public or not-for-profit sector, how could you establish the costs of an organisation which delivers a similar service?

3.4 DIFFERENTIATION-BASED STRATEGIES

When following a strategy of *broad differentiation* it is important to strike the right balance between providing unique benefits while minimising the additional cost of the product or service. Getting the balance wrong could result in the erosion of all superior profits. Honda seeks competitive advantage by following a differentiated strategy in terms of enhanced reliability and advanced engine and transmission technologies. Its competitive scope is broad, because it competes globally and across all market segments. Another example of a 'differentiation' strategy is the Swatch Watch that is available through retail channels such as jewellers, department stores and airport shops. To its broad market it is differentiated by its modern and unusual designs. As the designs have changed, a thriving collectors' market has developed.

The Porsche 911 Carrera Cabriolet – product of a strategy of differentiation

An organisation may choose a strategy of *differentiation focus* when a target segment has unique needs and is willing to pay a premium for the right product or service features. This strategy depends on the existence of segments whose needs are for products or services with greater functional or service features than those aimed at the broad market. Here, customers expect or are offered a comprehensive product package, including service features if needed. The competitor operating in this segment is likely to seek out sophisticated design and technologies, whether related to a product or a service. The manufacturers of high-performance cars such as Porsche, Maserati or Lamborghini, for example, are highly differentiated in their aesthetic design, their advanced handling and other sought-after features. They serve a small clientele of enthusiasts drawn from all over the world.

Since differential advantage depends on whether potential customers value their relationship with the supplying organisation, the scope for being differentiated is not restricted to extra features on the product or service. There may be scope for differentiating the organisation's relationship with its customers in many ways:

- delivering the product or service
- managing the customer's inventory
- financing to help purchase
- training new users

- removing barriers to the ordering process, trial periods, etc.
- establishing close partnerships with customers that facilitate just-in-time scheduling, open book accounting, joint efficiency seeking projects, organisational process development projects, and so on
- providing after-sales service.

These tangible aspects are accompanied by intangible qualities that potential customers weigh up in their evaluation of the relationship. For example, we noted previously that consumers exercise choice on the basis of the image they associate with a particular product, as is common in fashion goods. Or, to take a different example from financial services, there are investors who trade only in shares of companies that are deemed not to harm the environment.

A supplier, whether firm, charity or public service, and its customers are each party to an explicit or tacit contract of expected performance. Suppliers promise, and customers expect, that a product or a service will meet certain levels of quality, reliability, durability, safety and so on. The contract may be underpinned by regulatory constraints such as safety standards that today affect most products and services. Many complex products and services need to comply with both regulatory and voluntary criteria, otherwise there is a risk of chaos and reduced safety. Examples include standardised power socket dimensions, computer data protocols, car fuel lead levels and so on. However, while these performance criteria constrain differentiation in particular directions, such constraints are also very often sources of innovation. For example, without common standards, competitors' resources are often diverted to maintaining proprietary standards, and customers generally do not value proprietary standards. On the other hand, where there are common technical standards, competitors can focus their creativity on other areas that potential customers *are* likely to value.

In the same way, market segments are not just static structural characteristics of a market to be taken for granted. The reality is that market segments exist because of patterns to human behaviour, which organise and guide suppliers' thinking about how to differentiate themselves. People buy fashion accessories and cosmetics because they seek a particular identity. Segmentation is thus created and routinely maintained jointly by suppliers and buyers. While such segmentation can be stable over time, competitive forces lend segments a degree of fragility. This is a potential source of innovation, and fragility provides scope for further differentiation if the organisation is able to enlist potential customers in creating a new segment.

Activity 3.2

Think of several examples of organisations pursuing differentiation strategies. **Now read and make notes on Chapter 9 in the Set Book.** Do the organisations that you have identified in the previous part of this activity derive their differentiation advantage from the sources identified in the chapter?

How could you analyse the ways in which a competitor in your industry differentiates its product or segments its market? What might constitute differentiation advantage in the public or not-for-profit sectors? How would you identify such sources of differentiation advantage in not-for-profit organisations?

MINI-CASE: GENERIC STRATEGIES IN THE CAR INDUSTRY

Consider the competitive strategies adopted by car manufacturers serving the Western European market-place.

In the market for larger family and company cars, it is obvious that there is little differentiation between models such as the Nissan Primera, Peugeot 406, Toyota Avensis, Opel Vectra and Ford Mondeo. All have similar functionality and pricing is broadly the same. The manufacturers are primarily interested in selling significant volumes of these cars to benefit from scale-driven cost and learning advantages. These can seem to be best positioned as pursuing cost-based strategies (although only one, of course, can be a 'leader' – if we are to take the framework literally).

Staying in the larger family and company car market, there are other manufacturers charging a premium for cars which might be best described as brand differentiators, selling across the market but selling additional distinctive features. Rover, for example, has been driven by its lower volume to stress its traditional image, exemplified by its nostalgic grille on the premium-priced Rover 600. The same underlying design of car is sold by Honda as the Accord, with a premium being charged for the brand image of engineering excellence and reliability built up by the company. In the same way, cars such as the BMW appeal to those in the broad market who value the record of 'build' excellence BMW have built up.

We have already discussed cars such as the Lada and Hyundai which generally appeal to lower income segments who are willing to sacrifice functionality. These cars tend to rely on older technology: in Malaysia, Proton cars have similarly relied on technology acquired from Mitsubishi. Perhaps a more interesting example is the Fiat Cinquecento, a new technology small car designed as a city car with restricted functionality and using the locational advantage of being built using low-cost labour in Poland. In the same way, Mercedes and Swatch have a joint venture to build a city car for the next century.

In the differentiation focus section of the matrix, there is a group of cars which add luxury and prestige to the value-package purchased by consumers of very large family and company executive cars. These are cars such as Mercedes (any saloon), Jaguar, the BMW 525, the Alfa Romeo 166 and Saab 9–5. Another group of cars that are sold to distinct segments who are willing to pay a premium are the sports cars, such as the Mazda MX-5, BMW Z-3,

The Rover 618 (left) and Honda Accord (right) – two cars with the same underlying design aimed at different market segments

MGF, Fiat Barchetta and Alfa Romeo Spider and GTV. This last group of cars differs in that the segment is interested in particular features (sporting abilities and image) and is willing to sacrifice some functionality (passenger space, luggage carrying, protection from the weather) to obtain it.

If we now allocate these examples of generic strategies to Porter's framework, we can plot them as in Figure 3.2.

Competitive advantage

	Lower cost	Differentiation
Broad target	Cost leadership • Ford Mondeo • Opel Vectra • Toyota Avensis	Broad differentiation • Rover 600 • Honda Accord • BMW 318
Narrow target	Cost focus • Lada Samara • Proton • Fiat Cinquecento	Differentiation focus • Mercedes-Benz • Mazda MX-5 • Alfa Romeo GTV

(Competitive scope)

Figure 3.2   Examples of generic strategies in the Western European car market

3.5   GENERIC STRATEGIES IN PERSPECTIVE

In Porter's view, the choice of generic strategy depends on the forces within the industry structure. The competitive environment tends to weed out inappropriate competitive strategies and their organisations on the basis of survival of the fittest. You have already encountered alternative views in Book 4 about the sources of competitive advantage. The Porter framework does, however, help in the assessment of the relative strengths and weaknesses of competitors and therefore suggests what strategy a new entrant might follow to position itself, or how an established firm could reposition itself. In assessing the possibilities, a firm would need to consider a range of issues including:

- Are there 'differentiators' that are serving a segment at unnecessarily high costs?

- If there is no lowest cost producer in the sector and no apparent differentiation among competitors, does this mean that there is room for a 'differentiator' or 'cost leader'?

- Is there a fundamentally different way of competing that would reward a new entrant?

Stable industry environments, for example, may encourage cost advantage from scale and experience economies, as they move toward standardisation practices. Unstable environments may encourage differentiation more than cost advantage. For example, rapid and continual technological change in the information technology and telecommunications sectors is characterised by an ever-growing range of products and services. In this environment, new firms enter and leave the industry at a high rate, due to intense competitive rivalry and rapid technological change that often makes products obsolete before they can recover their investment.

In public sector and not-for-profit organisations, such as local government or public health care, broad cost-driven strategies are usually practised on the grounds of equity. It is not usually possible to obtain a differentiated service by payment of a premium, although there might well be a willing market. This may be seen as queue-jumping in an environment where services are rationed. During the current move towards privatisation and market-based reform in these sectors, private providers focus almost exclusively on providing differentiated service such as higher standards of hospital food, more frequent or convenient uplift of waste by local authorities and so on. It could be argued that raising consumer sensitivity to differentiable services will lead to increased sensitivity to value for money, and also, by contrast, to the idea of paying extra for extra services.

Activity 3.3

What generic strategies is your organisation pursuing? Different units in your organisation may be pursuing different strategies but, using Porter's ideas, identify these strategies and list the reasons for your categorisation.

3.6 PROBING AND ELABORATING THE GENERIC STRATEGIES

Porter's generic strategies are clearly useful for understanding competitive advantage and they have been very influential. Nevertheless, it is important to critically evaluate their strengths and weaknesses.

Bowman and Asch (1996) find significant problems in practice with the static nature of Porter's analysis in a complex and dynamic world. For example, cost leadership is often confused with competing in low-price segments and so the question of *where* to compete can be misleading if combined with the question of *how* to compete. It is irrelevant to compare Hyundai with Jaguar because they compete for different customers. Hyundai competes with firms who are perceived by the customer to offer competing products, such as Lada.

Bowman and Asch also suggest that inputs can get confused with outputs. Customers do not particularly care about the input side of a strategy, which is invisible to them. A cost leadership strategy, or even a low-cost producer strategy, is unlikely to be identified as such by the consumer. Cost leaders can gain superior profits from an average market price for an average product, based on their lower costs. Following this practice, cost leaders would probably enjoy an average market share and not gain the volumes necessary to secure 'experience curve' benefits, another route to reducing costs.

In the same way, it appears that not all 'differentiators' command or demand premium prices. Some 'differentiators' actually increase market share instead. Differentiation in the airline industry – for example, by British Airways or American Airlines – has usually been aimed at increasing the number of passengers carried at similar prices to competitors. This is because the high fixed cost and capacity availability structure of running aircraft flights encourages airlines to maximise overall revenues, rather than a notional profit margin per passenger.

There are other dangers in using the generic strategies framework in too literal or rigid a manner. First, it is a static classification device. It takes no account of the way advantage is created and destroyed over time, in the way we discussed in Book 3. Secondly, there is a danger in trying to force organisations exclusively into one box or another. There needs to be a finer grain of analysis in practice to identify what an organisation's underlying sources of advantage actually are. This is why the Set Book chapters detail the sources of advantage that can underpin cost- and differentiation-based generic strategies. Organisations may even gain overall advantage by pursuing *both cost and differentiation advantages*, while being the leader in neither.

For example, the greatest profits in the UK supermarket sector during the period 1985–1995 were consistently achieved by Sainsbury. During this period, Sainsbury charged premiums over most competitors for own-label produce. They were not, however, the largest premiums in the sector. Sainsbury also pursued a low-cost strategy based on operational and managerial efficiencies, experience and scale benefits. They were not, however, the lowest-cost producer. Sainsbury was neither the leading differentiator nor the cost leader. By a careful blend of both strategies, however, the retailer achieved a period of prolonged competitive advantage resulting in superior profits.

Miller (1986) suggests that, in order to achieve differentiation, cost advantage and focus, we must consider how the organisation's fixed and current assets are being used. For example, in order to achieve a cost advantage, the organisation's assets tend to be selected and organised to maximise efficiency – Miller calls this *asset intensity*. But for a differentiator to achieve superior returns, there is an observed tendency to squeeze the maximum variety out of the minimum of assets, which he calls *asset parsimony*.

Miller also suggests that 'differentiation' can either be based on advantage from (a) product innovation or (b) marketing and branding. Mintzberg *et al.* (1995) go further in highlighting the role of price as a means of differentiating the value package offered to customers. They identify a total of six types of differentiation strategy:

- price
- image
- support
- design
- quality
- undifferentiated (or non-differentiated).

These differentiation strategies are, of course, often mixed and combined with one another. For example, the cosmetics industry, in selling perfumes, offers an interesting example of the first two strategies, *price* and *image*. The industry often reminds its critics that it is in the business of offering people an image, or identity. Particular fragrances and colours deliver particular identities at a price that is itself part of the image. Unlike standard consumer products, the industry was not prepared to compete on price. One beer brand (Stella Artois) has also promoted itself on the grounds that it is 'reassuringly expensive'.

A competitor may differentiate itself through the *support* or complementary products it provides to customers and this could take many forms: technical training, maintenance, finance, home delivery. The *quality* of the product or service also offers scope for differentiation. In Europe, washing machines from Miele, Bosch and AEG stand out from their competitors, not on features or support, but instead on the perceived *quality* and *design* of their construction. Through quality and image, they are able to command premium prices. Designer-wear, such as jeans, shirts, belts, scarves, watches, bags and other accessories with well-known brand labels, appeal to those who wish to be identified as connoisseurs of unique design.

Finally, there are many firms that get by *without differentiating* themselves in any form. Copying what the competitors are doing is an undifferentiated strategy. For some firms this is a conscious choice, but for others it is the result of managerial inability to be creative or innovative.

In addition, Mintzberg *et al.* also propose four characteristic markets, which provide a finer grain of analysis than broad or narrow focus:

* unsegmented
* segmented
* niche
* customised.

A chauffeur driven taxi service at Heathrow Airport – an example of targeting a niche market

Some firms look for an *unsegmented* mass market, others *segment* the broad market, and some target a particular *niche*. The provision of public transport exemplifies the spectrum of possibilities. At the unsegmented end of the market are the buses and trains. The market is also segmented with competitors offering taxis and different classes of air travel (club, business, first, economy). Niche markets include taxis specialising in chauffeur hire to airports or for weddings, and very discriminating and wealthy customers receive *customised* travel arrangements that can combine private jets, chauffeured limousines and escorted sightseeing or shopping.

Mintzberg's four market definitions combine with the six strategies of differentiation of the product or service to suggest a matrix of possibilities, some more likely than others. For example, a customised market strategy probably demands a customer-support differentiating strategy, while differentiating on low price and quality would normally not support a customising strategy.

Activity 3.4 _____

Mintzberg's four characteristic markets and six strategies of product or service differentiation imply a matrix of up to 24 combination strategies. Construct a blank matrix of this type. Now review the matrix to determine whether particular strategies being followed by your own organisation can be allocated to any of the 24 locations.

Discussion _____

Your organisation may follow multiple strategies. In this case, perhaps you have filled in six of Mintzberg's strategy combinations. You may, however, feel that your organisation has a single well-defined strategy. If we take the example of a chauffeur hire taxi serving a niche market, it is likely that a selection of differentiation strategies may all be in place: image, quality and support (complementary services such as confirmation of flights, alliances with hotels, etc.) are all likely to be evident, although design is relatively standardised within a limited choice of brand vehicles. While price may not be an obvious source of differentiation for chauffeur hire taxis, this may depend on the density of competition in the geographic market served. If a chauffeur taxi hire company wants to win a contract for ten cars at an all-day wedding, it may well have to offer a lower price.

Finally, it is unlikely that you completed the matrix with 24 different strategies followed by your organisation. It may well be that some of the combinations seem unlikely or impossible strategies to follow in your industry. If this occurred to you as you completed the matrix, you may wish to reflect on the lessons of strategic group and strategic space analysis that you encountered in Book 3. Unlikely or impossible industry strategies can always be revisited to consider whether they could be a source of competitive innovation if conditions change.

3.7 INNOVATION AS A SOURCE OF COMPETITIVE ADVANTAGE

Innovation is of interest to the strategist for two main reasons. First it can be a threat to the returns derived from existing products and services. Second it can be a source of advantage for innovating organisations and can cause radical shifts in industry structures. This is what Schumpeter (1934) calls 'creative destruction'. Examples of this phenomenon are abundant in such innovations as the printing press, the steam engine, the railways and the semi-conductor. One idea that runs through our earlier discussion on generic sources of competitive advantage from either a low cost or a differentiation perspective is that both can involve innovation.

From a cost perspective the capability to design products with a low build cost, and to develop or improve process technologies, were identified as key drivers of this form of advantage.

Differentiation advantage can also be based on innovative design and utilisation of new science, for example the Swatch series of watches.

Thus innovation has the potential to be a strategic option for all forms of organisation. For example, in the service sector, organisations can possibly derive advantage through the application of technology to either their offering or their processes. Such an example is the case of Direct Line, the insurance company that applied information and communication technologies to eliminate a source of cost – brokers' commissions – and to add value for the consumer through differentiation in the form of being able to give prompt approval for repairs to begin.

In this section we will explore these ideas in more depth to build on the discussion in Book 4, which looked at how the capability to innovate can be built.

What is innovation? Robert Grant in the Set Book essentially follows Freeman (1982) who suggests that an invention is an idea, a sketch or a model for a new or improved device, product or process, which may or may not lead to a technological innovation. An innovation is really only accomplished with the first economic transaction involving the new product or service.

It is clear that some innovations do not have the radical transforming impact that we suggested in the opening to this section. We suggest that the majority of them are what can be termed incremental in nature. They are the result of, or actually are, the marginal improvements of the product or service offering. Each is the outcome of a development trajectory that is both coherent and cumulative. Such an incremental trajectory has been shown over time to be capable of even greater technical progress and productivity increases than major transforming innovations. Banbury and Mitchell (1995) conclude that the incremental product innovation is crucial to business survival and to performance for firms already established in a product market.

In some cases it has been found that the arrival of a radical new idea actually stimulates a period of innovation in the older technologies. This is known as the steamship phenomenon because the arrival of the steam-driven vessel inspired a flurry of innovation in sailing ships as they strove to compete.

The strategic management of innovation must take account of the fact that innovations may be interdependent and have a systemic quality. The adoption of any innovation may depend on *complementary innovations* occurring in the market-place, as with the example of virtual reality computer games and simulations requiring powerful PCs. Freeman (1982) suggests the term *new technological systems* to describe constellations of innovations that are technologically and economically interlinked. Technological interdependence is evident, for example, between petrochemicals, synthetic materials and plastics, and the innovations in process machinery required to produce them. Organisational and institutional innovation are also vital components of new technological systems. For example, the availability of consumer credit is an essential component of the creation of markets for new consumer products such as cars or televisions, as is the presence of appropriate skills in the workforce to enable the adoption of product and process innovations.

We now have three categories – incremental innovation, radical innovation, and new technological systems, which include complementary innovations. Can this analysis account for all types of innovation, from organisation-level product and process improvement through to economy-wide transformations? Freeman suggests that a fourth category is needed. He calls this a change of *techno-economic paradigm*, a cluster of innovations and new technological systems, as well as associated organisational and institutional changes. The key characteristic of innovations in the techno-economic paradigm is that they pervade the whole economy. They must therefore meet the following criteria:

- clearly perceived low and rapidly falling costs
- apparently unlimited supply over a long period
- potential for use and application throughout the economic system, both directly and indirectly, in products and processes.

These criteria were met by the techno-economic paradigm surrounding oil and petrochemicals, which underpinned the post-war economic boom, and, according to Freeman, are met today by the ICT techno-economic paradigm.

This results in a *typology of innovations*:

- incremental
- radical
- new technological system (including complementary innovations)
- techno-economic paradigm.

To these four we must, of course, add process innovation for, as we mentioned in the opening paragraph of this section, organisations also invest heavily not only in developing new products but also the ways in which they transform inputs into outputs.

When making the distinction between product and process innovation we need to be aware that the two types of innovation may have a dynamic interdependence over time. Strategic advantage may be gained by exploiting this interdependence. For example, the major banks developed electronic funds transfer (EFT) as a process innovation to speed up the transfer of money between branches, and then between banks. The productivity benefits and cost savings that resulted from the reduction of paper transfers were significant. The first phase, focused on automation of back-office tasks (basic data processing) enabled the UK banking sector to improve productivity to a 4.5 per cent annual growth rate by the early 1970s, when the volume of banking transactions was growing by 8 per cent per year. As the demand for banking services slowed from the mid-1970s, the banks continued to invest in ICTs at an increased rate over the period 1975–81. In a period of enhanced competition, innovative banks turned their ICT investment to improving the quality of services. The EFT systems were process innovations that also provided the infrastructure upon which new products could be based. In particular, they enabled the banks to introduce ATMs (automatic teller machines) that provided customers with 24-hour cash withdrawals, balance checks, and other services via the 'through-the-wall' computer terminals at their branches. This is also an example of a classic economy of scope, to which you were introduced in Book 4.

Quickly read through Chapter 11 in the Set Book and complete Activity 3.5.

Activity 3.5 _____

As you read the chapter, consider the following questions:

1   Noting the examples of innovations used in Chapter 11 of the Set Book, would you say this account provides a comprehensive coverage of innovation? What is missing or downplayed?

2   Note the pattern of technology development and dissemination suggested in Set Book Figure 11.1. What, in your view, does the Set Book consider to be the driver of technological innovation?

3   Recalling previous books, what are the implications of network effects, technological uncertainty and the importance of complementary resources for the strategic management of innovation in any organisation?

4   Is 'innovation' synonymous with 'R&D'? Which parts or functional areas of the organisation should or should not be concerned with innovation?

Discussion _____

1   Chapter 11 mostly concentrates on product innovations, largely ignoring process innovation. The examples tend to be the more notable innovations towards the 'radical' end of the product innovation spectrum, with little reference to incremental innovations – which are far more numerous.

2   Figure 11.1 suggests that innovation is driven by advances in knowledge and invention. The 'demand side' (i.e. the market) is portrayed as a recipient of the innovation, but has no input to the innovation process. This is essentially a 'technology-push' model.

3   This a big question. You will recall in Book 4, when we discussed the notion of organisations having resources and capabilities, the latter included the capability to access and utilise resources from outside the organisation. The common theme that unites the implications of network effects, technological uncertainty and the importance of complementary resources for innovation, is that organisations do not develop innovations in a vacuum. They must be able to access technology and knowledge from external sources, share risks, ensure the presence of resources they do not own (e.g. an electricity supply network for electric car makers), and consider how they might help other complementary suppliers develop the network externalities that would make their own products ands services more attractive.

4   *Innovation is a broader concept than that circumscribed by the notion of R&D. The R&D department is clearly a major locus of innovative activity in large organisations (small organisations do not tend to have R&D departments). However, remember that innovation assumes that the product, process or service has reached the market, or is commercially useful. For manufactured products, therefore, the production engineering and manufacturing departments would have been involved well before the product reaches the market. We should also assume that finance, marketing, sales and maintenance departments will have been involved in product design, since they will have to sell and maintain it at a profit. So too, personnel and staff development will have been involved, particularly if recruitment or training is required. The answer, therefore, is that all functional areas of the organisation may be involved in innovation, although the input of some might be indirect.*

Having discussed the various factors to be considered in formulating potential strategy options for your organisation or business unit, we will now go on to consider how managers may choose between them, and with what consequences.

4 STRATEGIC OPTIONS FOR PRODUCTS AND MARKETS, OLD AND NEW

The need for a finer grain (or deeper, more detailed level) of analysis when choosing strategy extends beyond elaborating types of cost, differentiation and focus strategies. It goes beyond identifying detailed sources of advantage. Managers must be prepared to grapple with the details of how strategy will be implemented, how growth will be achieved. Embedded in the development of a strategy are many choices:

- which markets or segments to penetrate or develop
- which new or related products and services to develop
- whether to diversify or divest activities
- how best to exploit and lever existing capabilities and whether to develop new capabilities.

Some of these options are most clearly presented in the Ansoff (1965) product/market matrix shown in Figure 4.1 below.

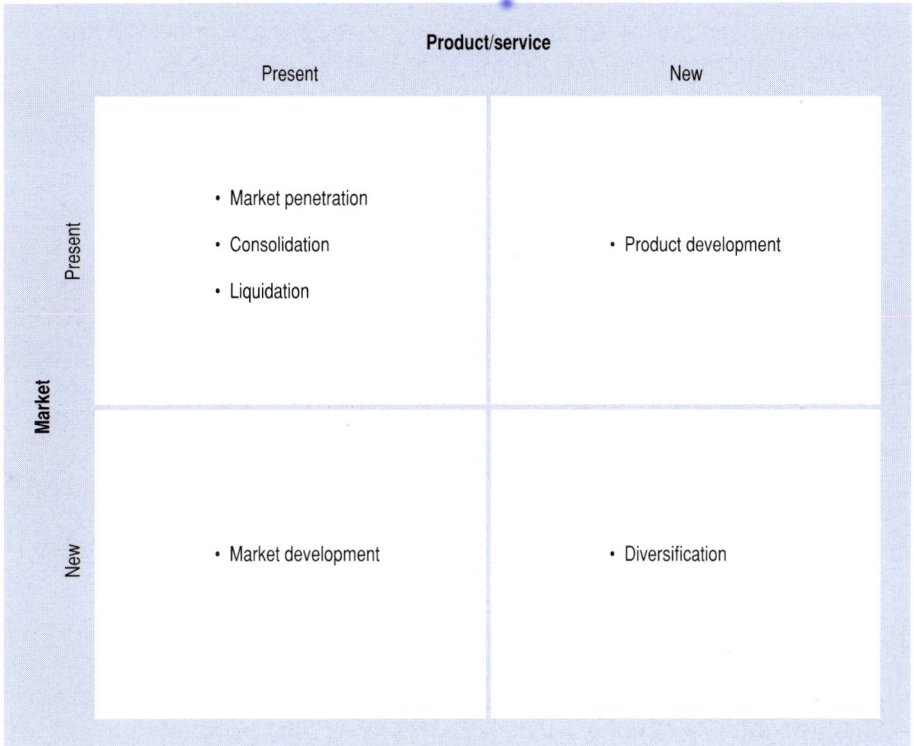

Figure 4.1   Ansoff's matrix (after Ansoff, 1965)

This matrix considers options for strategy based on two dimensions: the products or services the organisation sells and the markets it serves. In each case, it looks at the two states of 'what products and markets do we currently sell and serve' and 'which products or markets may we wish to move into in the future'. Let us consider each quadrant in turn – note that the three strategies in the upper-left quadrant are discussed individually.

4.1   PRESENT PRODUCTS, PRESENT MARKETS

4.1.1   Market penetration

A firm is pursuing a strategy of market penetration when it decides to grow its existing market share using existing products or services. The success of this strategy depends on the prospects for growth in the sector and the firm's success in exploiting competitive advantage or changing the basis of competition within the industry.

Among the alternative routes to growth, market penetration appears to carry the lowest risk. The organisation is (or should be) familiar with its products or services and with customer requirements. But there may be scope for a better understanding and for encouraging latent customer needs to emerge. The market should be able to support the generation of superior income streams from operations.

A growing market clearly invites a market penetration strategy. In contrast, in mature or static markets there will be established competitors, some of whom will be exploiting scale- or experience-based cost advantages. Successful market penetration in these conditions may depend on whether there is scope for a differentiation strategy, or whether the entrenched competitor's cost advantages can be undermined by a different and lower-cost way of competing – otherwise, a strategy to grow market share could simply result in a damaging price war. In the more extreme case where the market is in decline, and where competitors are leaving, a market penetration strategy may be an appropriate way of 'harvesting' the remaining opportunities in the sector, as we discuss more fully in Book 9.

4.1.2   Consolidation

Consolidation of competitive position requires different actions, depending on whether the market is growing, mature, or in decline.

- In growing markets, firms need to grow at least in line with the sector's growth rate. Failing to do so may result in an uncompetitive cost structure that hinders the firm's ability to invest in additional resources to improve its competitive position. Consolidation may also be necessary immediately after an acquisition or merger, since management needs time to assess how best to combine the strengths of the two entities.

- In mature markets, competitors' market shares are established and relatively stable. Competitors may seek to defend their position by increasing product or service quality, while at the same time seeking internal efficiency gains, perhaps introducing more automation to achieve cost reduction. Promotional campaigns are common ways of defending positions in relatively undifferentiated product types such as confectionery, soap powders or commodities.

- In declining markets, competitors may be liquidating their assets, while others may be acquiring those assets. Should one hold on for a turnaround in the industry's fortunes, or get out as quickly as possible? Harrigan and Porter (1983) suggest that firms in a declining industry should see it as an opportunity, and adopt an appropriate 'end-game' strategy. 'Harvesting' in such circumstances would involve maximising cash flow from existing market share by minimising new investment, cutting maintenance and promotion, reducing the product range, reducing customer support, closing down some distribution channels, and so on.

4.1.3 Liquidation

Total withdrawal from a market is referred to as liquidation because all assets are sold. It involves the closure of all activities related to that product/market territory. This option is often pursued where it has been concluded that profitability targets just cannot be met and resources would be better deployed elsewhere (or, indeed, returned to stakeholders). It may be that the market is in decline or that there has been inadequate management attention because of competing priorities. From the perspective of corporate strategy, rather than business strategy *per se*, a particular business is an asset to be bought and sold. Thus, a particular business may be divested because there are more profitable ventures elsewhere with a closer strategic 'fit' to which resources may be reallocated. The manner of divestment need not be a straightforward sale to another company. Alternative divestment routes such as management buy-outs by the existing management team were very popular during the 1980s and 1990s.

4.2 PRESENT PRODUCTS, NEW MARKETS

4.2.1 Market development

Here, the organisation takes its existing products, services and ventures into new markets. These may be defined geographically, or in terms of definable customer needs. A market development strategy may be an appropriate way of securing a foothold in a sector that is currently small or emerging, yet promises significant growth over the long term. When the firm has little influence over the development of a new sector, however, this may be a high-risk strategy.

Market development can reflect a corporate strategy rather than a business unit strategy. For example, Procter & Gamble, Unilever and Johnson & Johnson all provide a range of household cleaning products worldwide. They are credited with strong brand marketing expertise because they have worked hard at building brands as a way of differentiating their products. For these companies, market development is driven by corporate strategy, of which building global brands is a key source of product differentiation for what are essentially commodity products.

A market development strategy into new markets need not necessarily be closely related to the existing market provided there is a strategic link. A British bank's move into New Zealand, for example, might hinge on whether or not it can utilise its own expertise to help the New Zealand bank to grow, and what scope there might be to enhance its own expertise through learning how the New Zealand bank competes. This would depend, of course, on the banks' own internal capability for sharing such learning.

4.3 NEW PRODUCTS, PRESENT MARKETS

4.3.1 Product or service development

Product development can be a strategic route to growth in established markets where existing product ranges do not fully exploit the available opportunities. It can be a real source of competitive advantage to offer a complete product range, for example, as described in Mintzberg *et al.*'s (1995) differentiated strategy of 'support'. Product development is a central feature of business strategy for manufacturers of consumer electronics, such as audio-visual and kitchen appliances. In the fashion business, clothing retailers and manufacturers are usually bound to an annual cycle of anticipating fashion trends, designing, showing, manufacturing and selling them within one of two seasons – autumn/ winter and spring/summer.

Customers routinely make their preferences known to the providers of products and services, and this is then used to guide product development. For example, supermarkets stock a wide range of products, partly as a result of shoppers asking for certain items. Among national supermarket chains, there are often regional differences in what is offered, reflecting variation in the ethnic mix of local populations. In other industries, product development is more accurately described as 'application' development, where competitors look for customer-specific problems and provide tailored solutions: for example, many cable manufacturing firms compete on the basis of the technical sophistication of their cabling technology, claiming low transmission loss, security from radio signal interference, physical flexibility and so on. Technical innovation may require close development work with industrial customers. For example, in producing bespoke 'umbilical cords' that allow robots to perform specialised functions in the car assembly process; or in the cable harness that runs through a car's steering column, connecting functions on the steering wheel to the car's electrical network.

Regional or local government must also remain sensitive to social trends and adapt the provision of products and services appropriately. For example, in managing local economic growth, the regional government must assess in what ways the local infrastructure is inadequate: the variety of local industries; the employment opportunities available locally; communication and transport networks; the mix of skills available within the community; and the proportion of the population of school age or unemployed. The regional government will need to consider what kinds of inward investment incentives would be appropriate for attracting which industries; what training initiatives and support services for the unemployed are most likely to help create new employment; what additional commercial accommodation, schools or housing are needed, and so on.

4.4 NEW PRODUCTS, NEW MARKETS

4.4.1 Diversification

Strategic growth through diversification can be in related or unrelated businesses. If we regard Benetton primarily as a designer and manufacturer of fashion clothing, then its ownership of some retail outlets could be regarded as a related diversification into retailing. We may also refer to this as 'forward vertical integration' because Benetton has acquired control of a business activity that lies nearer to the end user market than its core activity as a manufacturer. In contrast, a firm may choose to 'integrate backwards' towards the raw material or other supply inputs that go into making its own products. Finally, if the firm acquires a provider of complementary products or services, this is referred to as 'horizontal integration', as when an accounting firm acquires a legal practice and begins to offer legal advice; or an advertising agency acquires a public relations firm, or an airline acquires a chain of travel agents to sell complete holidays.

There are many reasons why a firm may choose to diversify, including the opportunity to reduce input costs by finding and controlling a new source of raw materials, or by controlling a unique resource, perhaps a design consultancy. Horizontal integration of otherwise independent businesses can lead to a combined value that is greater than the sum of the parts – the effect known as 'synergy' (which we will discuss at greater length in Book 10). Another reason for diversification might be that the firm sees the industry that it is currently in as a declining one, or one where it can no longer make superior returns. Occasionally, firms make a scientific discovery that has no apparent use in the existing product market and actively look for potential new applications.

A strategy of diversification for a public or voluntary organisation may, for example, focus on alternative sources of resource acquisition to enhance or expand service delivery. This is well established in higher education, although the idea of universities appealing on a charitable basis for resources is not always well accepted by the service receivers (such as undergraduate students) who may feel that central government should provide the resource. However, the principle of private endowments for some professional posts or specific research projects is very common.

Diversification clearly carries significant risk and uncertainty, and Biggadike (1979) found that diversification took an average of eight years to show a positive net income stream. Often the strategic thinking behind an acquisition is muddled and unsound, and only partly supported by internal or external data. Many acquired diversifications never show a positive return on investment and are subsequently divested.

4.5 EXAMPLE: NEW AND OLD IN RETAIL BANKING

We can now illustrate the discussion up to this point in Section 4 by applying the Ansoff product/market matrix to a specific example: the strategies of a typical commercial retail bank. Faced with a choice as to how to grow its business, it may choose to pursue all six of Ansoff's strategies for products and markets:

- *Market penetration* – may involve the opening of new branches in areas of lower customer penetration, or promotional initiatives to attract key new customers (e.g. students or teenagers or high net-worth private clients).

- *Consolidation* – may mean the introduction of customer databases and information automation to process queries and transactions faster and more accurately.

- *Liquidation* – might involve the sale or closure of branches in depressed areas or geographic regions where a critical mass of customers cannot be achieved.
- *Market development* – could mean the bank opening branches in overseas markets where none currently exist, because growth prospects in those markets are more attractive or synergies can be achieved in services sold to international customers.
- *Product development* – may involve the bank in offering telephone banking. Although the core features of telephone banking may be similar to branch banking, it does offer a development of product for customers in its convenience and flexibility (for example with 24-hour operation).
- *Diversification* – might mean the bank sets up a direct-sell telephone-based insurance company, selling or acquiring car or home insurance with no reference to the bank's existing branch network.

If we were to map these strategies onto Ansoff's matrix, the following would result:

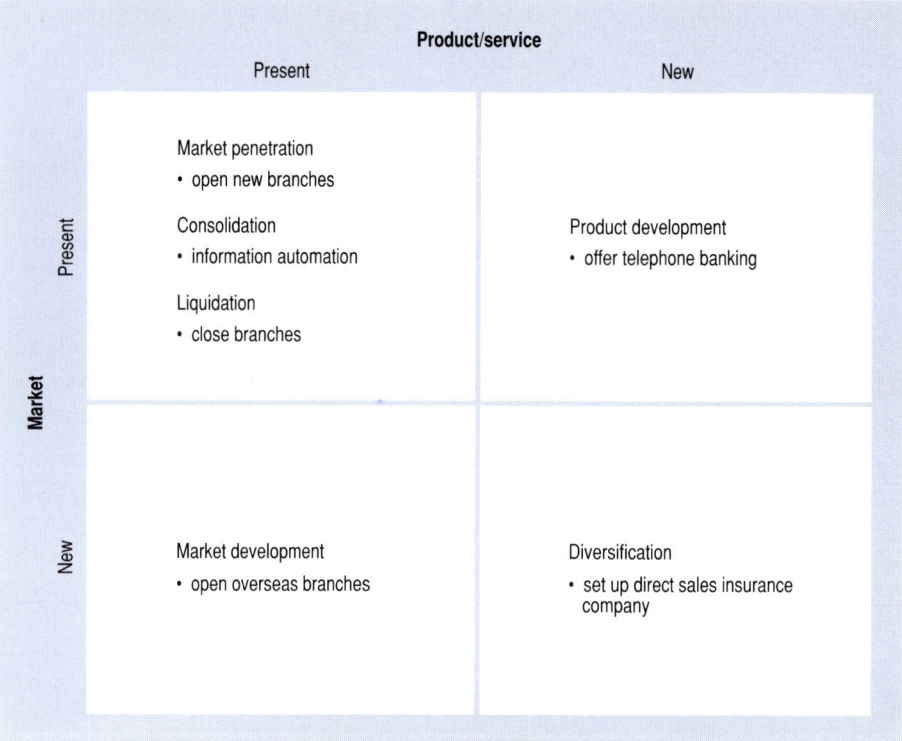

Figure 4.2   Strategies of a commercial retail bank mapped onto Ansoff's matrix

4.6   BOUNDARIES AND THE CHOICES BETWEEN OLD AND NEW

The Ansoff matrix provides us with a useful way of further selecting suitable product and market strategies, in support of generic strategies, to exploit an organisation's sources of advantage. It reinforces the point that competitive strategies cannot simply be made at an abstract, generic level. The implementation of that strategy at the product/market level must also be considered.

It is, however, important to realise that this level of detailed analysis in choosing strategy goes beyond simply considering the two dimensions of products and markets. A host of other choices must be made. For example, does our strategy require us to acquire new resources or strategic assets, or can the strategy be developed by exploiting those we already have? Book 4 identified the importance of distinctive capabilities, routines and skills as sources of advantage. Must these be developed or acquired anew, or do we intend to leverage our existing sources of advantage in new markets? Do we have to develop entirely new or amended technologies to operate our new strategy? An organisation may be faced with the inevitability of changing its capabilities, resources or technologies if it is to develop entirely new sources of advantage or alter an apparently stable industry structure for its own benefit.

These choices between pursuing a strategy in old or new markets, using old or new products, resources, capabilities or technologies, also raise a related set of questions discussed in Book 4. Does the organisation attempt to own the resources itself or merely obtain access to them? Can other organisations provide the skills and capabilities more effectively? Does the organisation try to replicate, initiate or license a proprietary technology? Does it rely on agents or partners to provide sales cover in some markets (as Glaxo did with Zantac)?

These are questions about the boundaries of the organisation. They imply choices about whether an organisation acquires assets, resources or capabilities (or even entire companies) or develops them internally. This is the 'make or buy' decision discussed in Book 4 when transaction cost economics were considered. The obverse of a decision to acquire or develop internally might equally be the outsourcing dilemma: retain or divest? Such boundary questions cannot be limited, however, to make or buy decisions. Increasingly, organisations are seeking access to resources and capabilities through devices such as joint ventures and collaborative networks. The benefits of relational and classical contracting discussed in Book 2 are important to these types of decisions. Further, in joint ventures and collaborative networks, the boundaries of the organisation are no longer clear-cut (if they ever were). Decisions must then be made about how these boundaries, networks and ventures are managed.

These topics, discussed in part in Books 2 and 4, will also be covered in Books 9 and 10, but you should be aware at present that they are all important strategic decisions about the fine grain of strategy, necessary to its successful formulation and implementation.

5 TESTING STRATEGIC OPTIONS AND STRATEGIC CHOICES

5.1 INTRODUCTION

We have discussed the importance of identifying an organisation's sources of advantage as having key importance in choosing strategy. We have also considered generic ways of classifying strategies to exploit those sources of advantage, and the need for a more detailed level of analysis and choice if strategies are to be implemented successfully. Choices about which segments to target, which markets to enter, what products to produce, what resources and capabilities to develop, whether to develop strategies alone or in alliance and so on, are all important to strategic success. We will next consider how we might evaluate strategic options that are open to us.

5.2 THE TESTS OF SUITABILITY, FEASIBILITY AND ACCEPTABILITY

Johnson and Scholes (1988) suggest three sets of generic testing criteria: suitability, feasibility and acceptability.

Suitability

The *suitability* of a proposed strategy can be assessed by the extent to which it matches the needs identified from a strategic analysis. Such a test of suitability is sometimes regarded as a test of consistency with the environmental or resource analyses and their fit with the organisational objectives.

- Obviously, the proposed strategy should address the strategic problem or opportunity identified in the strategic analysis. Does it overcome an identified resource weakness or environmental threat?

- Next, the strategy should capitalise on the organisation's identified resources and capabilities and the way they relate to external opportunities.

- Finally, the strategy should fit the organisation's objectives, such as required rates of return on capital, profitability measures and other, non-financial, performance indicators.

Feasibility

The test of *feasibility* of a proposed strategy will consider how well it would work in practice and how difficult it might be to achieve. The questions to be asked would include:

- Can the strategy be resourced? Even the most brilliant strategy cannot be implemented if, for example, the organisation's financial position is too weak to raise capital.

- Can the organisation actually achieve the required level of operational performance, say in quality and service levels? Would a strategy aimed at reducing costs in manufacturing run into problems associated with inadequate managerial resource, insufficient numbers of trained staff, or inadequate process and product technologies?
- How will the competition react and how will the organisation cope with that reaction? For example, a strategy to increase market share by reducing prices may lead to fierce competitive reaction.

In considering the feasibility of a strategy, however, there is a danger of ignoring the challenge of strategic stretch and leverage (Prahalad and Hamel, 1994) discussed in Book 1. Feasibility should therefore reflect the challenge as well as the test of ambition.

Acceptability

Johnson and Scholes' final evaluation criterion is *acceptability*. This addresses the issues of how stakeholders might feel about the expected outcomes of the strategy – typically in terms of risk, profitability, reward, ethics and the effect on relationships. Meeting reasonable stakeholder expectations is clearly a crucial test for acceptability in a strategy. Test questions include:

- What will be the financial or cost–benefit performance? Is there an unacceptable risk of endangering overall liquidity or affecting capital structure?
- Is there a risk that the organisation's relationships with its stakeholders could be unacceptably affected? Is the proposal likely to alienate employees, institutional shareholders, existing customers or clients, or governmental organisations?
- What is the effect of the proposed strategy on the internal systems and procedures? Even if feasible, will there be additional strain on staff?

The three tests of suitability, feasibility and acceptability provide an initial set of screening tools for strategic choice. They prompt managers to be explicit about the underlying rationale behind proposed strategies and to assess the associated risks and uncertainties. The criteria also guide the softer process of assessing how acceptable the proposed strategies might be to stakeholders.

5.3 THE TESTS OF CONSISTENCY, CONSONANCE, ADVANTAGE AND FEASIBILITY

It is usually helpful to test proposed strategies from a number of perspectives. Rumelt (1995) suggests the four tests of 'consistency, consonance, advantage and feasibility'. He acknowledges that it may be impossible to demonstrate conclusively that a particular business strategy can, or will, work, let alone be an optimal strategy. He points out, however, that all proposed strategies can be tested for four types of critical flaws. As will be seen, there is some overlap with the criteria of Johnson and Scholes.

Consistency

Rumelt suggests a *consistency* test: the proposed strategy must not present mutually inconsistent goals and policies. You may feel that failing this test is unlikely, but it may be a particularly necessary test for emergent strategies since these will not have been explicitly formulated and may have formed over time in an *ad hoc* fashion. Even deliberate strategies may contain compromise arrangements between power groups.

Inconsistency in strategy is not simply a flaw in logic. A key function of strategy is to provide a coherent framework for organisational action. Rumelt cites the practical example of high-technology firms that face a strategic choice between offering customised high-cost products and standardised low-cost products. If senior management does not enunciate a clear and consistent view of where the firm stands on these issues, there will be continuing conflict between sales, design, engineering and manufacturing people. The same situation might arise in a public-sector organisation where specialised interests conflict with general goals and where priorities in allocation of resources are difficult: for example, which medical treatments should be publicly funded, or whether pre-school, primary or secondary education should be allocated additional available funds.

Rumelt then goes on to argue that an organisation relates to its environment in two main aspects:

1 It must match and be adapted to the environment – the products or services must create more value than they cost.

2 It must compete with other organisations that are also trying to adapt and prosper.

Consonance

Rumelt therefore proposes a test of *consonance* that focuses on the creation of social value: to evaluate the economic relationships that characterise the business and determine whether or not sufficient value is being created to sustain the demand for the strategy in the long term.

The major difficulty in evaluating consonance is that most of the critical threats or substitutes that come from the external environment will also threaten the whole industry. Management may be so focused on existing competition that the threat is only recognised after the damage is done. Rumelt also points out that many forecasting techniques do not reveal potentially critical changes that arise from *interaction* among combinations of trends. For example, supermarkets came into being only when home refrigeration allowed shoppers to buy in bulk. Similarly, retail parks depend on an increase in car ownership. The key to the test of consonance is to grasp why the organisation exists and the basic economic foundation that supports and defines the business, and then to study the consequences of key changes.

Advantage

Rumelt's third test is about competitive *advantage* or whether the organisation can capture enough of the value it creates. As you learned in Book 4, competitive strategy is the art of creating and exploiting those advantages that are most telling, enduring and most difficult to duplicate. The strategy must provide for the creation and/or maintenance of a competitive advantage in one or more of three roots:

- superior skills

- superior resources
- superior position.

Feasibility

Rumelt's final test of strategy is *feasibility*. This was discussed in Section 5.2 and we do not need to repeat it here.

5.4 TESTING FOR EFFICIENCY, EFFECTIVENESS, ECONOMY AND EQUITY

Public and private not-for-profit organisations may often choose to test proposed strategies against objectives which are founded on the 'four Es': efficiency, effectiveness, economy and equity.

There can be conflicting objectives if, for example, both efficiency and equity are to be served. By its nature, equitable service distribution has a tendency to be economically inefficient. For example, the cost of granting planning permission for a building or an extension can vary widely, depending on the nature of the property. Despite this, a standard charge is usually made, so that low-cost permissions effectively subsidise high-cost ones. In the same way, the environmental health department of a local government organisation may wish to keep domestic cleansing costs down by collecting every two weeks, instead of once or even twice a week. This could be in a conflict with a parallel objective of, say, reducing rat populations or presenting a pleasant appearance for tourists.

Activity 5.1 _____

Grant (1995, p. 26) describes four critical elements that he thinks should feature in a successfully formulated strategy, which can be summarised as:

- goals that are simple, consistent and long-term
- a profound understanding of the competitive environment
- an objective appraisal of resources
- effective implementation.

Test your own organisation against these elements. Does your organisation have all four elements of these tests of a successful strategy? If not, do you still consider your organisation's strategy successful? Are there any further critical elements for successful strategy formulation that you have identified?

5.5 RISK AND UNCERTAINTY IN STRATEGIC CHOICE

Strategy is about charting a course for the future: will governments alter legislation? How will competitors react? Will war break out in one of the countries where business is carried out? Strategic choice must always be made in the face of such risk and uncertainty. You should be well aware of the difference between risk and uncertainty.

Risk is concerned with assessing the probability of foreseen outcomes.

In contrast, *uncertainty* is to do with outcomes that may be unforeseen, or those which are foreseen but against which a degree of estimated risk cannot be set.

Running a successful ice-cream vending operation demands a careful assessment of elements of risk and uncertainty

For example, suppose you are offered the chance to buy an ice-cream van for £5,000. If the weather is good, historical records show that you will make a return on capital employed of 20 per cent; if fair, 15 per cent; if poor, around 5 per cent. You also know that there is a 30 per cent chance of the weather being good, 60 per cent fair and 10 per cent poor – based again on historical records. You are now in a position to assess three trading scenarios and assign a probability to each. In contrast, some very unpredictable event could occur, for example you may discover that the ice-cream van you have bought provides the security on the previous owner's loan; it cannot be legally sold and you must return it! This is a situation of *uncertainty* and you cannot ascribe it a probability. For a second example, a new film carries the *risk* of loss if cinemas are less than 50 per cent full – the break-even point. However, there is always the unpredictable *uncertainty* that the film fails to gain a cinematic release (although video release may recoup some of the loss).

Assessing uncertainties and weighing up risks is a difficult, often personal, process and very dependent on the business environment. In making choices about strategy, acceptance of different degrees of risk is often a matter of an individual manager's (or group of managers') personal preferences. Some individuals are very risk-averse, others take risks almost as a matter of routine. In fact, Wilde (1982) suggests that:

- tolerance to risk affects the way in which people assess information
- people behave so as to maintain a certain level of subjective risk at all times.

For example, in countries where the wearing of seat-belts in cars is compulsory by law, drivers appear to adjust their average driving speeds upwards, merely re-creating the previous risk/safety ratio.

Strategic risks that would be acceptable in one industry, such as PC manufacture, would be quite unacceptable in another, such as health care or aerospace. Quinn (1978) feels that perceived risk is largely a function of an individual's knowledge about a sector or industry. This raises the question as to whether managers entering new industries are best equipped to assess the risks and uncertainties of it. For example, would managers used to predicting stable revenues in public monopoly utilities be best placed to identify the risks and uncertainties of, say, software design and manufacture.

There are modelling techniques available which may *help* managers to make these judgements, but it is important to note that strategy can rarely be *optimised* in this way, as the variables are usually too complex. You have to use your judgement to determine the optimum strategy.

Judgement may involve 'satisficing' and compromise. For example, in most organisations there will be a drive to attain the lowest possible cost, in order to yield the highest possible added-value. Alternatively, the strategic intent might be to maximise market share without regard (within limits) for the cost. You will appreciate that there may well be trade-offs in the face of conflicting objectives, some of which will be measurable, as with finance or market share, and other objectives will be expressions of stakeholder preference. Measurement of success in strategic situations is frequently concerned with reaching the most acceptable solution in the face of conflicting objectives, inadequate resources, or unfavourable attitudes.

5.6 FUTURE MODELLING AND SCENARIO PLANNING

Although strategic optimisation can rarely be achieved through modelling, it can be valuable to use future modelling and risk management techniques, such as scenario planning. Read the following passage, which is adapted from Tapiero (1988).

> Future modelling is a basic activity which consists of transforming a set of possible and future-oriented events into a coherent whole. This is complicated, because it requires a very clear understanding of the causes of change; that is, we seek to establish not only causal links between events, but how these links are maintained over time. In planning, we face an unmanageable number (indeed an unlimited number) of possible futures. Therefore, if we are to make a reproduction of the future in the present, we must determine a substitute for it.

> This substitute is not what will necessarily occur; it is our guess about what may occur. When managers' intentions are combined with such guesses about the future, then we engage in learning, adaptation and, more generally, in uncertainty reduction, i.e. we replace a string of unknown events by another (or the same) string of events with an altered likelihood of occurrence. In this manner, managers seek to influence and possibly control the risks of the environment within which they function. This is called risk management.

Whenever a model for the future and a reduction of uncertainty has been achieved, alternative courses of action can be tested for their future impact. By manipulating the model on the basis of credible assumptions, we obtain credible time paths of the variables with which we are most directly concerned. [...] Managers' intentions are combined with such guesses about the future in an information-gathering, learning and adaptation process. The plans are then adjusted as necessary to achieve the desired risk–return ratio.

Planning in this sense is at the core of a great many managerial activities. To render relevant choices more manageable and to gain more information concerning the impact of an action upon the future, we need information.

Tapiero describes a rational approach to risk management and future modelling. He emphasises the management intention, not to forecast the future, but to estimate the range of outcomes and their associated probabilities.

It is also important not to confuse the basic risk inherent in any strategic option with strategic options that are designed to reduce risk. For example, when an organisation enters a new market or launches a new product, it might adopt a strategy that is perceived as low-risk, such as the use of joint ventures or licensing of technology. Here, one of the strategic intentions is to reduce risk. Of course, the decision still carries with it a basic risk.

Capabilities in systematic risk management may, indeed, be at the very heart of some businesses, for example life assurance, liability insurance or market-making in futures exchanges. Other companies may benefit from access to superior skills in the routine management of future risks and uncertainties, for example hedging foreign currency realisations.

Future modelling capabilities such as scenario planning can also give some organisations an advantage in dealing with uncertain but rapid or discontinuous change. For example, scenario planning has been pioneered and developed by the oil company, Shell (de Geus, 1988). In February 1986, the price of crude oil collapsed from $27 per barrel to $8 at its lowest, before settling back at a range of between $13 and $19 for the next ten years. This was an unimaginable catastrophe in the industry. Two years earlier, however, Shell executives were asked to consider the impact of a $10 price on the company. Initially incredulous, the executives had, however, settled back to produce plans of how the company would survive. These scenario plans are widely credited with giving Shell an advantage in reacting quickly and effectively to the price collapse.

5.7 RISK, REWARD AND SUPERIOR PROFITABILITY

Strategic choice should take into account the risks associated with different strategic options. These risks may not be quantifiable but they can normally be categorised into high, medium or low. (You may have met risk projection in earlier studies in the use of the capital–asset pricing model, in which the riskiness of corporate activity is related to the pricing of an organisation's shares and, thus, the financial rewards of shareholding.)

The whole issue of stakeholder objectives (as discussed in Book 2) and their attitudes to risk–return relationships, sets the context in which strategic choice has to take place. One way of characterising the different financial goals of different stakeholders, and the different financial rating with which they will be primarily concerned, is set out in Figures 5.1 and 5.2. The purpose of these figures is not to debate the precise location of different stakeholder groups (which *is* clearly a matter of debate), but to understand the implications of trade-offs between risk and return.

Clearly, in the real world there is a relationship between risk and return – other things being equal, people will demand higher returns from more risky investments of resources. Thus the pattern of expected normal returns runs from the top left-hand corner of the matrix to the bottom right. This does not, however, stop stakeholders seeking to further maximise their returns while minimising their risks. This is why the stakeholders on the matrix are not distributed evenly along a straight line (Figure 5.1). The concerns of the different stakeholders will, in turn, lead them to place emphasis on different measures of financial performance (Figure 5.2).

Day (1990) argues that such financial reward evaluation of strategic choice will be credible only if stakeholders address three fundamental issues that determine the pay-off from a strategic choice:

- the prospects for superior profitability
- the chances that superior profitability will be realised
- the acceptability of the risk–reward ratio.

These three issues are discussed in turn below.

Figure 5.1   Matrix showing the relationship between stakeholder goals and risk/return

	Risk tolerance	
	Higher	**Lower**
Maximise returns	• High return on equity • High leverage acceptable • High turnover growth aim • Fixed cost bias in corporate costs	• High return on total capital • High leverage unacceptable • Lower turnover growth to avoid cash problems • Prefer variable cost bias
Indifferent above predetermined threshold	• Growth in turnover • Growth in asset base • High leverage acceptable	• Low growth • Low leverage • High quick ratio • High current ratio • Stable markets

*(Left axis label: **Return objective**)*

Figure 5.2   Effect of risk/return attitudes on ratios

In this course, you have encountered two main views of how *the prospects for superior profitability* can be assessed. Superior profits can be achieved:

1 relative to organisations in other industries, by entering an attractive industry or by altering the structure of an industry to make it more attractive

2 relative to firms in the same industry, by achieving and sustaining a competitive advantage based on distinctive resources and capabilities.

In practice, the strategic choices facing most managers pursuing superior profits will tend to focus on improving profits by achieving competitive advantage. These choices can be related to the tests of consonance (the creation of 'social value') and advantage proposed by Rumelt in Section 5.3. This is because the combined effect of exit barriers from the existing industry or sector, and entry barriers into the new industry or sector, usually make such movements unrealistic.

The chances that superior profitability will be achieved is the second of Day's fundamental issues. Given that the opportunity promises superior profits, what chance does the intended strategy have of being realised? Does the organisation have the skills and necessary resources or, if not, can the deficiencies be overcome without too much cost or delay? If the superior profits derive from a competitive advantage, is this sustainable? These concerns are clearly related to Rumelt's test of feasibility in Section 5.3. Feasibility considerations are also related to the overall uncertainty of the project and are not to be confused with risk.

The third of Day's fundamental issues is *the acceptability of the risk–reward ratio* as discussed in Section 5.7. The importance of relating investment risk–return profiles and trade-offs back to the objectives and risk–return profiles of stakeholders, demonstrates again the relationship between Day's focus on risk–reward ratios and both Johnson and Scholes's acceptability test (Section 5.2) and Rumelt's consistency test (Section 5.3).

6 SUMMARY AND CONCLUSION

This book has concentrated on choice in strategy and identified a number of tests of options and criteria which will help an organisation choose an appropriate and successful strategy. In particular, the importance of strategy as a means of exploiting sources of advantage has been affirmed as a key consideration in strategic choice.

The book deliberately avoids discussion of the organisational and social processes by which strategic choices are made, as these issues are dealt with in Book 6. Choices in strategy could, for example, be made using a 'linear' planning approach such as the model proposed by Andrews discussed in Book 1. It is quite possible to take the ideas the course has discussed so far and map them on to Andrews' model, as shown in Table 6.1:

Table 6.1 Strategy formulation using Andrews' corporate planning process	
Andrews' stage	**Where discussed**
• identification of organisational objectives	Book 2
• appraisal of the external and internal environment	Books 3 and 4
• formulation of several alternative strategies	Book 5
• evaluation of these alternative strategies against objectives and in the context of resources available and management values; followed by strategy selection	Book 5
• implementation of chosen strategy	throughout the course

Book 1 also pointed out, however, that analysing or formulating strategy is likely to be an iterative process, in which actions can occur simultaneously and without the explicit intention of the organisation and its management. Mintzberg (1994) has categorised academic schools of thought on how strategy is made and strategic choices taken. He noted two main categories of perspective that seek to explain the same observable personal and organisational behaviours of strategy process.

1   *Prescriptive* – seeking to prescribe the ways of making choices about strategy. It attempts to define, through a rational process, what should happen in strategy.

2   *Descriptive* – seeking to describe the organisational strategy-making process; this rationalisation is done with hindsight after strategy has been made. It explains strategy 'as it is rather than how it should be'.

Ohmae (1984) has written persuasively about the boundary between the rational *prescriptive* approach to making strategy and the *descriptive* approach. Synthesising successful business strategies never results just from rigorous analysis, but from a particular state of mind. Insight and a drive for achievement fuel a thought process that is creative and intuitive rather than rational. Ohmae acknowledges the role of analysis; indeed, strategists could hardly do without it, but they use it to stimulate the creative process, test the resulting ideas and ensure successful execution of high-potential 'wild' ideas. No matter how difficult or unprecedented the problem, a breakthrough to the best possible solution can come only from a combination of rational analysis (based on the real nature of things and imaginative reintegration of all the different items into a new pattern), and by the exercising of individual thought and judgement. Ohmae believes that great strategies, like great works of art or great scientific discoveries, although they all call for technical mastery in the analysis, must originate in insights and judgements that are beyond the reach of conscious analysis.

As a student of strategy, you will encounter both prescriptive and descriptive accounts of how choices are or can be made in strategy. You need to be flexible enough to recognise the elements and the merits of both approaches and be prepared to advance your own individual thoughts.

REFERENCES

Ansoff, H.I. (1965) *Corporate Strategy*, McGraw-Hill, New York.

Banbury, C.M. and Mitchell, W. (1995) 'The effect of introducing important incremental innovations on market share and business survival', *Strategic Management Journal*, Vol. 16, pp. 161–182.

Biggadike, R. (1979) 'The risky business of diversification', *Harvard Business Review*, May/June.

Bowman, C. and Asch, D. (1996) *Managing Strategy*, Macmillan, Basingstoke.

Day, G.S. (1990) *Market-driven Strategy Process for Creating Value*, The Free Press, New York.

de Geus, A. (1988) 'Planning as learning', *Harvard Business Review*, March–April.

Freeman, C. (1982) *The Economics of Industrial Innovation* (2nd edn), Frances Pinter, London.

Grant, R. (1995) *Contemporary Strategy Analysis* (2nd ed.), Blackwell, Oxford.

Harrigan, K.R. and Porter, M.E. (1983) 'End-game strategies for declining industries', *Harvard Business Review*, July/August.

Jarillo, J-C. and Martinez, J.I. under the direction of Stevenson, H.H. (1988) 'Benetton SpA', Harvard Business School Case 9-389-074.

Johnson, G. and Scholes, K. (1988) *Exploring Corporate Strategy* (2nd ed.), Prentice-Hall, Hemel Hempstead.

Kay, J. (1993) *Foundations of Corporate Success*, Oxford University Press, Oxford.

Miller, D. (1986) 'Configurations of strategy and structure: towards a synthesis', in Asch, D. and Bowman, C. (eds) *Readings in Strategic Management*, Macmillan, Basingstoke.

Mintzberg, H., Quinn, B.J. and Ghoshal, S. (1995) *The Strategy Process*, Prentice-Hall, Hemel Hempstead.

Mintzberg, H. (1994) *The Rise and Fall of Strategic Planning*, Prentice-Hall, Hemel Hempstead.

Ohmae, K. (1983) *The Mind of the Strategist*, Penguin, Harmondsworth.

Porter, M.E. (1980) *Competitive Strategy*, The Free Press, New York.

Porter, M.E. (1985) *Competitive Advantage*, The Free Press, New York.

Prahalad, C.K. and Hamel, G. (1994) 'New strategy paradigms', *Strategic Management Journal*, Vol. 15, Special Issue.

Quinn, J.B. (1978) 'Strategic change: logical incrementalism', *Sloan Management Review*, Vol. 1, p. 20.

Roussel, P.A., Saad, K.N. and Erickson, T.J. (1991) *Third Generation R&D: Managing the Link to Corporate Strategy*, Harvard Business School Press, Boston, Mass.

Rumelt, R. (1995) 'The evaluation of business strategy', in Mintzberg, H., Quinn, B.J. and Ghoshal, S., *op. cit.*

Schumpeter, J. (1943) *Capitalism, Socialism and Democracy*, Allen and Unwin, London.

Smith, R.J. (1994) *Strategic Planning and Management in the Public Sector*, Longman, London.

Tapiero, C. (1988) *Applied Stochastic Models and Control in Management*, North-Holland, Amsterdam.

Wilde, G.J.S. (1982) 'The theory of risk homeostasis', *Risk Analysis*, Vol. 2, No. 4, pp. 209–225.

ACKNOWLEDGEMENTS

Grateful acknowledgement is made to the following sources for permission to reproduce material in this book:

Photographs

Page 16: © Lada Cars; *page 17:* © Porsche Cars GB Ltd; *page 19:* (Rover 618) © Rover Group; *page 19:* (Honda Accord) © Honda Motor Europe Ltd; *page 23:* courtesy of Tristar Cars; *page 40:* Mike Levers/Open University.

Figures

Figure 3.1: Porter, M. E. 1985, *Competitive Advantage: Creating and Sustaining Superior Performance*, p. 12, figure 1.3, Simon & Schuster; *Figure 4.1:* Ansoff, H. I. 1968, *Corporate Strategy*, Table 6.1, McGraw-Hill © 1968 H. Igor Ansoff.

PUTTING PROCESS INTO STRATEGY

Author: Kevin Daniels

CONTENTS

1 INTRODUCTION

So far in this course, we have examined the nature of strategy in Book 1 and looked at the purposes and objectives of organisations in Book 2. In Books 3, 4 and 5 we focused upon techniques for analysing the organisation's environment, resources and capabilities and formulating strategy. These can help you to judge the best course of action for your organisation and to choose the most appropriate strategy.

This book is about what these techniques do not help you to analyse: for instance, how decisions are taken and how strategies are formed. Forming[1] new strategies implies change. Change involves people and time, as the people within and around an organisation adjust to transition. As we have already seen in Book 2, there are many stakeholders within an organisation, each with different perspectives and objectives. The task for the strategist is to weigh these perspectives – to develop the most appropriate strategy, not just by considering economic analyses but also on the basis of stakeholder objectives and how best to manage the time between forming and implementing the strategy.

This book is about developing an awareness of the so-called 'softer' issues of strategy, such as managing the timing and pacing of strategies, and the role of leadership, culture and politics. These issues are as important as conducting strategic analysis correctly. The book aims to develop your ability to manage issues such as these – at departmental[2], business, or corporate level. In short, this book is about the *process* of strategy and the importance of strategic thinking.

To study this book you need:

Course Reader
Audio Cassette 1

1.1 LEARNING OBJECTIVES OF THIS BOOK

To help you develop an understanding of process, we begin by looking at two fundamental properties of process – time and change. In particular we will look at the role of time in both obtaining organisational benefits and causing organisational disasters. We next look more closely at strategic decisions, patterns in strategic decisions and how strategies are developed in organisations. We then look at how organisations can learn from decisions, and how this can improve future decision-making. Finally, we shall discuss the importance of organisational context in shaping the most appropriate form of decision-making.

After studying this book, you should be able to:

- distinguish between strategic analysis, strategic choice and strategy implementation
- recognise the importance of time as a source of competitive advantage
- state the characteristics of strategic decisions
- use tools to help with the political aspects of strategy formation
- describe different processes of strategy development
- describe the processes and importance of strategic thinking
- recognise the importance of organisational learning, and describe how it can be encouraged.

2 STRATEGY PROCESS, TIME AND CHANGE

Figure 2.1   Argenti's model of the corporate planning process

In Book 1 we discussed some different approaches to understanding strategy. One was the planning approach, which is very useful for distinguishing between the stages in the process of strategy. Figure 2.1 shows one such planning approach. Argenti (1980) identifies five distinct phases through which organisations *should* progress in strategic management. Organisations should set targets, identify gaps that will emerge between targets and the current strategy, appraise both the external and internal organisational environments, formulate a new strategy on the basis of the strategic appraisal, and implement the strategy by drawing up action plans and budgets. Roughly, Argenti's five phases can be grouped into three: strategic analysis (target setting, gap analysis and strategic appraisal), strategic choice (strategy formulation) and strategy implementation.

Argenti, like other proponents of the planning approach, suggests that analysis should precede choice and choice precede implementation. In reality, most organisations fail to do this. A more realistic picture of the strategy process is given in Figure 2.2. Figure 2.2 shows that strategic analysis consists of environmental analysis and assessing resources and capabilities. Strategic choice consists of identifying strategic options, evaluating them and selecting the best option. Strategic choice also requires evaluation of the expectations of different stakeholder groups and dealing with them. Strategy implementation involves allocating resources, organisation restructuring and managing change and culture.

Figure 2.2   A realistic model of strategy process (adapted from Johnson and Scholes, 1993)

Figure 2.2 illustrates some important principles of strategy that are mentioned briefly here. These include the distinction between *deliberate* and *emergent* strategies and an *incremental* approach to strategy. We discussed deliberate and emergent strategies in Book 1, and we will revisit them briefly in Section 3.2. We will also discuss incremental approaches in Section 4.2.

Most importantly, Figure 2.2. shows that analysis, choice and implementation overlap. This raises many possibilities. First, in some organisations, the classic planning approach does occur, where analysis leads choice and choice leads implementation – such that a *deliberate* strategy is the result. In other organisations, choice can lead analysis and implementation, such as where a group of managers decide to change the organisation to meet their own objectives, and conduct rigorous analysis to justify the decision to other stakeholders after the decision has been made and is in the process of implementation. Further, the figure illustrates that implementation can lead choice and analysis. Consider for instance a supermarket chain, where staff at one store are forced to cut prices through fierce local competition. Finding the price cuts attract more customers, other stores copy the pattern. Eventually, top management notice these changes, contract an economics consultancy to investigate pricing policy, and then after a full strategic analysis, decide to continue with the new accidental or *emergent* strategy of price differentiation throughout all the stores. Finally, Figure 2.2 illustrates that analysis, choice and implementation often proceed together, with the preferred choices influencing implementation and analysis, analysis influencing choice and implementation influencing analysis and choice. In this way, organisations may *incrementally* move through the process of strategy – as the strategy adjusts to changes in analysis, choice and implementation.

Reflection

What drives the strategy process in your department or organisation – analysis, choice or implementation? Do any of these stages overlap? Is the pattern constant?

Showing strategy process as three distinct, yet overlapping parts tells us that ordering is an important part of it. The ordering of each part of the process can be influenced by structures and control systems (Book 7), and politics and culture (Book 8). Knowing which stage precedes the other stages may help us to understand the strategy process in a particular organisation. For instance, if implementation is leading the strategy but there is resistance to change, it may be useful to switch to a process where analysis of internal resources and capabilities leads strategy. Or, if analysis produces few answers, it may be time to experiment and try implementing something on a small scale to see what happens. The process can be managed by looking at the progress being made in each stage and the ordering of each stage.

Organisations can learn from current strategy to form and implement future strategy. For instance, not only does implementing a strategy help develop skills in change management, it can also provide important feedback on strategic analysis ('Did we know before the change effort precisely what management skills would be needed to bring about change? Are we able to analyse for this in the future?'). Similarly with strategic choice ('Were the expectations of stakeholders fully taken into consideration?', 'Did we identify those strategic options that became visible as the organisation changed?'). Organisational learning is an important part of the strategy process, and we will examine this in greater detail in Section 6 of this book.

2.1   TIME AS A SOURCE OF COMPETITIVE ADVANTAGE

In the previous section, we saw that the strategy process can be divided into three components – analysis, choice and implementation – and that any one of these components can precede the others. Therefore, implicit in the notion of strategy process is the notion of time – the time it takes to move from one component of the strategy process to another or the time it takes to learn skills in each of the components. Indeed, we saw at the beginning of the book that understanding the role of time in the strategy process is important to understanding the strategy process as whole.

Time has always been important in managing strategy, but today its importance is even greater. The increasing pace of technological, competitive and managerial innovation means that staying ahead of competitors or keeping abreast of societal changes is more difficult than it has been in the past. Some industries are now described as 'hypercompetitive' – where strategic manoeuvring and innovation are so fast that the industry is never stable and any competitive advantage is soon eroded (D'Aveni, 1995). In an influential article, George Stalk notes that:

> The best competitors, the most successful ones, know how to keep moving and always stay on the cutting edge.
>
> Today, time is on the cutting edge. The ways leading companies manage time – in production, in new product development and introduction, in sales and distribution – represent the most powerful new sources of competitive advantage.
>
> (Stalk, 1988, p. 41)

While concepts such as just-in-time manufacturing are clearly relevant to his argument, Stalk notes that doing *everything* more quickly – manufacturing or service delivery, sales and distribution, innovation and strategy – is important for developing advantage. Stalk illustrates this with the example of head-to-head competition between Honda and Yamaha, shown in the mini-case below.

MINI-CASE: THE H-Y WAR

In the late 1970s, Japanese companies exploited flexible manufacturing to the point that a new competitive thrust emerged – the variety war. A classic example of a variety war was the battle that erupted between Honda and Yamaha for supremacy in the motorcycle market, a struggle popularly known in Japanese business circles as the H-Y War. Yamaha ignited the H-Y War in 1981 when it announced the opening of a new factory which would make it the world's largest motorcycle manufacturer, a prestigious position held by Honda. But Honda had been concentrating its corporate resources on the automobile business and away from its motorcycle operation. Now faced with Yamaha's overt and public challenge, Honda chose to counterattack.

Honda launched its response with the war cry 'Yamaha wo tsubusu!', ('We will crush, squash, slaughter Yamaha'!) In the no-holds-barred battle that ensued, Honda cut prices, flooded distribution channels, and boosted advertising expenditure. Most important – and most impressive to consumers – Honda also rapidly increased the rate of change in its product line, using variety to bury Yamaha. At the start of the war, Honda had 60 models of motorcycles. Over the next 18 months, Honda introduced or replaced 113 models, effectively turning over its entire product line twice. Yamaha also began the war with 60 models; it was able to manage only 37 changes in its product line during those 18 months.

Honda's new product introductions devastated Yamaha. First, Honda succeeded in making motorcycle design a matter of fashion, where newness and freshness were important attributes for consumers. Second, Honda raised the technological sophistication of its products, introducing four-valve engines, composites, direct drive, and other new features. Next to a Honda, Yamaha products looked old, unattractive, and out of date. Demand for Yamaha products dried up; in a desperate effort to move them, dealers were forced to price them below cost. But even that didn't work. At the most intense point in the H-Y War, Yamaha had more than 12 months of inventory in its dealers' showrooms. Finally Yamaha surrendered. In a public statement, Yamaha President Eguchi announced, 'We want to end the H-Y War. It is our fault. Of course there will be competition in the future but it will be based on a mutual recognition of our respective positions.'

Honda didn't go unscathed either. The company's sales and service network was severely disrupted, requiring additional investment before it returned to a stable footing. However, so decisive was its victory that Honda effectively had as much time as it wanted to recover. It had emphatically defended its title as the world's largest motorcycle producer and done so in a way that warned Suzuki and Kawasaki not to challenge that leadership. Variety had won the war.

Time-based competitive advantage

The strength of variety as a competitive weapon raises an interesting question. How could Japanese companies accommodate such rapid rates of change? In Honda's case, there could be only three possible answers. The company did one of the following:

1 Began the development of more than 100 new models 10 to 15 years before the attack.

2 Authorized a sudden, massive spending surge to develop and manufacture products on a crash basis.

3 Used structurally different methods to develop, manufacture, and introduce new products.

In fact, what Honda and other variety-driven competitors pioneered was time-based competitiveness. They managed structural changes that enabled their operations to execute their processes much faster. As a consequence, time became their new source of competitive advantage.

(Stalk, 1988, pp. 44–5)

Stalk draws an important lesson from the H-Y war – managing time is crucial for strategic success.

Examining your organisation with tools such as the value chain (Book 4) can help you to identify areas in which operations and the links between operations can be made faster. But Stalk talks of speeding the innovation process too. For this he recommends small but regular improvements in products or services and product development teams working in a cross-functional manner. Most importantly for us, Stalk discusses fast strategy as a source of competitive advantage and strategic success. How can the strategy process be managed to confer advantage? We will look for answers to this question in Section 2.2. In his recommendations for speeding innovation, Stalk is effectively recommending an incremental approach within a decentralised structure. As you will see in Book 7, however, decentralised structures are not always wholly appropriate for organisations.

2.2   MANAGING TIME IN STRATEGIC CHANGE

Speeding the strategy process can help to achieve advantage and strategic success. There are two clear ways of doing this: to complete each phase of the strategy process faster, and to conduct each phase of the strategy process simultaneously with other stages. Eccles (1993) discusses how both may be achieved in the context of strategic change. He is concerned with how organisations can implement strategies and change more quickly by considering the whole of the strategy process – not only the implementation of strategic change. He recognises that strategy is both about time and change, and about formulating the most appropriate strategy.

Eccles recommends that managers should examine 14 factors during strategic change. Each of these 14 factors is accompanied by one or more questions. If change is to be successful, then managers must be convinced that they have answers to each of these questions. The 14 factors plus questions are shown in Table 2.1. Eccles suggests that managers should draw up a table that shows the organisation's current capability on each of the factors, the organisation's chances of enhancing that factor and the importance of that factor.

Table 2.1	Eccles' factors of strategic change	
Category	**Factor**	**Question(s)**
Purpose and initiative	1 The contemplative executive	Have we a champion?
		What dedicated group will drive this through?
	2 Single goal	What are we trying to achieve?
		Where are we trying to get to?
	3 Clarity of purpose	Why are we doing this?
		Is the logic clear?
Concordance and trust	4 The illusion of unity	Are we agreed on this?
		Do people accept the plan?
	5 How open to be?	Is there enough trust and shared agreement?
		How much should we reveal?
How much should we reveal?	6 Communication	Do we talk and listen to each other? Do people understand?
Leadership, capabilities and structure	7 Proportionate responsibility	Are we ready and willing to lead?
	8 The limitations of empowerment	How much do we help people to act responsibly?
	9 Teams and leaders	Is it clear who is to be responsible for what?
	10 Structure and culture	Are we organised sensibly to pursue our goal?
Building on action and success	11 Creating winners	Do we reward commitment, success and meritorious failure?
	12 Fast change, initial acts and early successes	How shall we show that it works?
		How shall we gain momentum and enthusiasm?
		How can we best make speedy progress?
	13 Caring for casualties	How shall we treat the injured?
	14 Managing unintended consequences	Can we adapt and learn?
		How shall we cope with contingencies?
		How resilient and flexible are we?

(from Succeeding with Change, *Tony Eccles, McGraw-Hill, 1993. Reproduced by kind permission of McGraw-Hill.)*

For managing time in the strategy process, Eccles suggests 'shrinking' each of the three components of the strategy process and increasing the 'overlap' among these components (cf. Figure 2.2). Shrinking means spending less time on each activity – being over-cautious about analysis, choice and implementation can slow the strategy process considerably. Increasing overlap means conducting different phases of the strategy process simultaneously – such as tentatively accepting initial analyses and implementing strategies on a trial basis in limited areas. Both 'shrinking' and 'overlapping' should lead to increased speed in the strategy process, and strategic change in particular. However, Eccles warns against changing too quickly – allowing inadequate time can be as disastrous as taking too long over strategic change. It is important to consider strategic change carefully if it is to be quick – and the required speed will change with the circumstances.

Activity 2.1

Think of an example of change in your own department or organisation. Answer the questions in Table 2.1.

How can your department or organisation enhance capability on each of these 'factors', and how important are these factors for implementing the change?

Does answering these questions help you to suggest ways in which to quicken the strategy process for your organisation or department?

If so, what are these suggestions and how did the questions help you to make these suggestions?

If not, why do you think Eccles' recommendations do not apply to your department or organisation?

Like Stalk with innovation, Eccles is offering a recipe for strategic change. As we have seen earlier, however, with the planning models of Argenti, organisations do not necessarily follow the recipes of academic writers. While managers can try to mould the strategy process to their own recipes or those of academics and consultants, it is also important to manage the strategy process as it evolves by taking advantage of emergent strategies.

Eccles implies that either being too fast or taking too long can lead to strategic failure. Being too fast may result from insufficient analysis, or consideration of options; or trying to implement a change without the necessary resources to do it quickly. Being too slow may come from a reluctance to change the organisation. In both cases, the results are the same – the most appropriate strategy is not implemented. This can lead to strategic degeneration and inferior performance. Once this has happened in an organisation, it is easy for it to happen repeatedly. Figure 2.3 illustrates this process, which is known as strategic drift (Johnson, 1988).

Figure 2.3 shows that errors in implementing the most appropriate strategy lead to divergence between environmental change and organisational change. At first, managers will not act upon this divergence – because the discrepancies between environmental and organisational change are too small for them to notice. Managers take subsequent strategic decisions on the basis that the previous strategies are still appropriate. That is, through 'top-down' information processing (recall

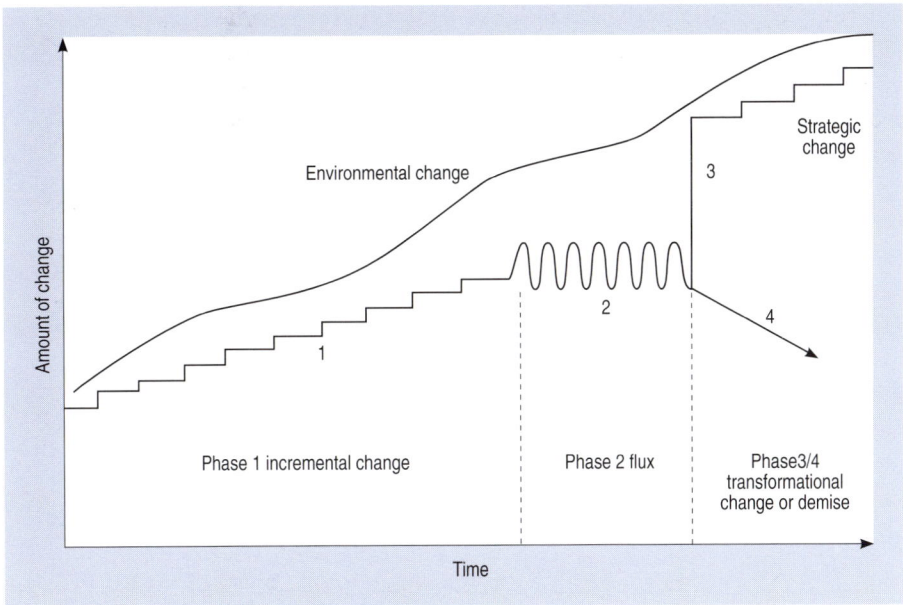

Figure 2.3   The risk of strategic drift (Johnson, 1988)

Book 1), managers only attend to information that is compatible, or consonant, with their model. Information that is not compatible, that is dissonant with this model is ignored; in some cases the bearer of the information is ridiculed, scapegoated or otherwise sanctioned. Johnson (1988) reports that a marketing manager in a retail firm was ridiculed for commissioning a market research report that indicated performance was deteriorating, when all the other managers 'knew' that this was not the case. As important information is ignored, the divergence between organisational change and environmental change becomes greater and greater. At this point, not only has the organisation 'drifted' from the environment – but managers' mental models have too. These points are illustrated in the quotes from hospital managers shown in Box 2.1.

BOX 2.1

'The management consultants found it difficult to persuade the strategy makers that the existing view (that everybody was doing everything well and that what they were doing was what needed to be done) was not necessarily correct. There just wasn't any information, either for or against, on the topic. We undertook rational business planning ... but it could be argued that planning decisions were made with limited information, based on the prejudices and preferences of top management ... There has been an over-dependence on historical signals and accepted wisdom.'

'The present signs are that many of our buyers [GP fundholders (local doctors), district health authorities, purchasing officers], and even the ultimate consumers, do not necessarily want a major part of what we offer. One GP fundholder has employed its own physiotherapist to treat its patients. Many GPs are sending their patients to slimming clubs rather than referring them to our dieticians. Increasingly, it seems, our customers do not see us as an automatic first point of referral.'

'Senior managers were surprised when they discovered that the private sector was poaching our service users. It had never dawned on them that this type of activity could take place and they had never thought about checking for competitive activity.'

Managers only notice the divergence when there is so large a difference between predicted and actual performance that it cannot be ignored. This can occur when there is a salient signal from the environment. In the private sector, such a signal could be a rapid drop in credit rating. In the public sector it could be avoidable public discontent. For charities, it could be a failure to respond to a major crisis such as an earthquake. At this point, managers enter a state of flux and attempt to revise their mental models about what the organisation should be doing. This inevitably leads to some confusion as different options surface and conflicting ideas are presented for a new strategic direction. At the end of this stage, either organisational performance continues to deteriorate under the weight of conflicting prescriptions for a new strategy, or managers must attempt ambitious and radical change embracing fundamental changes in mental models. Radical change only works if (a) the organisation is capable of making this great change and (b) it isn't too late anyway. If neither condition is met, organisational collapse in one form or another may well follow.

Activity 2.2

List (a) the advantages and (b) the disadvantages in attempting to increase the speed of the strategy process in your own department or organisation.

Discussion

One advantage is being able to access markets or resources faster than others. Being able to change more quickly also means that change can take place more often, enabling more frequent innovation and allowing the organisation to match changes in the strategic environment more easily. Speeding up the strategy process can also have a number of disadvantages – most notably not taking enough time to analyse the environment to make sure that the a new strategy is really necessary and the organisation has the resources to successfully execute it. In the long term this could mean strategic drift, as hurried analysis means environmental demands are not identified – which could eventually lead to strategic failure, or a difficult, radical change in strategy at best.

3 STRATEGIC DECISIONS

At the heart of strategic management lies the concept of making decisions to reach objectives (Simon, 1977). We saw in Book 1 that strategic decisions involve major organisational change – for example, decisions concerning technology, restructuring and launching new products. But strategic choices are rarely the result of one-off decisions (recall Figure 2.2). Strategic decisions are more likely to occur as a series of related decisions that are less extensive in scope than the final strategic decision (Pettigrew, 1990). These minor decisions can take place at any part of the strategy process. For example, strategy involves deciding which information is most important, which stakeholders are most influential and which control mechanisms and budgets are needed to implement the change.

Each individual decision passes through three phases (Mintzberg, Raisinghani and Theoret, 1976):

1 recognition that a decision needs to be made

2 a search for relevant information

3 narrowing down the options and making the final choice.

Figure 3.1 shows these phases, and that while it is possible to go through the stages of making a strategic decision sequentially only once, this is rare.

Figure 3.1   Stages in strategic decisions

Decisions need to start with the recognition that a decision needs to be made – but after that, decisions do not have to follow the order above. For instance, after recognition, managers may find relevant information that reveals another type of decision needs to be made, returning the decision process back to the recognition phase. A series of decisions often passes through these stages many times before a final strategic decision is made. Sometimes, unexpected and creative insights can help to accelerate the process towards the final decision (Langley *et al.*, 1995). We will return to the importance of insight in strategy in Section 5.

Langley *et al.* show a number of ways in which a pattern of decisions can lead to the final strategic decision. These are:

- *Nesting* – This occurs when a large decision is broken down into smaller decisions. For example, a local government authority may know it needs to build a major new road. It will first have to make decisions about which route is politically acceptable, the amount, of 'acceptable' environmental damage, where a road can best influence the district's economic prospects, how funding can be obtained, and the size and quality of the road construction, etc.

- *Snowballing* – This occurs when minor decisions, taken with no relevance to strategy, escalate into a strategic decision. For instance, a decision to launch a new advertising campaign may lead to a decision to reposition the product in the market, which may lead to a decision to develop a new product, which then leads to a decision to acquire a smaller company that has expertise in developing such new products.

- *Recurrence* – This occurs when essentially the same decision is taken over again. The decision for Du Pont to adopt a multi-divisional structure (which you will learn more about in Books 7 and 9) was rejected three times before its final acceptance (Chandler, 1962).

Langley *et al.* also warn that decisions on seemingly unconnected issues can also influence each other. A decision to relocate an organisation may preclude developing new services because of resource constraints. Conversely, deciding not to relocate may enable new product development as resources become free.

'The beginning of a strategic decision is often characterised by informal meetings and speculation'.

The Rolling Stones. In January 1963 Brian Jones wrote to the BBC looking for an opportunity for his band to make a broadcast. His letter contains what is in effect a classic mission statement:

'I am writing on behalf of the "Rollin' Stones" Rhythm and Blues band.... The band's policy is to play authentic Rhythm & Blues music, using outstanding exponents of the music such as Howling Wolf, Bo Diddley, Jimmy Reed, etc. etc. Within our self-imposed limitation we have a large repertoire covering R & B styles from the early country blues influenced R & B, to the far more commercial sound of Rhythm & Blues of the 1950s and 1960s ...'

Since strategic decisions often involve many related decisions, they can take a long time, although, as we have seen earlier, time can be a source of advantage. Hickson *et al.* (1986) looked at 150 strategic decisions and found that many decisions take several months to make – with some decisions taking up to four years. Besides repeating the same stages of the decision process, there are other reasons why strategic decisions take a great deal of time. The first reason is the long time that may occur between recognising the need for a decision and beginning to gather information and organising meetings between stakeholders. Impediments and delays are other reasons why strategic decisions take a long time. Hickson *et al.* found that impediments and delays can come from the following sources:

- *Sequencing* – waiting for priority in the order of attention. For example, managers may believe other issues to be more pressing.

- *Co-ordinating* – waiting for resources to become available, that is, waiting for people to get together.

- *Timing* – waiting for the right time, for example, an opportune moment to introduce the issues to different stakeholder groups.

- *Searching* – waiting for information to arrive. For example, waiting for the results of strategic analyses.

- *Problem solving* – investigating that which is not understood. For example, action learning to determine possible outcomes by experimentation.

- *Supplying* – awaiting the availability of resources. In some public sector organisations, cash resources only become available at certain times of the year.

- *Recycling* – reconsidering earlier actions in the decision, as shown in Figure 3.1.

- *Internal resistance* – active opposition from inside the organisation, such as trade unions or middle management.

- *External resistance* – active opposition from outside the organisation, such as customers, environmental lobby groups, local government, other organisations.

Of these nine sources of delay, Hickson *et al.* found that problem solving and external resistance were the most frequent.

3.1 TYPES OF STRATEGIC DECISION

Not all strategic decisions are alike. Indeed, it would be surprising if decisions about restructuring were the same in every organisation and if product development decisions were the same as acquisition decisions. Hickson *et al.* grouped the decisions they studied into three categories – *constricted, sporadic* and *fluid*.

Constricted decisions tend to involve many sources of expertise, but no great effort is made to acquire other sources of information. These types of decision have less scope for negotiation between stakeholders, and involve fewer formal meetings. Middle, rather than senior, managers often take the final decision. Box 3.1 describes a constricted decision.

BOX 3.1: CONSTRICTED DECISION

A decision to modernize an insurance company was made in this way. On the surface it was merely a commitment to updating and centralizing the data processing for the main line of business, vehicle insurance, but [...] its significance for those concerned was in a wider context. The company had been taken over by a larger firm, and, despite assurances, its top managers recognized that there was a risk of its business being absorbed into that of the parent and the company being obliterated as a working organization.

They realized that the best defence was for the parent company's management to see the subsidiary as a good profit-earner which should not be disturbed. The company was already in a leading position in its sector of the market, so that the range of insurance offered and the sales approach were felt to be as good as possible. Any move to ensure continued profitability and, equally important, to sustain an image as a vigorous up-to-the-minute enterprise had therefore to be in the direction of improving administration and organization.

The decision process circled around the chief executive within whose purview it legitimately came, never far out of his hands. There was no committee work, not even a special task force or group to work out details. Approval from the board of directors sitting as a board was not needed, though individual directors knew what was in the wind. The motor insurance department, the claims department, and other departments where appropriate, produced analyses of the existing system and what would be required of any new system. Externally, IBM were quick to offer their sales and advisory services, the insurance industry trade association was contacted about experience elsewhere, and some of the larger brokers who handled business for the company confided what competitors were doing. In just a few months, with no real delays, it was decided that a reorganization of the administration based on centralized microfilm records ought both to raise earnings by improving the premium-to-expenses ratio, and improve efficiency in the field by speeding up the calculations of premiums and cover sent out to sales agents. This, it was felt, would go as far as anything else could do to ensure company autonomy.

(Hickson et al., 1986, p. 123)

Sporadic decisions are characterised by delays and impediments; the involvement of experts but variability in the quality of the information available; informal interaction and negotiation, especially between personal contacts; a great deal of time to reach a decision; and the involvement of senior management in the final decision. Box 3.2 shows an example of a sporadic decision.

BOX 3.2:   SPORADIC DECISION

It was a sporadic process that brought the management of a nationalized industry to the decision to buy a one-third share in a firm that was a large purchaser of its products. This decision was an attempt to ensure future sales in a situation where either other interested parties might take complete control of the firm, or the firm might go out of business. Two multinational oil corporations, a multinational chemical corporation, and another very large nationalized industry were all involved, as well as the prospective subsidiary itself and the local government for its area. The prospective subsidiary wanted assured funds for expansion, and all the other interests wanted to expand or at least to protect the firm's demand for their own products. The local government, on the other hand, resisted expansion on ecological grounds.

The decision-making process in this nationalized industry moved in fits and starts. Spasms of work by departmental staff to produce forecasts of future output and costs, and to give estimates of the investment the subsidiary might make in new plant if it received an injection of fresh capital, and similar spasms of hectic toing and froing amongst senior managers, were broken by pauses whilst the reactions of the other powerful interests to reports and proposals were awaited. The financial grounds for injecting new capital by means of a takeover were very much in doubt. Time passed while successive reports and proposals were tossed backwards and forwards between the organizations concerned, and renegotiated to suit their differing interests, until after 18 months an agreement was reached. The board of the nationalized industry made a commitment to take a one-third share in its customer firm, along with one of the oil corporations and the other state-owned industry, each of which also took one-third. A difficult uneven process came to an end.

(Hickson et al., 1986, pp. 118–9)

Fluid decisions often have fewer delays and impediments, less involvement by experts, variability in the quality of information gathered, more meetings, more scope for negotiation, involvement of senior management in the final decision and relatively less time to make the final decision. Box 3.3 gives an example of a fluid decision.

BOX 3.3: FLUID DECISION

...the decision in a metropolitan municipality to venture into the realms of chance by launching a lottery to augment the normal funds from local taxpayers and the national government. In not much more than a month, following the return of the leader of the council from a holiday during which he had become enthused by the idea, the proposal for a lottery was manoeuvred through a local government committee structure that was not prepared for it. With the main opposition party lukewarm and probably inattentive, outright resistance coming only from within a minority third party, and with officials failing to find any causes for procedural delays, the proposal went through the Management Board of senior officials, the Finance Committee of the municipal council, the full council, and into the hands of a specially created Lottery Sub-Committee in no time, including having gained the necessary permit from the authorities regulating gaming. It seems significant that the influential individual who brought the idea back from the seaside was both leader of the controlling party in the full council, and chairman of the vital Finance Committee.

This was a fluid process conducted properly and openly via formal meetings and committees, yet so smooth and fast as to be over probably before many politicians and officials had fully grasped the implications of what was happening.

(Hickson et al., 1986, pp. 120–1)

Reflection

Think of a recent strategic decision taken in your own department or organisation. How would you categorise that decision? What features of the decision led you to your conclusion? What delays and impediments disrupted this decision? What speculation circulated about the decision before formal action began?

3.2 DESCRIBING DECISION PROCESSES

We have seen the importance of decisions in strategy, and the way in which several smaller decisions can lead to a larger strategic decision. This illustrates that there is a role for managerial choice at many stages in the process of strategy. However, to notice a strategy through patterns in *managerial choice*, it is necessary for the decisions to be both *intended* and *consistent* (Mintzberg, 1983). That is, strategists must take decisions to realise an objective and persevere in their attempts to reach that objective in all parts of the process of strategy. However, if conscious management thought and action is not driving strategy, it does not have to be intended. Organisations can have a strategy without a single member of the organisation choosing that strategy (Mintzberg and Waters, 1990). For instance, the external environment may force strategies upon some organisations, or strategies can evolve as an organisation adapts to changing circumstances (as you will see later in this book). It is this distinction, between managers playing an active part in choosing strategy and managers being more passive in the choice of strategy, that underlies Mintzberg and Waters' deliberate/emergent continuum (1985), that you encountered first in Book 1.

Some organisations are more likely to be able to choose strategies in a deliberate manner than others. Mintzberg and Waters consider deliberate strategy to be more common in bureaucratic and centrally controlled organisations. They think emergent strategy is more common in less hierarchical and decentralised organisations. Just because an organisation is more likely to have emergent, rather than deliberate strategies, does not mean that managers have no influence over strategy. It means that the nature of the influence changes – managers must be aware of emergent patterns of decisions to craft these into a suitable strategy.

Activity 3.1

Think about emergent patterns of decisions in your department or organisation. How do these influence strategy? Write down how these emergent patterns could determine the strategic direction of your department or organisation.

Mintzberg and McHugh (1985) consider that getting the best out of emergent strategies involves taking a 'grass roots' approach to strategy. They note six lessons from grass roots strategies:

1   Strategies grow initially like weeds in a garden; they are not cultivated like tomatoes in a hot house.

2   Strategies can take root in all kinds of strange places, virtually wherever people have the capacity to learn and the resources to support that capacity.

3   Strategies become organisational when they become collective, that is, when the patterns proliferate, to pervade the behaviour of the organisation at large. Weeds can proliferate and encompass a whole garden; then the cultivated plants may look out of place. The same holds true of emergent strategies.

4   The process of proliferation may be conscious but need not be; likewise it may be managed but need not be.

5   Organisations experience periods of convergence, punctuated by periods of divergence. Periods of continuity in strategy are interrupted by periods of change where, through experimentation and renewal, new strategic themes emerge.

6   To manage the process is not to preconceive strategies but to recognise their emergence and intervene when appropriate. Managers need to create a climate within which a wide variety of strategies can grow. They can do this by establishing flexible structures and supporting ideologies, and by defining broad, guiding (umbrella) strategies.

4 PATTERNS IN STRATEGIC DECISIONS: PROCESSES OF STRATEGY DEVELOPMENT

We have seen already that strategic decisions are rarely the product of isolated decisions, but come from a stream of preceding decisions. Similarly, Mintzberg and Waters (1985) give a definition of strategy as 'a pattern in [a] stream of actions'. There are different processes that influence how decisions and actions are taken, and these can remain constant within an organisation and across decisions. Whether a strategy is deliberate or emergent will depend very much on the processes that develop strategies.

You have seen the planning models of Andrews and Argenti, who recommend that managers should take a very deliberate and rational approach to developing strategy. Using planning tools, managers should be able to develop a rational and optimal strategy based on objective consideration of the information gathered. Then by applying methods, such as the strategic control systems described in Books 7 and 9, managers should be able to implement strategy in the most effective and efficient way. However, a truly planned and deliberate approach to strategy development remains nothing more than an intention for many organisations.

Why then is a truly planned approach to strategy so difficult? One answer lies in the mental or cognitive abilities and motives of managers themselves. In Book 1, you encountered the concept of 'top-down' information processing by applying mental models based on past experience and beliefs. People use 'top-down' processing for two reasons. First, it is quick and easy. We don't have to spend time gathering information and deciding which is the most important – our experience tells us what is important. Secondly, many management situations are too complex for us to give our attention to every piece of information – there is only so much that we can pay attention to. As a simple example, if you read on a train, as you concentrate on the words on the page you are probably unaware of many of the things that are going on around you – for instance the discussion of two people sitting opposite you. Since there is only so much we can take in, we have to ignore some information to be able to pay attention to other pieces of information – our mental models help us to decide which information to pay attention to. By observing managers selectively attending to some pieces of information and not others, Simon (1957) developed the concept of *bounded rationality* – people make decisions on the basis of the information that they attend to.

Bounded rationality explains how cognitive abilities limit the extent to which we are able to adhere completely to planning approaches to strategy development. As you saw in Book 2, managers' motives may differ from the motives of other stakeholders, such as shareholders, employees, union leaders, the local community and politicians. In pursuing their own objectives, whilst balancing the objectives of other powerful stakeholders, and attending to only a limited amount of information, managers often *satisfice* (Cyert and March, 1963) – that is they take a decision that is not optimal, but good enough in the light of conflicting goals.

However, despite the limitations on the planning approach to strategy in reality, planning as an activity can be useful for many reasons. Langley (1988, 1990) has found that organisations do indeed use planning to gather information for developing strategies. However, Langley has also found that organisations also use planning for:

1   *Public relations* – in which strategic planning is intended to impress or influence outsiders, such as securing backing from shareholders.

2   *Direction and control* – by integrating control mechanisms into planning systems or by using planning as a filter for selecting initiatives.

3   *Symbolism, sidetracking and serendipity* – Here, planning is initiated: (a) to give the impression of a willingness to act, (b) to delay a final decision; or (c) to keep analysts occupied.

4   *Group therapy* – which involves the communication of strategic visions and participation by people at all levels. Langley (1988) noted that this might be the most important function of strategic planning.

Langley's view that planning can be used to 'sidetrack' decisions, or as 'group therapy', illustrates the importance of the objectives of differing stakeholders in the strategy process. Because there is often conflict between stakeholder objectives and bargaining between stakeholders, strategy is a political process.

4.1 POLITICAL STRATEGY FORMULATION

MacMillan (1978) defines politics as the process that takes place when one or more 'actors' attempt to structure a situation so that their individual goals are promoted. An actor can be an individual, a group, an organisation or a nation. He argues that planning approaches to strategy ignore the political implications of actively attempting to restructure the organisation and the environment. That is, attempting strategic change may meet with resistance – either from within or outside the organisation.

In practice, many managers informally incorporate political considerations in their responses to the realities of organisational behaviour as they know it. However, MacMillan refers to political strategy *formulation* – for MacMillan, incorporating politics into strategy should be a deliberate process.

To formulate strategies that incorporate political issues it is necessary to:

1   analyse the power and influence of each stakeholder group

2   determine who are allies and who are opponents

3   negotiate with allies

4   formulate offensive and defensive strategies to deal with opponents.

Points 1 and 2 are aspects of *political analysis*; points 3 and 4 are aspects of *political strategy formulation*[3]. In the following sub-sections, we shall examine the nature of power and influence, how to determine power and influence for each stakeholder group, how to select allies and predict opponents, the process of negotiation and how to formulate offensive and defensive political strategies. You will return to these issues in Book 8.

4.1.1   Political analysis: power and influence

MacMillan (1978) draws a useful distinction between power and influence. He defines power as the capacity to restructure actual situations, influence as the capacity to control and modify the perceptions of others. Power and influence, in combination, determine political capability.

The exercise of influence and power can be considered in terms of a continuum in which a manager may move from, for example, a neutral style to more overt use of power. The following illustrates, in very simple terms, such a progression.

- 'This is something for your unit, Bill.' – Neutral drawing of attention.
- 'This is the situation and I suggest you do so and so.' – Reference to the needs of the situation.
- 'As your superior I am telling you to do this.' – Influence sought by reference to formal authority.
- 'I'm moving you on to another section.' – The manager has demonstrated power to restructure the actual situation.

Effective managers seldom need to move to the 'power' end of this continuum with their own staff and colleagues. In other circumstances, however, overt use of power may be more important in achieving desired results. For example, if several competing developers are bidding for the same plot of building land, the successful bidder will be the one who has the necessary purchasing power to outbid the rivals.

As we have seen in Book 2, Morgan (1986) has identified the following power bases within the organisation, which are among the most important sources of power and influence. To recap and expand on what we said there, these power bases are:

1   *Formal authority* – This is a form of legitimate power that accompanies a position. It arises because people recognise that the effective operation of the organisation requires some individuals to exercise rights in using the organisation's resources, to decide what is done and who should do it.

2   *Control of scarce resources* – Those who own or control resources will be in a position of power relative to those who depend upon those resources. Important resources include money, materials, technology, research and personnel.

3   *Organisational structures and procedures* – As you will see in Book 7, organisations can be configured to give power to some areas of the organisation and take it away from others. Within a decentralised structure, for example, semi-autonomous divisions may be ultimately controlled by the centre retaining authority for all resource commitments above a certain value.

4   *Control of decision processes* – Controlling which committees take which decisions, and who sits on those committees, is a subtle means of controlling and influencing the outcome of decisions.

5   *Control of knowledge and information* – Having sole knowledge of an important process means that others are dependent on you for controlling that process. Professional bodies secure power by deliberately controlling access to their specialised knowledge through stringent entry criteria.

6   *Boundary management* – Power may be created by monitoring and controlling the transactions that take place at the interfaces between

different sections of an organisation, or between the organisation and the outside world. Transactions across boundaries may be encouraged or blocked, by boundary managers to promote certain interests.

7   *Ability to manage uncertainty* – Where people are uncertain of a course of action, those with the skills or contacts needed to resolve the perceived problem can increase their power base.

8   *Control of technology* – A wide range of people develop personal power on the basis of their knowledge and skilful exploitation of specific technologies.

9   *Alliances and informal networks* – Influential friends, membership of networks and social contacts within and outside the organisation can all provide sources of power. Much of the activity associated with networks of contacts is based on mutual dependency and exchange.

10 *Countervailing power* –Whenever power becomes concentrated in relatively few hands, that concentration of power legitimises the power of others as the opposition. This is particularly the cases in democratic, consensus or collegial organisations. There is also a tendency for opposing forces to co-ordinate their actions to redress the imbalance.

11 *Symbolism and the management of meaning* – The use by a leader of evocative language, symbolising competitors as the enemy, using such positive words as 'challenge', 'opportunity', 'vision', 'champion', emphasising and visibly rewarding desired achievements, are all ways of reinforcing the beliefs of the leader and inculcating these in others. Establishing a strong shared culture provides a power base for the leader in that internal value differences are reduced and the energy that might otherwise be dissipated by internal conflict can be channelled in directions that are considered to be more productive.

12 *Gender power* – Organisations often operate in ways that enable men to achieve positions of power more easily than women. Gender-related biases are often created and maintained on a day-to-day basis, not only by obvious discrimination but also in less visible ways – encouraging stereotypical masculine behaviour such as aggression, etc.

It is useful to determine the extent to which each stakeholder group possesses each source of power when making an assessment of political capability. Such an assessment may also enable you to identify which stakeholder groups are dependent upon other groups for important resources – and therefore which stakeholders are likely to be influenced or coerced by other groups.

As a simple example at the individual level, consider the introduction of new information technology for keeping records in a small general medical practice. There are three stakeholders – Diane, the senior partner, Julie, the medical secretary and Andrew, the junior partner. The three stakeholders have the following sources of power and influence.

Diane:
- Formal authority – she is the senior partner
- Control of scarce resources – as senior partner, she controls the budget

Julie:
- Control of knowledge and information – as secretary she knows whether new information technology will help with keeping records

Andrew:

- Ability to manage uncertainty – Andrew's sister is a software engineer helping Andrew to understand how the new technology works
- Symbolism and the management of meaning – Andrew is very quick to remind the others that other medical practices have adopted this technology.

It is better to secure as many sources of power as possible – and usually the most useful allies and the most dangerous opponents are those who have the most power. In this case, Diane and Andrew are more or less evenly matched, but Julie has access to only one power base. One power base may outweigh others: in some organisations control of resources could be more important than symbolism; in others formal authority could be the most important power base. As you will see in Book 8, the culture of an organisation influences the usefulness of power bases.

It is little use having access to a wide power base without the knowledge to use it. Sometimes the most skilful political players make better use of few resources than seemingly stronger opponents. The legend of Robin Hood is one example: Robin was able to evade capture from the stronger Normans by using his influence with the peasantry. All guerrilla leaders use this tactic.

Activity 4.1

Think of a problem facing your department or organisation at the moment. Apply Morgan's 12 bases of power to assess the political capability of three of the major stakeholder groups which are interested in solving that problem (e.g. senior management, middle management, employees).

4.1.2   Political analysis: allies and opponents

One way to secure a larger power base is to enlist the help of allies. Allies are likely to share similar objectives to your own group – or can be persuaded or forced to share similar interests. Opponents on the other hand do not wish your objectives to be achieved. In this sub-section, we shall examine some tools to help choose allies and predict likely opponents. The *actor/issue matrix* is one of these tools.

The actor/issue matrix

This helps you to identify the objectives of each stakeholder group – and therefore identify which stakeholders share similar objectives (potential allies) and which stakeholders have objectives incompatible with your objectives (potential opponents). The actor/issue matrix can be illustrated by thinking about the example of the medical practice we have just encountered (see Table 4.1). In the matrix we have listed three issues that are likely to be of direct concern to one of the three participants. We can then go on to consider what the attitude of each participant is likely to be to each of these issues.

We can see from Table 4.1 that Diane is likely to oppose the introduction of new technology, but Julie and Andrew are likely to assist the implementation of new technology. Therefore, Julie and Andrew may become allies.

Table 4.1 Actor/issue matrix			
issue/actor	**Diane**	**Julie**	**Andrew**
loss of status derived from personal knowledge of patients	*		
opportunity to acquire new skills		*	
easier access to information			*

The relationship matrix

An extension of the actor/issue matrix is to consider the relationships between stakeholders. Which actors are in day-to-day contact with one another? Are you aware of support that some regularly give to others? Are some of the actors on poor terms with one another? If so, for what reasons? These factors can be represented on a relationship matrix and can help you to decide which groups are most likely to help each other by forming coalitions.

Suppose in our example that we also know that Diane and Andrew are not on good terms, and that Julie is Diane's niece. We could represent these relationships as shown in Table 4.2. This table modifies the conclusions reached through the actor/issue matrix. While the strained relationship between Diane and Andrew is likely to increase Diane's opposition to new technology and increase Andrew's advocacy of new technology, the relationship between Diane and Julie indicates that we need to know more about Julie's relationship with Andrew if we are to predict how she will behave.

Table 4.2 Relationship matrix			
Actors	**Diane**	**Julie**	**Andrew**
Diane	–	niece/aunt	strained
Julie	niece/aunt	–	
Andrew	strained		–

The actor/issue and the relationship matrices are useful for identifying potential alliances amongst stakeholders – who are most likely to support one other. Coalitions are most likely to form when stakeholders have good relationships and share the same objectives. They may still form between stakeholders who are not in particularly close contact if they have many of the same objectives, but this is less likely. In this case, if coalitions form, they will usually disband as soon as the political battle is won or lost.

MacMillan recommends that managers *should* form coalitions and alliances. But remember, those who oppose you may also form coalitions and alliances!

Having identified possible coalitions of allies and opponents, you can combine this information with the sources of power of each stakeholder group in a *force field analysis*. This gives a final indication of the forces for change, the forces against change and who are likely to be the most useful allies and the strongest opponents.

Force field analysis

Force field analysis is based on the idea that in situations where change is planned there will be forces for and forces against the change, and together these determine the present equilibrium. These supporting and opposing forces are represented on a diagram in which the length of the arrows representing the different forces corresponds to their perceived strength – which can be determined through applying Morgan's 12 bases of power.

In our example, we know that Diane opposes the new technology and Andrew advocates the new technology. We are unsure about Julie: although she would like to acquire new skills, her relationship with her aunt may prevent her from actively helping Andrew. Figure 4.1 shows a force field analysis for our example.

Figure 4.1   An example of a force field analysis

Activity 4.2

Thinking of the problem you identified in Activity 4.1, use the actor/issue matrix and the relationship matrix to determine which groups are likely to oppose each other over the solution to this problem. Use force field analysis to determine which alliance is likely to be the most powerful.

There is sometimes a temptation to secure change by increasing the force with which it is being pushed through. For example, Andrew might try to form an alliance with Julie to tip the power balance in his favour. However, this may well lead to increasing opposition and deteriorating relationships if Andrew is not careful. The skilful tactician may achieve better results by carefully analysing the reasons for, and sources of, opposition and finding creative ways to reduce one or more of them to swing the balance of forces in his/her favour. Thus, Andrew might try to repair his strained relationship with Diane. This is discussed in more detail below.

4.1.3 Political strategy formulation

Having completed the political analysis, the political strategy formulation can proceed. The steps are as follows:

1   Set tentative objectives which you hope to reach by acting independently against the opposition. In our example, for Andrew this might mean persuading Diane to talk to his sister about the advantages of new technology.

2   Select potential allies. Since Andrew and Diane are evenly matched, both will be looking to secure an alliance with Julie.

3   Use independent political capability as a bargaining base in negotiations with allies. Andrew might use his political capability to persuade Julie that new technology can help her to acquire new skills. Diane might use her formal authority as senior partner and aunt (or may use her control of the budget) to promise a pay increase to secure Julie's compliance.

4   Do not accept any agreement with an ally that achieves less than acting alone. In our example, neither Andrew nor Diane can resolve the issue alone.

5   Select a combination of allies for each critical decision area. Julie's overall objective is to acquire new skills, so for this decision Andrew might be her best ally. In future decisions Diane's control of financial resources may make her a better ally if Julie needs funds to attend a training course.

6   Match the combined strengths and weaknesses of an alliance against the strengths and weaknesses of the opposition. As we have already seen, whoever secures Julie's support will have the strongest political capability.

Activity 4.3 _____

Still thinking of the same problem as in the last two activities, work through the six steps of political strategy formulation for the stakeholder group that you identify with the most to determine the best alliance for this stakeholder group.

4.1.4 Negotiation for alliances

The next step is negotiation with potential allies. MacMillan (1978) proposes the following procedure in preparing for any negotiation:

1   Collect relevant facts relating to the negotiation. This can be done with the tools for political analysis.

2   Classify the facts according to the issues that are likely to arise during negotiation. Returning to the medical practice, Andrew might decide that Julie is likely to raise issues concerned with obtaining the relevant training to use the new technology. Andrew must use his ability to manage uncertainty to reassure Julie that installing the new technology does mean she will have to undertake some form of training. Andrew is also aware that Julie is likely to mention both her relationship with Diane, and Andrew's strained relationship with Diane.

3   Clarify and prioritise the objectives of the negotiation. Andrew's objective during negotiation will be to persuade Julie to mention to

Diane that: (a) record keeping will be far more efficient with new technology; and (b) technology cannot replace the personal relationships Diane has cultivated with many of her patients.

4 Choose the sequence to be used in discussing the issues. Andrew decides that he should begin by chatting casually to Julie about expanding her skills, and then to mention that new record-keeping software could help her to develop her computer literacy skills, as well as do her job more efficiently. After agreeing that the new technology requires some form of training, Andrew decides that he should mention that his poor relationship with Diane means that she is more likely to listen to Julie.

5 Choose the strategy to be adopted for the negotiation. Andrew's knowledge of the new technology means that he can promise Julie some form of training – which he intends to introduce to awaken her interest in the technology. Andrew is also able to use symbolism and the management of meaning. He decides that if Julie is reluctant to talk to Diane on the promise of training alone, then he can attempt to persuade Julie that the new technology means that she will gain skills that will make her employable, not only with other medical practices, but in a wide range of other organisations.

The outcome of successful negotiations will be the formation of an alliance.

Activity 4.4 _____

Work through these five steps to formulate a plan for negotiating with a potentially important ally for the problem you used in the last few activities.

4.1.5   Offence and defence

The final step in political strategy formulation is to develop offensive and defensive plans. Offensive plans may be adopted to exploit the weaknesses and erode the strength of the opposition and defensive plans to counter attempts by the opposition to exploit the alliance's weaknesses and erode its strengths.

If the opposition is strong, the alliance may have to bargain by attempting to manipulate the situation through its power and influence, and then accommodate the prevailing situation to achieve the most favourable position.

In political strategy formulation three factors must be borne in mind.

1 *Timing* – Whenever possible, actions should be taken when the alliance's own capability is at its strongest and the opposition's is weakest.

2 *Information* – To prepare and time offensive and defensive plans, it is important to secure good information about opponents' plans, commitments, alternatives, values, internal changes and problems.

3 *Options available* – An alliance may be able to improve its own position by reducing opponents' options, and increasing its own options in critical areas. This may be possible by bringing influence to bear on the opponents' customers, suppliers, alliance partners and so on.

In the medical practice, Andrew decides that Diane's formal authority is at its strongest at the time of Julie's annual appraisal, which takes place in September. Diane also employs a firm of accountants to check the financial health of the practice in February. The accountants' report is available to Andrew – which makes Diane's control over financial resources weaker at this time of year. Andrew's political capability is weakest when he is on holiday. He usually takes his holidays in the summer, to coincide with the school holidays. Since his own political capability is weakest in the summer, Diane's formal authority is strongest in late summer and her control of financial resources weakest in February, Andrew decides his best time to act is soon after the accountants' report. Andrew knows that Diane's birthday is in early March, and that Julie's family always give Diane a birthday party. Andrew therefore decides that the best time to persuade Julie to talk to Diane is just after her birthday party – when Diane will (hopefully) be favourably disposed to Julie, and her formal authority and control of financial resources are weakest.

In this example, Andrew has used the information about Diane's birthday party, the budget and Julie's appraisal to time his offensive strategy when Diane's political capability is at its weakest, and his at its strongest. He has attempted to narrow Diane's options, by making it less likely that Diane will refuse to consider the new technology at all. Because of the timing of the offensive, Diane's predisposition to Julie means that, at worst, Diane may decide to look into the issue further. However, Andrew also needs a defensive strategy: Diane may decide to take her time investigating the new technology and delay a final decision until the summer, when she is strongest. One way would be for Andrew and Julie to use their political capability to keep pressure on Diane to come to a quick decision. However, Diane may not react too well to pressure. A better defensive plan could be for Andrew to accommodate the prevailing situation and make concessions in other decision areas to repair his relationship with Diane.

4.2   POLITICS, PLANNING, INCREMENTALISM AND LOGICAL INCREMENTALISM

Developing a strategy is often a very imprecise process. This is because of the tendency to satisfice rather than optimise; an inability to pay full attention to every piece of information because strategic information is complex and ambiguous; and the bargaining and negotiation between stakeholders that surrounds strategic decisions. This means that the strategist is often unable to develop a strategy in a 'once and for all' manner, but must often try new ideas – both to stretch the limits of the strategist's own knowledge of the potential of various strategies and to elicit the opinions of stakeholder groups. Thus strategy development can be an *incremental* process – where ideas are tried, negotiations take place, consequences are assessed and then the process starts over again. There are two forms of incremental strategy development:

- Lindblom (1959) describes *incrementalism* as an approach to strategy that involves working through problems and remaking strategy over and over again in response to changes. An incremental approach to strategy development evolves from a stream of decisions taken in an iterative manner, as we discussed in Section 3. In this way, the incremental approach to strategy tends to produce emergent strategies

– but top management commitment to these strategies is low, since they may need to change.

- Quinn (1980) describes *logical incrementalism* as a process in which the strategist has an idea for a suitable strategy, but has neither the information nor the political support to implement that strategy. Strategic planning is very important in this process – it allows the strategist to gather information that may help to support the strategy. Informal discussions with colleagues from many different departments are important. These discussions help build support and consensus, and provide information to re-shape the strategy. As managers gather information through planning systems, sub-systems and discussion, the details of the strategy begin to emerge. Eventually, after much refinement and usually much time, a strategy is implemented. Throughout this process, the strategist retains a broad strategic view and, if the basic idea is a good one, keeps the same general idea. Unlike incremental strategy development, *logical* incremental strategy development does not result from a stream of satisficing decisions, but is a more deliberate process that is more likely to produce an *umbrella* strategy.

Since both incrementalism and logical incrementalism rely on informal discussion and bargaining – albeit to a greater or lesser degree – the danger of strategic drift is very real for organisations using these strategy development processes (Johnson, 1988). While concerned with internal negotiations, strategists may be too busy to notice changes in the external environment.

4.3   ALTERNATIVE EXPLANATIONS OF STRATEGY DEVELOPMENT: LEADERSHIP, CULTURE AND ENFORCED CHOICE

So far in this section we have looked at strategy development as a planned process, a political process and an incremental process – however, strategy can develop in at least three other ways – through *leadership*, through *organisational culture* and by *imposition from external forces*.

4.3.1   Leadership

The role of the strategist does not only involve interpreting strategic analyses, bargaining with stakeholders and taking decisions – the strategist can have a great impact as a leader. In some cases, senior managers are the strongest force driving strategy development (Noel, 1989), using their political capability to realise their vision for the organisation. Strategic leadership requires more than the obsessions or strength of will of senior managers, it requires an understanding of the appropriateness of different leadership styles (Pettigrew and Whipp, 1991).

Strategic leadership styles can be distinguished by the extent to which they are more participative or more authoritarian. The more participative strategist is likely to attempt to *influence* other stakeholders during the strategy process. A more authoritarian strategist will try to impose strategy on others by using *power* rather than influence. Kotter and Schlesinger (1979) have noted that strategists can choose from seven different approaches in developing strategy. These seven approaches cannot clearly be divided into participative or authoritarian approaches, but on the whole, a more participative strategist may tend to:

1   *involve* stakeholders in the decision process and allow them to *participate* in strategic decisions

2   attempt to *educate* other stakeholders of the benefits of a new strategy through *communication*

3   *support* other stakeholder groups by helping to *facilitate* their own interests

4   *negotiate* with other stakeholders to reach agreement.

In contrast, a more authoritarian strategist may:

5   attempt to *manipulate* different stakeholders by selective use of information

6   *co-opt* stakeholders on to key decision making groups to give the illusion of participation and to obtain the endorsement of these stakeholders – but without actually adjusting for the opinions of these stakeholders

7   *coerce* stakeholders by making threats – for example denying promotion to middle managers unless they comply.

While an authoritarian style may be useful in some circumstances and a participative style in others, we often have our own preferred style of leadership. It is important to adapt our styles to suit the circumstances. Kotter and Schlesinger recommend that more authoritarian approaches are useful to implement a new strategy quickly, although such approaches carry the risk of future problems due to resentment and a lack of trust. More participative approaches are useful for building trust and commitment. However, participative approaches are time-consuming and they can be expensive.

The importance of strategic leadership goes beyond choosing the most appropriate leadership style. Strategic leaders can have a great impact on the culture of an organisation (Schein, 1992). Managing the culture of an organisation is a difficult, some would say impossible, process – but strategists can influence culture. Creating strategic visions and missions that other members of the organisation can understand and agree with is only part of the process. Leading by conspicuous example and selectively promoting or recruiting managers who 'fit' the preferred culture are other examples of how strategists can influence the culture of an organisation. Organisations such as IBM, Matsushita, General Motors and Marks and Spencer have all had powerful and influential founders, whose actions and strategic visions continued to influence the strategies of those organisations long after they had left. This illustrates not only the power of successful strategic leadership but also the power of organisational culture over strategy.

Left to right: Michael Marks, Thomas Spencer, Simon Marks. Organisations such as Marks and Spencer have had powerful founders, who continued to influence their strategies long after they had left. Michael Marks, having fled the pogroms of Tsarist Russia, set up a trestle table in Leeds' Kirkgate open market two days a week in late 1884. In 1886 he moved to the indoor market and erected a sign over his stall: 'Don't ask the price, it's a penny'. This became the basis of the successful 'penny bazaar' formula. (Michael's son-in-law Harry Sacher wrote: 'one of the effects of a fixed price is to set the trader always on the search for greater variety and better value at that price'.) In 1894 Marks invited Thomas Spencer, book-keeper and cashier for Isaac Dewhirst, a nearby wholesaler from whom Marks bought reels of cotton, to become his business partner. Simon Marks, Michael's son, who was only 19 when his father died in 1907, struggled over the next few years to take control of the family business, which was becoming highly profitable despite increasing competition (particularly from F.W. Woolworth – see Book 1). Simon became company chairman in August 1916, a post he held until his death in 1964. Simon Marks, with his brother-in-law Israel Sieff, introduced the policy of buying directly from manufacturers in the 1920s. One of the first of these was the Leicester-based clothing firm Corah, whose St Margaret trademark gave them the idea for St Michael. The business Isaac Dewhirst founded, now the Dewhirst group of companies, are still major partners of M & S today.

4.3.2 Culture

We will look at culture in more detail, and how culture is derived and changes, in Book 8. The culture of an organisation represents a shared recipe for action. This recipe develops as the organisation grows. It is not only influenced by founders and prominent senior managers, it also develops from the shared experience of managers. Myths and stories of organisational heroes (often senior managers – but not always) communicate this collective experience. This collective experience means that managers within an organisation often develop similar mental models of the most appropriate strategies and the strategic environment (Daniels *et al.*, 1994). Strategies that are not consistent with shared mental models may meet with resistance, because managers may:

- not understand the new strategy
- refuse to implement a strategy that they believe will not work
- refuse to implement a strategy that reflects a strategic vision they do not agree with.

Box 4.1 gives an example of the role of organisational culture in strategy development.

BOX 4.1:   THE ROLE OF CULTURE IN STRATEGY DEVELOPMENT

After working for a small manufacturing company for four years, Monique was promoted from manufacturing director to managing director. Although the company enjoyed an excellent reputation, Monique had realised for some time that the company needed some new and innovative products within the next few years, since competitors were investing heavily in research and development. Many of the managers had been working for the company since it was founded about 20 years previously and regarded Monique as a newcomer who really did not understand how the company worked, although they also realised that Monique was talented both as an engineer and a manager. Nevertheless, Monique did persuade other senior managers to start developing a new strategy based on a more innovative product line. At first, everyone publicly stated that they supported the new initiative; but when the change in strategy began to affect organisational members, there was resistance to the strategy. Some of the managers stated that the company was not in the market for selling 'hi-tech gadgets', but for selling good quality traditional tools. However, most of the managers resisted the change because they did not believe that they had the right experience to develop products using new technologies. Even though Monique had been initially confident in the quality of her staff, she resorted to systematically appointing young engineers from outside in key manufacturing positions to bring about the necessary changes in attitudes.

4.3.3   Enforced choice

We have seen throughout this book the importance of managerial choice – since taking strategic decisions and developing strategy is about managerial choice. However, some organisations have less latitude than others in the strategic options they can choose from – as illustrated in the 'imposed' strategy on the deliberate–emergent continuum of Mintzberg and Waters (1985 – see Book 1). Writers such as Hannan and Freeman (1989) argue that the external environment severely limits managers' choice of strategies – the best that managers can do is to attempt to match their strategies to the constraints of the environment. Economic forces such as exit barriers constrain organisations from leaving unattractive industries; or powerful buyers may force organisations to adopt just-in-time manufacturing. Economic forces are not the only sources of constraint: local or national governments often force public-sector organisations to adopt strategies that they would not normally even consider (such as the restructuring the United Kingdom's National Health Service which many stakeholders, including powerful professional elites, opposed).

4.4   STRATEGY DEVELOPMENT 'PROFILES'

The ways of looking at strategy development pattern processes that we have discussed are complementary – an organisation may have an incremental approach to strategy development, but still be strongly influenced by its culture. Explanations of strategy development processes have been described by many different writers, and Bailey and Johnson (1995) have synthesised these explanations into an integrated model of strategy development. They propose that there are six dimensions of strategy development which correspond to the six areas we have discussed here. These dimensions are labelled:

1   *Planning* – Developing strategies from rational, planning approaches.

2   *Political* – Strategy develops as a result of political interactions between stakeholders.

3   *Incrementalism* – Developing strategies in an incremental manner. Combined with planning, this dimension produces logical incrementalism.

4   *Command* – Strategies are linked to a particularly powerful leader, or to a strong leader's 'vision' or 'mission'.

5   *Cultural* – Strategy develops from the shared mental models of managers, which are influenced by their shared experience.

6   *Enforced choice* – Strategies are imposed on organisations by external forces.

Bailey and Johnson suggest that every organisation can be characterised by the extent to which each of these processes operate. To help to do this, they have developed a 'strategy development profile'. This is illustrated in Box 4.2, which compares the profiles of two different organisations. The nearer the position of a process to the outer edge of the circles in Figures 4.2 and 4.3, the more that process characterises strategy development.

BOX 4.2:   STRATEGY DEVELOPMENT PROFILES FOR TWO DIFFERENT ORGANISATIONS

The example in Figure 4.2 is a common configuration of processes seen within the public sector. The process of strategy development is characterised by the dominant external influence of the environment and by the internal influence of cultural and political forces. This local government division sees its freedom of strategic movement to be severely limited by central government legislation, expectations and financial control.

However, political activity in the form of negotiation and bargaining within the organisation are important factors in issues concerning the implementation of the strategy, for example in the prioritisation of strategic tasks, or in the allocation of financial resources. In fact, in this part of the process the highly influential and deterministic external environment directly impacts on the internal power structure of the organisations. It is those groups who deal with the external environment and who operate as boundary spanners, who attain greatest influence over the operational aspects of the strategy. Controlling externally derived resources and information, it is these groups who could restrict or delay the implementation of the present strategy.

The process of strategy development in this organisation could present substantial problems for change. It appears that what strategic change there is, is dictated by forces outside the organisation and through internal power struggles or political negotiation. Such a combination does not bode well for repositioning strategy if the operating environment were to change rapidly, for example by becoming more competitive. There are however organisations that have faced such circumstances who have appeared to change the processes that drive the strategy within their organisation.

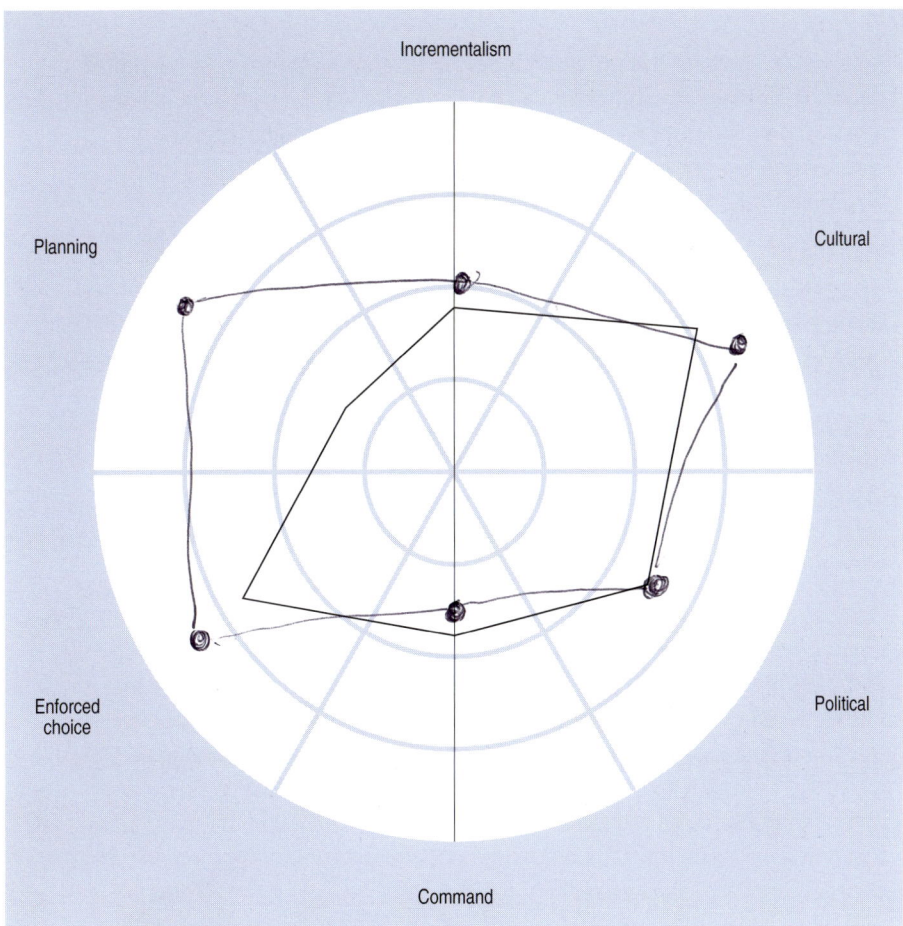

Figure 4.2   Archetypal public-sector organisation

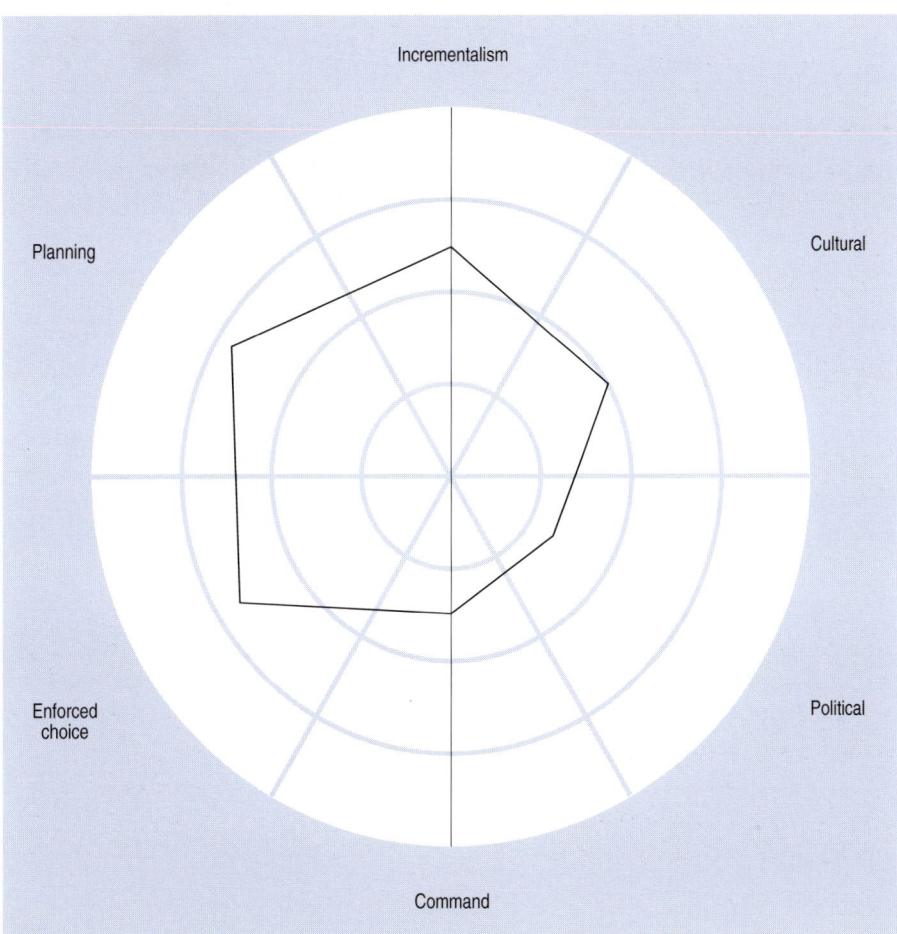

Figure 4.3   Transitional public-sector organisation

Figure 4.3, showing the profile of an organisation in transition between the public and private sector, is an illustration of this. Under these conditions strategy development is perceived to be related to the planning and incremental dimensions though still under the influence of the external environment as depicted by the enforced choice dimension.

In particular, planning is perceived by the organisation's members to be a major influence over the process of strategy development. This is seen to relate particularly to the existence of definite and precise strategic objectives and the assessment of potential strategic options against explicit objectives. However, planning in this instance is seen to be moderated by an adaptive approach to strategy development. New strategies deliberately build on existing strategies, with small continual changes to strategy ensuring that the organisation keeps in line with its operating environment. Indeed strategy is seen to emerge gradually as the organisation adjusts its strategy to match changes in its market place.

Such contrasting patterns from two organisations operating in a similar environment pose interesting questions. Do the forces shown to be dominant in the transitional organisation represent what the members feel are the forces which will facilitate a smooth transition into the private sector, rather than a reflection of the processes actually at work? Do the organisation's members perceive that with an archetypal planning process in place any potential problems associated with transition can effectively be planned out: that planning somehow diminishes the cultural and political forces so typical of public sector organisations?

(Bailey and Johnson, 1995)

Reflection

Which of the six dimensions of strategy development best characterise your own department's or organisation's approach to strategy development? Remember that you can characterise departments or organisations by more than one dimension.

As Box 4.2 illustrates for public-sector organisations, you can probably point to a number of influences on the strategy development processes that operate in your department or organisation. As you will see later in this course, organisational structure and systems (Books 7 and 9) controls the type, as well as the strength of organisational culture and politics (Book 8). These can all influence the formation, choice and implementation of strategies.

5 STRATEGIC THINKING

So far in this book, we have examined the nature of the strategy process and how to adapt the process to differing circumstances – whether through political action, using the most appropriate leadership style, or building organisational culture through symbolic action. We have emphasised the role of choice in many areas of the strategy process – not least in strategic decision-making. Also, we have emphasised the importance of mental models. All this implies that one core area of the strategy process is the mental activity of strategists. We now return to the area of strategic thinking.

Read the chapter by Daniels and Henry, 'Strategy: a cognitive perspective', in the Course Reader.

Daniels and Henry look at many areas of mental processes that are relevant to how individual managers approach strategic issues. They draw attention to the distinction between bottom-up and top-down processing and the importance of mental models. Developing suitable mental models is an important issue in strategic thinking, since this helps decision-making in some circumstances. Top-down processing is not appropriate in every circumstance for example. In some contexts, such as where the environment is static and there is time to consider the issue carefully, bottom-up processing might be a useful substitute. Other contexts do require the application of top-down processing, despite the risks of cognitive bias. Daniels and Henry suggest that discussions with colleagues may help to overcome such bias – this is why strategic decisions are often taken by 'boards' or 'top teams'.

Daniels and Henry draw attention to different styles of learning, creativity, problem-solving and decision-making. They consider that different cognitive styles are suited to strategic thinking in different circumstances. For example, creative cognitive styles, such as the 'innovator' or 'diverger' styles, may be more suited to rapidly changing situations that require quick thinking.

Although they mention the role of collective experience in developing mental models and the importance of discussions to avoid cognitive bias, Daniels and Henry concentrate on individual cognitive processes. However, strategic thinking occurs in a social context – strategists rarely act alone. For example, managing strategy involves forming coalitions, anticipating the objectives and intentions of others and crafting the cultural context of an organisation. Strategic thinking is more than just selecting the right mental model or cognitive style, it is about being 'heedful' of the actions and mental models of others (Weick and Roberts, 1993).

In her interview, Anne Huff reflects on the importance of strategic thinking as an individual and a collective social activity. She considers how diverse mental models can be combined into a 'collective mind' that guides the strategy process within an organisation, but also warns against the danger of 'groupthink': of becoming uncritically collective.

Now listen to the audio track by Anne Huff on strategic thinking. (AC1 Side 1)

6 ORGANISATIONAL LEARNING

In Section 5, we saw the importance of learning and expertise in developing appropriate mental models and insight. Indeed, part of the popularity of post-experience management courses, such as the MBA, is that they both enable managers to learn from the experience of others and give a framework within which managers can learn more from their own experiences. An organisation that can learn from its past mistakes and successes is likely to perform much better than an organisation in which no learning takes place. Organisations that learn more successfully than others are likely to build more capabilities and a greater store of tacit knowledge (Book 4). In this section, we shall look at organisational learning in more detail.

The term 'organisational learning' is, strictly speaking, false: organisations cannot learn – only people can learn. Walsh and Ungson (1991) consider that there are six sources of information within an organisation from which people can learn. Together, they call these six sources 'organisational memory'. These six components of organisational memory are:

1   *Culture* – Stories of organisational heroes, organisational symbols, shared behaviours and mental models are all sources of information which organisational members can use to guide their actions. For example, a story about entry into a foreign market contains information that may be useful for other international marketing activities.

2   *Transformations* – The process through which a product is made or a service delivered contains information that organisational members can copy. For instance, the process of repairing a photocopier contains information that development engineers can build into new photocopiers.

3   *Structures* – Each part of an organisation contains specialist knowledge. For instance, a planning department may contain predictions of future economic or political trends. This information may be available to other departments to help in planning their activities.

4   *Ecology* – The physical layout of offices and work places reflects information about the status of particular individuals or departments, and the relationships among them. For instance, two business units situated close to each other may reflect their dependence upon each other in a horizontal strategy.

5   *External archives* – This refers to information that is either publicly available (such as audit reports) or the personal recollections of former organisational members.

6   *Individuals* – People within an organisation have their own knowledge and mental models. They can communicate this knowledge to others – either verbally or through their actions.

Managers can use each of these sources of information to stimulate their own learning – or the learning of other organisational members. In some cases, the aspects of organisational memory are observable to outsiders –

so managers can learn by observing organisations that have pioneered certain processes such as total quality management. As organisational members draw upon these sources of information, an organisation can appear 'to learn' as people acquire new skills and information.

Of the six aspects of organisational memory, watching the actions of individuals may be the most important for organisational learning (Laland, 1993). Senior managers in one company may learn by closely watching the mistakes and successes of a competitor company. Within an organisation, individuals learn from each other. If one person does something that improves performance, others may begin to copy that person – either because they wish to improve their own performance, or because the new behaviour is rewarded and valued by key stakeholders. In this way, new routines may develop in an organisation that improve its performance. Other organisations may not be able to copy these routines, since they may be invisible to them, or only have been able to emerge from the context of one organisation, in which case the routines become a distinctive capability.

Box 6.1 illustrates 'organisational learning' by a number of people imitating the behaviour of one individual.

BOX 6.1: AN EXAMPLE OF 'ORGANISATIONAL LEARNING'

James worked as a commissioning editor at a publisher, specialising in technical material. Unlike other commissioning editors in the industry, James believed he had a duty to ensure the best deal for authors. James quickly got a reputation amongst authors, who became more likely to approach James than others. This allowed James to choose the best manuscripts available, without having to chase people. Seeing his success, other commissioning editors at James' organisation began to seek similar deals for authors in their specialisms. As a result, the publisher developed a distinctive reputation for high-quality technical books.

Although senior[4] managers can set umbrella strategies and reward those behaviours that they desire the organisation to learn, for something to give advantage it must be specific to the organisation and competitors must not be able to copy it. As we suggested in Book 1, therefore, the knowledge distributed by management writers and academics is available to everyone. For such knowledge to potentially provide advantage, the learner must tailor it to his/her own organisation's context. Therefore, one of the paradoxes of 'organisational' learning is that it is often *emergent,* peculiar to that organisation's context.

Hampden-Turner (1993) has suggested that organisations can use the emergent properties of organisational learning to their advantage in forming strategy. He suggests that managers should develop and alter deliberate strategies as new information emerges from the implementation of such strategies. Over time, managers craft strategy incrementally by combining deliberate and emergent strategies. Hampden-Turner argues that emergent strategy without deliberate strategy leads to a situation where strategists no longer have control over the organisation. He also argues that deliberate strategy without emergent strategy will fail, since people will not implement a strategy without changing it to suit their own objectives and circumstances.

Activity 6.1

Read the following description of organisational learning among three competitors. In which organisations did organisational learning emerge to influence the formation of deliberate strategy? How did this happen?

COMPETITION AND INNOVATION AMONGST THREE MANAGEMENT CONSULTANCIES

In one sector of the management consultancy industry, the competitors were aware that innovation in the services offered had become the most important way to secure competitive advantage – the success of some of their rivals indicated as much. Within this sector, three different competitors set out to improve their innovation – each starting from a different point.

AOE had always prided themselves on their specialism in public-sector organisations – an area that had traditionally not sought innovative services. But, with changes in the public sector, this was no longer the case. AOE sought to expand its product range by developing staff and by selectively recruiting outsiders from more innovative consultancies who were sympathetic to AOE's focus on the public sector. Both these strategies enabled AOE to retain its traditional focus.

French and Partners had recent competitive success by aggressive acquisition of smaller competitors. It was not too surprising that French and Partners decided to engage in 'head-hunting' to 'buy in' innovative consultants. However, swamped by a much larger surrounding culture of success by aggressive acquisition, the new recruits failed to deliver on their potential.

Avia Consultants had for a long time been leaders in their market niche, but performance had begun to slide, despite high quality staff. Avia's senior partners decided that, on the basis of past successes, Avia's human resources were capable of becoming more innovative – if given the right incentives. Despite much persuading and some forcing, Avia's middle managers were not interested in changing their approach to business. Then, by chance, two new managers were recruited to high profile projects. These managers brought with them fresh approaches to old problems. On seeing new possibilities, the old managers began to seek out advice from the new recruits. More importantly, Avia realised that if it wanted to become more innovative, it needed more high-profile new recruits.

In neither AOE nor French and Partners did organisational learning emerge to influence the formation of deliberate strategy. In AOE's case, concentrating on the public sector had been successful in the past, and was likely to be successful in the near future. Consultants at AOE did not need to evolve radically new mental models – a slightly new innovative approach (learnt through training and the example of new recruits) may have been enough. French and Partners had come to associate aggressive acquisition with organisational success. They tried to repeat this by 'acquiring' innovative consultants. However, what works in one context may not work in another.

Avia learned through a process that was emergent. An unintended effect of recruiting two new managers to high-profile positions was that innovative new ideas became attractive to middle managers who had resisted change. The senior partners soon realised that they could help to bring about the necessary change by adopting a deliberate policy of recruiting more new managers. Avia's case illustrates Hampden-Turner's point that managers can learn from emergent strategies and blend them into deliberate strategies. However, the degree to which managers can combine the lessons learnt from emergent strategy into a deliberate strategy is clearly dependent upon the circumstances. For example, an organisation may not have time to wait for lessons to be learnt from emergent strategies. As we have seen, organisations may be forced into action by government legislation, changes in competition or other environmental forces ('hypercompetition').

Avia's case also illustrates the importance of rethinking mental models during organisational learning. Managers at AOE and French and Partners did not rethink their mental models – they modified their mental models slightly on the basis of their recent experience. This is known as *single-loop learning* (Argyris and Schon, 1978). Managers at Avia re-evaluated their mental models (which implied that internal development could bring more innovation) and changed these mental models in the light of the emergent successes of the newly recruited managers. This is known as *double-loop learning* (Argyris and Schon, 1978).

Single-loop learning (see Figure 6.1) is about changing the content of our mental models incrementally by adding information. In single-loop learning we learn directly from the consequences of our actions or the actions of others, but do not radically alter our mental models. In double-loop learning (see Figure 6.2), we reflect on the nature of our mental models that are guiding our actions, and revise them in a more radical manner. One important consequence of double-loop learning is that organisations are less likely to experience strategic drift, since the mental models that cause drift are constantly being re-evaluated and changed.

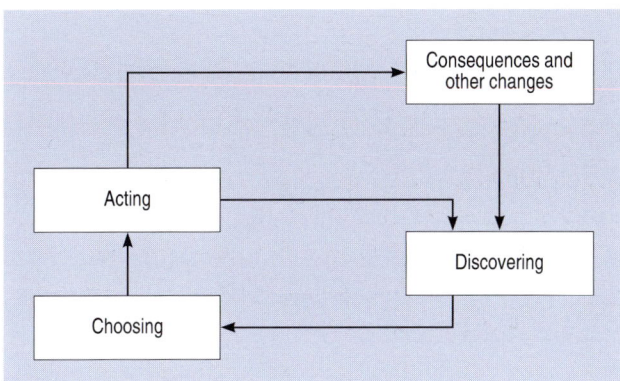

Figure 6.1   Simple single-loop learning

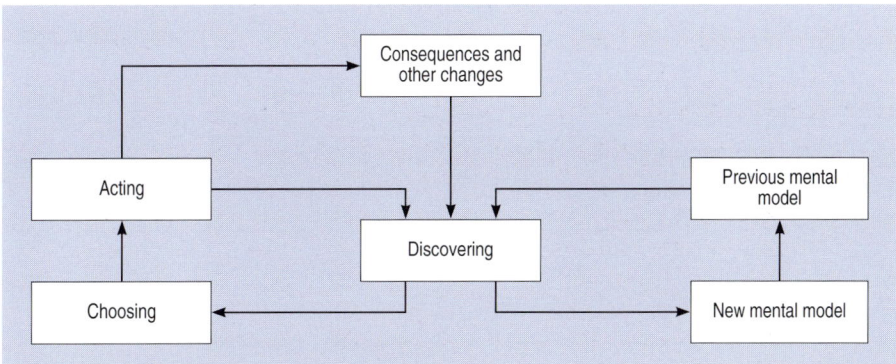

Figure 6.2   Complex double-loop learning

6.1   FROM ORGANISATIONAL LEARNING TO THE LEARNING ORGANISATION

All organisations learn to a greater or lesser degree. However, some organisations promote learning more than others, and these are often promoted as 'learning organisations'. Learning organisations seek to promote learning at all levels in the organisation in an attempt to benefit from greater organisational capability. Senge (1992) thinks that learning organisations are characterised also by the 'personal mastery' of their members. By personal mastery Senge means the ability to examine your own mental models to engage in double-loop learning.

We have already seen that individual learning is an active process. Learning organisations (Jones and Hendry, 1994) encourage active individual learning by:

- providing greater access to training for organisational members
- using participative management and flat organisational structures
- involving people at all organisational levels in the strategy process to create a shared strategic vision.

How can strategists encourage an organisation to become a learning organisation? Schein (1992) believes that it is possible to develop a 'learning culture' within organisations and that it is the responsibility of senior managers to encourage such a culture. So what then is a learning culture? Schein believes that the learning culture consists of the following *attitudes* and *beliefs*, shared by organisation members:

- The environment does not force strategic choices upon the organisation – the organisation can influence its strategic environment.
- Senior managers should encourage organisation members to solve problems proactively.
- Senior managers and experts can be questioned by other organisation members.
- Senior managers trust people within the organisation.
- There is no one best way of working. Sometimes it is best to work individually, sometimes it is best to work in groups.
- People look to the future, both the near future and the far future.
- Everyone must be able to speak to everyone else – communicating information is important for organisational success.
- Diversity in the organisation is good, provided everybody communicates with each other.
- The strategic and organisational environments are complex and difficult to analyse.

Schein believes such a culture would encourage people to experiment and to be open about their successes and failures, thus allowing solutions to *emerge* from organisation members.

Reflection

Think about Schein's recommendations. Which two are most appropriate for your department or organisation?

Whether every part of Schein's learning culture is appropriate for every organisation is open to question. Organisational learning is important for a range of issues but, for us, the most important aspect of organisational learning is that it can help managers to develop strategy. Learning must be an inherent part of the strategy process. Experience with each part of the strategy process enhances managers' mental models of managing strategy. Reflective strategists will try to revise their mental models frequently, using double-loop learning to challenge their assumptions. In so doing, strategists may learn to adapt strategy processes and their leadership style to suit changing circumstances. The ability to draw upon many styles may then be a source of advantage, leading to improved performance, growth and stakeholder satisfaction (Hart, 1992).

7 SUMMARY AND CONCLUSION

We have suggested that the context in which strategy is made influences the nature of the strategy process. Context refers to both the internal organisational environment and the external industrial and institutional environment, within which strategists have to develop strategies. Context is important to many of the concepts and ideas we have discussed in this book. For example:

- The ordering of strategic analysis, choice and implementation will depend on the context of the organisation.
- Balancing the need for careful consideration against speed in the strategy process is dependent upon context – some organisations have more time than others.
- How strategic decisions are taken, and whether strategies are deliberate or emergent depends very much on context.
- The development and appropriateness of strategies and configurations of strategy development styles, is dependent upon context.
- It is important to develop the right cultural context to encourage organisational learning.
- The appropriateness of 'top-down' or 'bottom-up' thinking, or different cognitive styles, depends upon the context within which strategic issues have to be diagnosed.
- Using different strategy development processes can help strategists to cope with changing contexts.

The first six books in this course have been concerned mainly with *generic* aspects of strategy. In many places the importance of context has been highlighted. Now that you have a broad appreciation of the nature of strategy, strategic analysis, innovation and strategy process, over the next four books you will develop your knowledge of strategy in different contexts.

NOTES

1 You may have noticed the term 'forming strategy' used in this paragraph. Elsewhere, people talk about strategy *formulation*. There is a distinction between the terms. *Formulation* implies a conscious and proactive attempt to plan a strategy, perhaps by using the tools discussed earlier in the course. Strategy *formation* implies that strategies can happen for many reasons, not just by planning, as we will see later in this book. Some writers on strategy use the term strategy *development*, which is the same as strategy *formation*.

2 We saw in Book 1 that strategy can have many levels – corporate, business or internal unit (departmental). Many of the concepts in this book can be applied to departmental, business and corporate levels of strategy. Therefore, many of the activities can be applied either to your organisation or department – whichever is more suitable.

3 *Political strategy formulation* refers to the procedures that are available to help managers use power and influence to secure decisions. *Political strategy formulation* can be incorporated into the wider processes of formulating or forming strategy at department, business or corporate level.

4 Senior managers can help their organisations to 'learn' new routines in two ways. They can lead by example – senior managers are very prominent organisational members and others tend to copy their behaviour, believing their behaviour to be appropriate. Senior managers can also reward those who initiate new routines, encouraging others to copy them.

REFERENCES

Argenti, J. (1980) *Practical Corporate Planning*, New York, Allen and Unwin.

Argyris, C. and Schon, D. (1978) *Organisational Learning: a theory of action perspective*, Reading MA, Addison-Wesley.

Bailey, A. and Johnson, G. (1995) 'The processes of strategy development', in J.L. Thomspon (ed.), *The CIMA Handbook of Strategic Management,* Oxford, Butterworth Heinemann.

Chandler, A.D. (1962) *Strategy and Structure: chapters in the history of the American industrial enterprise*, Cambridge MA, MIT Press.

Cyert, R.M. and March, J.G. (1963) *A Behavioral Theory of the Firm*, Englewood Cliffs, NJ, Prentice-Hall.

D'Aveni, R.A. (1995) 'Coping with hyper competition: utilising the new 7S's framework', *Academy of Management Executive,* Vol. 9, pp. 45–60.

Daniels, K., Johnson, G. and de Chernatony, L. (1994) 'Differences in managerial cognitions of competition', *British Journal of Management*, 5, S21–S29.

Eccles, A. (1993) *Succeeding with Change*, London, McGraw Hill.

Hampden-Turner, C.M. (1993) 'Dilemmas of strategic learning loops', in J. Hendry, G. Johnson and J. Newton (eds), *Strategic Thinking: leadership and the management of change*, Chichester, Wiley.

Hannan, M.T. and Freeman, J.H. (1989) *Organisational Ecology*, Cambridge, MA, Harvard University Press.

Hart, S.L. (1992) 'An integrative framework for strategy-making processes', *Academy of Management Review*, Vol. 17, pp. 327–51.

Hickson, D., Butler, R., Cray, D., Mallory, G. and Wilson, D. (1986) *Top Decisions: strategic decision making in organisations*, Oxford, Blackwell.

Johnson, G. (1988) 'Rethinking incrementalism', *Strategic Management Journal*, Vol. 9, pp. 313–27.

Johnson, G. and Scholes, K. (1993) *Exploring Corporate Strategy: text and cases* (3rd edn), London, Prentice Hall.

Jones, A.M. and Hendry, C. (1994) 'The learning organisation: adult learning and organisational transformation', *British Journal of Management*, Vol. 5, pp. 153–62.

Kotter, J.P. and Schlesinger, L.A. (1979) 'Choosing strategies for change', *Harvard Business Review*, March–April.

Laland, K.N. (1993) 'The mathematical modelling of human culture and its implications for psychology and the human sciences', *British Journal of Psychology*, Vol. 84, pp. 145–70.

Langley, A. (1990) 'Patterns in the use of formal analysis in strategic decisions', *Organisation Studies*, Vol. 11, pp. 17–45.

Langley, A., Mintzberg, H., Pitcher, P., Posanda, E. and Saint-Macary, J. (1995) 'Opening up decision-making: the view from the black stool', *Organisation Science*, Vol. 6, pp. 260–79.

Langley, A. (1988) 'The roles of formal strategic planning', *Long Range Planning,* Vol. 21, No. 3, pp. 40–50.

Lindblom, C.E. (1959) 'The science of muddling through', *Public Administration Review, Vol.* 19, pp. 79–88.

MacMillan, I.C. (1978) *Strategy Formulation: political concepts*, St Paul, MN, West Publishing.

Mintzberg, H. and Waters, J.A. (1985) 'Of strategies, deliberate and emergent', *Strategic Management Journal,* Vol. 6, pp. 257–72.

Mintzberg, H. and Waters, J.A. (1990) 'Does decision get in the way?', *Organisation Studies,* Vol. 11, pp. 1–6.

Mintzberg, H. (1983) *Power In and Around Organisations*, Englewood Cliffs, NJ, Prentice Hall.

Mintzberg, H. and McHugh, M. (1985) 'Strategy formulation in an adhocracy', *Administrative Science Quarterly,* Vol. 30, pp. 167–97.

Mintzberg, H., Raisinghani, O. and Theoret, A. (1976) 'The structure of unstructured decision processes', *Administrative Science Quarterly,* Vol. 21, pp. 246–75.

Morgan, G. (1986) *Images of Organisation*, Beverley Hills, Sage.

Noel, A. (1989) 'Strategic cores and magnificent obsessions: discovering strategy formation through daily activities of CEOs', *Strategic Management Journal* (special issue), Vol. 10, pp. 33–50.

Pettigrew, A. and Whipp, R. (1991) *Managing Change for Competitive Success*, Oxford, Blackwell.

Pettigrew, A. (1990) 'Studying strategic choice and strategic change: a comment on Mintzberg and Waters: "Does decision get in the way?"', *Organisation Studies,* Vol. 11, pp. 1–6.

Quinn, J.B. (1980) *Strategies for Change: Logical Incrementalism*, Homewood, IL, Homewood.

Schein, E.H. (1992) *Organisational Culture and Leadership* (2nd edn), San Francisco, Jossey Bass.

Senge, P.M. (1992) *The Fifth Discipline: the art and practice of the learning organisation*, London, Century Business/Doubleday.

Simon, H.A. (1957) *Administrative Behavior*, New York, The Free Press.

Simon, H.A. (1977) *The New Science of Management Decision*, New York, Prentice Hall.

Stalk, G. (1988) 'Time – the next source of competitive advantage', *Harvard Business Review,* July–August, pp. 41–51.

Walsh, J.P. and Ungson, G.R. (1991) 'Organisational memory', *Academy of Management Review,* Vol. 16, pp. 57–91.

Weick, K.E. and Roberts, K.H. (1993) 'Collective mind in organisations: heedful interrelating on flight decks', *Administrative Science Quarterly,* Vol. 38, pp. 357–81.

ACKNOWLEDGEMENTS

Grateful acknowledgement is made to the following sources for permission to reproduce material in this book:

Text

Pages 9–10: Reprinted by permission of *Harvard Business Review*. From 'Time – the next source of competitive advantage, by Stalk, G.', July–August, 1988. Copyright 1988 by the President and Fellows of Harvard College; all rights reserved; *Boxes 3.1; 3.2 and 3.3:* Hickson, D. J., Butler, R. J., Cray, D., Mallory, G. R. and Wilson, D. C. 1986, *Top Decisions: Strategic decision-making in organizations*, Basil Blackwell Ltd; *Box 4.2:* Bailey, A. and Johnson, G. 'The process of strategy development' in Thompson, J. L., 1995, *The CIMA Handbook of Strategic Management*, Butterworth-Heinemann

Figures

Figures 2.2 and 2.3: Johnson, G. and Scholes, K., 1993, *Exploring Corporate Strategy: texts and cases*, Prentice-Hall International (UK) Ltd; *Figures 4.2 and 4.3:* Bailey, A. and Johnson, G. 'The process of strategy development' in Thompson, J. L., 1995, *The CIMA Handbook of Strategic Management*, Butterworth-Heinemann; *Figures 6.1 and 6.2:* Stacey, R. *Strategic Management and Organisational Dynamics*, Pitman Publishing

Table

Table 2.1: Eccles, A., 1994, *Succeeding with Change: Implementing action-driven strategies*, reproduced with permission of McGraw-Hill

Photographs

Page 16: Courtesy of Popperfoto; *Page 34:* Reproduced by permission of Marks and Spencer Company Archives.

Organisational Capabilities: Structure and Systems

Authors: David Coleman and Eric Cassells

CONTENTS

1 INTRODUCTION

In Book 7 we examine the structural aspects of organisations and how these interact with strategy. Our approach, although treating organisational structure and systems at times separately, regards them as fundamentally integrated. Indeed, they also need to be seen in conjunction with *culture* and *power*, which are covered in greater depth in Book 8.

Often, when thinking about structure, the first thing that comes to mind is the organisation chart. But structure means more than the organisation chart or organigram. By structure, we mean the way the boundary around the organisation is drawn, and all the ways in which the activities of the organisation are divided up and then co-ordinated: the definition of individual positions and groupings; the extent of centralisation or decentralisation; and the degree of formalisation, etc.

Systems involve the types and flows of information used for planning, decision-making, co-ordination and control – especially those with significance for strategy. While these include formal systems, informal ways of passing information will also be important, as you will perhaps recall from your earlier studies of Mintzberg's (1980) ten managerial roles (and will certainly know from your own experience!).

One way of distinguishing structure from systems is to think of a house: the bricks, beams and floors are parts of the structure, while the systems include the heating, drainage and ventilation.

To study this book you need:
    Course Reader
    Set Book

1.1 LEARNING OBJECTIVES OF THIS BOOK

In Section 2 we examine a major contribution to the understanding of organisation structure which seeks to integrate a range of internal design features and external influences, and which seeks to go beyond the contingency theory approach.

Systems are addressed in Section 3.

Section 4 reviews the development of thinking about the relationship between strategy, structure and systems. Additionally, recent evidence of the extent of 'restructuring' is discussed.

Section 5 concludes by linking structure, systems and strategy together and by looking forward to the fuller treatment of culture in Book 8.

After studying this book, you should be able to:
- use Mintzberg's framework to identify basic structural components and the overall structural type of an organisation
- specify the contributions that systems and IT can make to strategy formulation and implementation
- recognise types of strategic control
- evaluate restructuring programmes in terms of their strategic merit

- describe the developing interrelationship between strategy, structure and systems as a basis for innovation and advantage
- predict two main trends in the development of new structural forms.

1.2 DIFFERENT CIRCUMSTANCES, DIFFERENT STRUCTURES

It is likely that in your previous studies you have encountered the contrast between the hierarchy structure and the matrix structure. Hierarchies have acquired a bad image – as being synonymous with 'bureaucracy' (which has become a pejorative term denoting rigidity and demotivation). Yet in the right, stable circumstances they can deliver a product or service efficiently and consistently: think of railways or banks. In changing environments, however, their rigidities count against them. A senior manager in a state corporation in Taiwan which is being prepared for privatisation recently waved expansively across his department in which rows of clerks stretched into the distance, each column with a section chief at its head like a human tableau of the organisation chart. 'This organisation is like one of those Chinese dragons', he said, 'you tweak the tail and 30 minutes later the head figures out something happened'. Increasingly, organisations searching for advantage from structure are seeking to escape from such problems of hierarchy by moving to other types of organisational structure such as the matrix.

Yet matrix structures are themselves often not the answer. Difficulties arise from increasing complexity as two, three or even more dimensions create confusion and stress in the managers seeking to build and implement strategies within them. New variants of matrix structures are emerging, as well as wholly new types of structure which we shall discuss in Section 4.

Burns and Stalker (1961) drew on the metaphor of the distinction between a machine and an organism to describe two perceived types of system: 'mechanistic' systems of management (appropriate for stable conditions) and 'organismic' systems (suitable for changing conditions). This is an example of what is known as the 'contingency' view: that factors such as external environment or production technology determine the form of organisational structure. In this view, the organisation is virtually passive in the adoption of a structure contingent on its circumstances. We shall explore this view, and others, before ending with a more proactive position. Indeed, the proposition underpinning this book is that organisations consciously design structures and systems to provide a basis for competitive advantage:

> Ultimately, there may be no long-term sustainable advantage except the ability to organise and manage. ...This action requires organisational learning and flexibility – in short, the development of organisational capabilities.
>
> *(Galbraith and Lawler, 1993, p. 3)*

1.3 REACHING FOR NEW STRUCTURES

We conclude this introduction with a mini-case to give you an opportunity to grapple with the issues of structure, systems and strategy. ABB is a much-admired European multinational. In 1996, for the third year in succession, it was voted Europe's most respected company in a

Financial Times survey. The article, featured as a mini-case below, describes the situation five years after ABB's formation by merger.

MINI-CASE: 'ABB MANAGERS STRIP FOR ACTION'

Since 1988, when Mr Percy Barnevik led Sweden's Asea engineering and robotics group into a merger with the venerable but flagging Swiss power engineering group Brown Boveri, the new ABB Asea Brown Boveri has hardly paused for breath.

But a new streamlined management structure unveiled by Mr Barnevik yesterday suggests that this uniquely multinational industrial group could move even faster in the future.

In the past five years, ABB has acquired some 60 companies all over the world, some of them, such as Combustion Engineering in the US, huge.

It has also marched boldly into eastern Europe, buying up rundown engineering companies and successfully injecting western management techniques. More recently, it has focused on fast growing Asian markets for its heavy infrastructure products.

Along the way, ABB managers have closed dozens of plants and, since the spring of 1990, eliminated more than 40,000 jobs. The group's non-recurring charges typically run at over $100m a year.

But it now can claim that its $32bn in annual sales are spread fairly evenly among the world's three main economic regions, whereas at the outset it was active mainly in European markets. It also claims to be the world's largest power engineering group whereas Asea and Brown Boveri were marginal players.

However, it is not only ABB that has changed. As Mr Barnevik observes, the creation of huge, rather protectionist, regional trading blocs has happened with surprising speed. The economic integration of central and eastern European countries into the European bloc is also proceeding apace. And the elimination of protectionist barriers between western European countries is accelerating.

For a group which produces heavy infrastructure equipment – from power stations to railway locomotives – these changes have a big impact on the way it should conduct its business.

One consequence has been faster growth of large turnkey projects. Developing countries have always tended to purchase infrastructure on a turnkey basis because they did not have the engineering skills themselves. Now developed countries are moving that way as well, as privatised utilities shed the huge in-house design and engineering bureaucracies that flourished under state ownership.

Mr Barnevik recalled yesterday that when ABB was formed, his main objective was to make managers within the group's thousands of operating units more responsible for performance. No fewer than 5,000 Profit centres were established.

The emphasis was on decentralisation and as few layers of middle management as possible.

He still likes those principles, but he and other ABB directors have found that they, and the management structures built to implement them, were not enough for the new environment in which they operate.

ABB managers have been fairly successful in preventing individual ABB companies from competing against each other for business, but they have failed so far to bring together all their resources for making bids on big turnkey projects.

Various group divisions supply most of the technology and equipment needed to build steel rolling mills and pulp and paper mills. However, as the know-how and marketing efforts are dispersed, ABB seldom makes effective bids for large integrated projects.

'We want to facilitate integrated system thinking', Mr Barnevik says. Thus, the power distribution and power transmission divisions are being combined. Most of the 'various activities' division is being put into an industrial plants division.

ABB has so far used the popular matrix management system, under which directors have both regional and line responsibilities. But in the new executive board, this is being simplified, with three directors having only regional responsibilities and four only divisional responsibilities.

Mr Barnevik said some board directors have been choking under the complexity of their responsibilities. The solution will be to push more tasks down to the next layer of management.

It remains to be seen how this will work out in practice. Mr Barnevik made clear that no management consultants had been used in the design of the new structure. 'We have enough management talent here that if we put our heads together, we should not need consultants.'

One thing is certain; the pace of change at ABB will remain brisk. Commenting on the group's decision to provide $500m for plant closures this year, Mr Barnevik said he was unhappy having to put large sums into the profit and loss account every year for non-recurring costs. 'A group like ours will have to live with restructuring as a normal part of its business. So we are doing this big move now, and then I hope to get out of the habit of reporting non-recurring costs.'

Asked what he thought an acceptable annual level of unhighlighted restructuring costs might be, he replied, 'about 1 per cent of invoicing'.

(*Source:* Financial Times, *25 August 1993*)

Activity 1.1

On the basis of your reading of the mini-case on ABB above, address the following questions:

How would you assess the external environment in which ABB operates?

What are the key elements of ABB's overall strategy?

What functions do the structure and systems need to perform?

How successfully do they do this?

Discussion

The environment is changing rapidly and unpredictably, with the development of trading blocs, European integration, privatisation, and growth in Asian markets. These have big implications for ABB, notably in ABB's need to tackle big, 'turnkey' projects.

The key elements of the strategy are: to become a larger player with a presence inside each of the trading blocs; to grow rapidly by acquisition; to respond to local needs through extensive decentralisation, yet at the same time to create 'integrated systems thinking'.

The structure and systems particularly need: to facilitate integrated systems thinking in a decentralised organisation, in which profit centres, geographically, culturally and technically distant, come together to win and deliver major projects; to permit continual restructuring, including simultaneous acquisition and 'downsizing'; to 'live with restructuring as a normal part of business.' Matrix structures are being modified.

ABB does not do this very successfully yet, according to Mr Barnevik. The structure has reduced internal competition, but has not yet found a satisfactory solution for harnessing collaboration across a decentralised structure.

The mini-case demonstrates well the dilemmas involved in designing a structure for an emerging multinational in a fast-changing environment. If ABB can pull this off, its structure and systems will potentially be sources of real advantage.

A large chemicals company which is highly decentralised recently encountered a similar dilemma. Individual operating locations buy large quantities of feed stocks, often from the same suppliers (who have become adept at spreading their most advantageous deals secured at one of the company's locations to all other locations). What should the chemical company's response be?

One possibility would be to ignore this – to take the benefits of decentralisation and ignore the downside. The trouble is that, dealing with really large and powerful suppliers, this is very expensive. An alternative would be to centralise purchasing – but this is cumbersome and negates the speed and flexibility of decentralisation. In fact, this company, like ABB, is developing a way of co-operating between the decentralised locations, by forming *ad hoc* negotiating teams to front discussions with major suppliers, combined with an information network showing who uses which supplier. Apart from occasional team-building activities and the development of a shared negotiating approach, the resulting network never meets collectively. No one knows whether it will work; as in ABB, it is a question of 'feeling your way'.

Both examples illustrate the importance of structure and systems in strategy.

2 STRUCTURAL COMPONENTS, CONTINGENCIES AND CONFIGURATIONS

2.1 INTRODUCTION

This section is largely based on a highly influential article from a classic work on organisation structure by Henry Mintzberg (1979) which consolidated all the 'contingency' literature in one model and went beyond contingency to suggest that organisations could to some degree choose their structures. You will be asked to read this article (in the Course Reader) and undertake some activities in order to evaluate his ideas. First it will be useful for you to read the mini-case 'Easton College'.

MINI-CASE: EASTON COLLEGE

Easton College began as a small commercial college serving a local demand for professional, business and secretarial courses. There were 34 teaching staff, about equally divided between two departments. The heads of these two departments reported directly to the college principal. The bursar, who also reported to the principal, ran a small department which dealt with routine administration and reprographics.

Easton College has recently experienced a period of considerable growth during which the number of teaching staff has more than doubled, and the range of courses offered has expanded. The college now competes for students with other educational institutions across the country. Postgraduate management courses and specialist short courses have been developed to meet the needs of large, locally based companies.

The staff of over 90 lecturers is now split into four schools, but they are also members of other groupings: 'discipline units', course development teams, research groups and any number of school and college committees. Whereas the early guiding principle tended to be 'have text book, will teach', staff are now expected to specialise in one discipline. The demand for specialisation stems from the significant changes in the college's portfolio of courses. In order to get approval from the external accreditation bodies, it was necessary to demonstrate a high level of competence amongst the lecturing staff. The staff group as a whole is now more highly qualified; whereas a lecturer with a master's degree used to be the exception, now it is the norm. To meet the increased administrative load which accompanied the expansion in student numbers and courses, greater secretarial assistance is available to all schools and a resource/reprographics department operates.

Activity 2.1 _____

Read the Introduction and Sections I and II of 'The structuring of organisations' by Henry Mintzberg in the Course Reader.

These sections introduce his overall argument, the six basic parts of the organisation and six co-ordinating mechanisms.

Draw a diagram representing the six basic parts of the structure of Easton College.

Add in any co-ordinating mechanisms. If you identify more than one, which do you think is most important?

Discussion _____

On the basis of the information provided, the basic parts would look something like Figure 2.1. (The co-ordinating mechanisms are shown in brackets.)

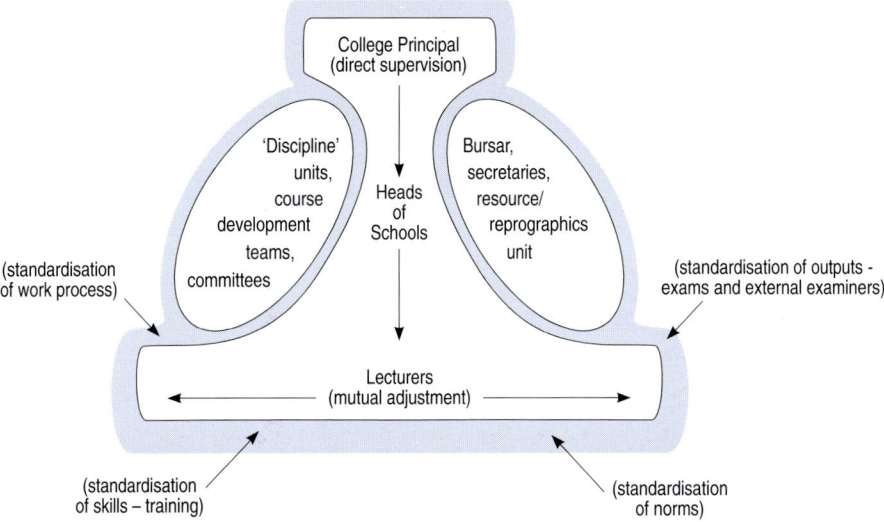

Figure 2.1   The structure of Easton College

Even with such a simple example, complexities begin to show up: lecturers appear both in the operating core and as key members of the technostructure. It seems possible to identify all six co-ordinating mechanisms, although the emphasis on the importance of lecturer qualifications suggests that standardisation of skills is the dominant one. Note also the standardisation of outputs, like skills, drawn on external professional rather than internal standards.

2.2 DESIGN PARAMETERS

Activity 2.2 _____

Now read Section III of the Course Reader article by Henry Mintzberg, 'The structuring of organisations', in which he identifies ten 'design parameters' that have an important influence on organisation structure. They are reproduced below. For each of them, try to identify examples from the Easton College mini-case.

Design parameter	Examples/comments
INDIVIDUAL POSITIONS	
1 Job specialisation	
2 Behaviour formalisation	
3 Training	
4 Indoctrination	
SUPERSTRUCTURE	
5 Unit grouping	
6 Unit size	
LATERAL LINKAGES	
7 Planning and control systems	
8 Liaison devices	
DECISION-MAKING SYSTEM	
9 Vertical decentralisation	
10 Horizontal decentralisation	

Discussion

Here are some ideas.

1 Job specialisation	*Lecturers increasingly 'horizontally' specialised by discipline; vertical enlargement*
2 Behaviour formalisation	*Lecturers required to teach courses to meet external client/examination demands*
3 Training	*Increasingly important for lecturers to be qualified*
4 Indoctrination	*Nothing explicit here; presumably new 'customer' sensitive culture would need to be accepted*
5 Unit grouping	*Four schools, also overlapping with other groupings in technostructure; also administrative support activities*
6 Unit size	*Four large discipline groups*
7 Planning and control systems	*Clear action planning systems in technostructure; performance control systems via principal and committees, also externally via exam results and accreditation*
8 Liaison devices	*A matrix structure and/or task forces in which lecturers lecture and also contribute to discipline units, course development teams, research groups and committees*
9 Vertical decentralisation	*Some decentralisation vertically via heads of schools*

10 Horizontal   *Considerable amount of this in links*
    decentralisation   *between lecturers, technostructure and*
                           support staff?

*The treatment of centralisation/decentralisation is more elaborated
here than in many accounts which just emphasise the trend to
decentralise. This section of Mintzberg's article is summarised in
Table 2.1.*

Table 2.1: Mintzberg's six types of decentralisation

Full centralisation ◄——————————————► Full Decentralisation

Type	I Centralisation	II Limited horizontal decentralisation	III Limited vertical decentralisation	IV Horizontal decentralisation	V Selective horizontal and vertical decentralisation	VI Decentralisation
Power shared by:	Strategic apex only	Strategic apex technostructure	Strategic apex, technostructure, middle line	Operating core	Strategic apex, technostructure, support staff, middle line	All members
Type of decentralisation (selective/ parallel)	None	Selective	Parallel	Parallel	Selective	Both parallel and selective
Co-ordinating mechanism	Direct supervision	Standardisation of work processes	Standardisation of work output	Standardisation of skills	Mutual adjustment	Standardisation of norms

It is interesting to note the range of factors Mintzberg includes in the
design parameters – he includes systems, decision-making and liaison.
Since he also includes ideology as one of the basic parts of the
organisation, this may be viewed as an attempt at an integrated
conceptual approach to structure, systems and organisational design (and
indeed, culture) as part of strategy.

2.3 MINTZBERG'S HYPOTHESES

Activity 2.3 _____

**Now read Section IV of Mintzberg's Course Reader article, on
situational factors.** Which of the hypotheses apply to the Easton College
mini-case?

Discussion _____

*Increasing age and size seem to be leading to more formalisation
(Hypotheses H1 and H2). There is considerable growth in
specialisation (H3) and some in unit size (H4). The technical
system is increasingly formalising the work of the operating core
(H6), and the evidence for increasing complexity supports H7. The
external environment appears to be increasingly dynamic and the*

College's markets becoming diversified (H9, H11). Evidence on power seems insufficient for us to comment.

Activity 2.4 _____

The final part of Mintzberg's Course Reader article concerns the 'pulls' on the organisation exerted by the basic parts, the tendency towards configuration and the six resulting structures.

 Read Section V of the article now.

Which are the dominant parts of the structure, the dominant pull on the organisation and the overall structural type of Easton College?

Discussion _____

The dominant part seems to be the operating core of lecturers, the dominant pull to be to professionalise. Overall it looks like a professional bureaucracy. Yet there are signs of more liaison devices than might be expected in a 'pure' version – perhaps a response to the changing environment?

Mintzberg suggests that, instead of an infinite variety of organisation types, the predominant pull will result in one of six structural types which he labels the simple structure, machine bureaucracy, professional bureaucracy, divisionalised form, adhocracy and missionary. Some characteristics of each are listed in Table 2.2, together with some typical examples.

Table 2.2:	Mintzberg's six ideal structural types					
	Simple structure	**Machine bureaucracy**	**Professional bureaucracy**	**Divisionalised form**	**Adhocracy**	**Missionary**
Key part	Strategic apex	Technostructure	Operating core	Middle line	Support staff	Ideology
Co-ordinating mechanism	Direct supervision	Standardisation of work processes	Standardisation of skills	Standardisation of outputs	Mutual adjustment	Standardisation of norms
Dominant pull to:	Centralise	Standardise	Professionalise	Balkanise	Collaborate	Evangelise
Decentralisation	None (centralised)	Limited horizontal	Horizontal	Limited vertical	Selective horizontal and vertical	Full decentralisation
Planning and control	Little	Action planning	Little	Much performance control	Limited action planning	Little
Liaison devices	Few	Few	In administration	Few	Many throughout	Few
Typical examples	Small owner-manager firms undertaking simple activities, e.g. small shops	Fast food chains; airlines; telephone banking	Hospitals; colleges; law firms	Large conglomerates	Creative advertising agencies; bespoke software boutiques	Kibbutz; Evangelical churches; revolutionary movements

Mintzberg argues that the structures will achieve an internal consistency of design parameters and also a consistency with external contingency factors such as environment and task. The argument goes beyond contingency theory, however:

> ...organisations can select their situations in accordance with their structural designs just as much as they can select their designs in accordance with their situations.
>
> *(Mintzberg, 1979)*

The nature of the internal design parameters and the external contingency factors will have an impact on those who make and implement strategy. We shall develop this relationship between structure and strategy further in Section 4.

2.4 APPLICATION AND EVALUATION

Activity 2.5

Now that you have completed reading the Mintzberg article, return to the ABB mini-case we used for Activity 1.1. On the basis of the information there, how would you classify ABB in terms of overall structural type?

Discussion

From the information in the mini-case, there appears to be strong selective vertical decentralisation, much need for mutual adjustment between operating units and a strong pull to collaborate to deliver 'integrated systems thinking'. The environment is changing rapidly and unpredictably. These are all strong clues for an 'adhocracy'. The modifications to the matrix structure and the references to divisions suggest, however, that there are also some elements of a divisionalised form. We would need to know more about the planning and control systems to be sure. In reality, ABB still seems to be reaching to create its own hybrid form of extreme decentralisation. Mintzberg's types are, after all, 'ideal' types and we should expect reality to be less elegant.

Activity 2.6

Think now about the organisation you work in (or one with which you are familiar) and complete the following tasks:

1   Draw a diagram to represent the basic parts of the structure, and include any co-ordinating mechanisms you can identify.
2   State which of these you consider most important.
3   Identify examples and evidence of the ten design parameters, including the nature of decentralisation.
4   List those of Mintzberg's 16 hypotheses which apply to the organisation.
5   Identify any of Mintzberg's six 'ideal' types to which it approximates.

Activity 2.7

Reflect on Mintzberg's Reader article. How useful do you find it is as a framework for describing and explaining structural differences?

Discussion

Certainly the treatment in terms of basic parts, co-ordinating mechanisms, design parameters, pulls and hypotheses provides a comprehensive framework for description. The detailed treatment of types of decentralisation goes well beyond simple 'centralised/decentralised' discussions we often read about.

The 'configuration' idea of a dominant pull is also persuasive – it seems unlikely that there could be an infinite variety of structural types. From the evidence of our examples it all seems, however, to be an elegant abstraction. The treatment of ideology could be more fully developed since there seem to be different kinds.

In his writing since the Course Reader article was published, Mintzberg has reported some empirical support for the existence of configurations. Organisations in Montreal in Canada were surveyed and classified by Mintzberg's MBA students as follows (Table 2.3).

Table 2.3	
Simple structure	25
Machine bureaucracies	13
Professional bureaucracies	8
Divisionalised	11
Adhocracies	9
Missionary	0
SUB TOTAL	66
Combinations of two or more	57
TOTAL	123
(Mintzberg, 1989)	

Mintzberg's approach provides a comprehensive framework for describing the components of structure. It suggests that, beyond contingency ideas, there is an element of strategic choice in structure and situation. 'Structure' is defined widely to embrace both systems and ideology. Contrasting, say, a simple structure and an adhocracy, it is evident that who is involved in making and implementing strategy and how they do it will be quite different.

2.5 STRUCTURE, SYSTEMS AND ADVANTAGE

We stated in Section 2.1 that the work of Mintzberg, which you have been considering, was a consolidation of the 'contingency' literature. This studies the relationships between organisational structures and design, and underlying variables such as the nature of the environment and the organisational task.

 You should now read the Set Book where Grant discusses structures and designs with a more explicit concern for the economies of structuring. Noticeably, Grant starts Chapter 6 with a quote from Galbraith and

Lawler, which explains our interest in considering structure and systems as an organisational capability:

> Ultimately, there may be no long-term sustainable advantage other than the ability to organize and manage.

> *(Galbraith and Lawler, 1993)*

Now read Chapter 6 of the Set Book on 'Organization structure and management systems'.

Activity 2.8 _____

As a final step, in considering Mintzberg's six structural configurations, try to fill in the spaces in Table 2.4 (we have included culture to prepare you for Book 8).

Table 2.4: Mintzberg's structural configuration: Strategy, Control, Culture and Environment						
	Simple	**Machine bureaucracy**	**Professional bureaucracy**	**Diversified structure**	**Adhocracy**	**Missionary**
Strategy						
Control systems						
Culture						
Environment						
Examples						

How would you position your organisation (or one with which you are familiar) within Table 2.4?

Are any of the dimensions not consistent?

3 STRATEGY AND SYSTEMS

3.1 INTRODUCTION

In this section we focus on the role of systems, to which you were introduced in the Set Book, which provide information for decisions and control at a strategic level.

Empirical evidence on formal systems was provided by Daft and Macintosh (1984) in a study of 86 companies. They found the same six sub-systems, although differing in form and scope, frequently occurring.

For strategy formulation at senior level:

1 *Strategic plans* – Analysis of an organisation's position within the industry, products, competition, economic trends.

2 *Long-range plans* – Typically five-year financial projections.

Management control systems used by middle managers to implement strategy and evaluate performance:

3 *Annual operating budgets* – Estimates of profits, expenses, assets; issued monthly or quarterly, showing variances.

4 *Periodic statistical reports* – Covering headcounts, new orders, delinquent account ratios and similar issues.

5 *Performance appraisal* – Evaluation of the performance of individuals.

6 *Policies and procedures* – Policy guidelines and operating procedures.

Besides the separation between strategic and operational level sub-systems noted above, Daft and Macintosh also found that the systems used by middle managers, although broadly complementary, were not designed in that way. There is, however, a suspicion that their sample may have contained particularly hierarchical organisations with deliberate, planned strategies and clear separation of strategy and implementation.

Systems provide information for strategic analysis and implementation, and are crucial to managing the central dilemma of simultaneous co-ordination and specialisation. Think back to the Benetton example in Book 4, in which Benetton's information systems connected up with many suppliers, enabling Benetton to make rapid changes in response to changing customer tastes. Given the trend towards decentralised structures which deliver speed, but at the risk of fragmentation and duplication, the information systems function (in a manner reminiscent of the body's central nervous system), may provide the means for managing the tension: ABB's 'integrated systems thinking' is a good example.

The range of systems is wider than might be supposed. Band and Scanlan (1995) identify the following:

• structural devices, e.g. internal audits

• management information systems – notably financial reports and decision support tools, including project management

• budget and profit planning processes

- human resource management arrangements, such as recruitment skills development, performance management and the use of incentives
- research and development programmes
- work practices and norms, such as technology support, use of work teams, quality management techniques and provision for innovation
- explicit organisational values
- use of external instruments, such as performance benchmarks, periodic evaluations by consultants.

Note the inclusion of values and human resource management in Band and Scanlan's list. Cultural issues – which we address in Book 8 – interrelate closely with systems and strategy. Human resource systems such as the methods for describing jobs, appraising and rewarding performance, and providing careers for individuals, can either support strategy or undermine it. Imagine the impact of strongly individual financial incentives in a situation where collaborating with others is important. Such contradictions are common in many organisations. The information requirements of different organisation structures are also very different – contrast a strict, formal hierarchy with a freewheeling, lateral 'adhocracy'.

Information technology (IT) has had a major impact on extending the choice of potential organisation structures. One of the benefits of hierarchical structures is the reduction of interfaces between individuals for decision-making and co-ordination. IT systems now permit the multiple interfaces required in a lateral structure through e-mail, computer conferencing, intranets, relational databases and other types of networking. Telecommunications also permit organisations to be location-free: geographical proximity is no longer required. Control systems become increasingly automated through use of IT, with important organisational implications:

> 'With this new technology it is easier for operators to take on a managerial role because we have more data. There are data every few seconds on everything that is going on. Plus, managers don't have to be standing guard over you to find out what's happening. They can come back in 10 days and, from the computer, they can see everything that happened. This eliminates the middleman.'
>
> *(Factory worker, quoted by Zuboff, 1988, p. 265)*

Savage (1990) describes how parallel networked processing units, no longer dependent on a central processing unit, can work simultaneously and interactively on different aspects of the same application.

> This makes it possible for departments to work in parallel: design engineers, manufacturing engineers, and marketing specialists can look at the same drawings, process plans and market projects at the same time, even if they are widely separated in distance.
>
> *(p. 79)*

The purpose of systems is not only to enhance possible strategic directions, but also to co-ordinate and control. Control raises particular issues in strategy, and it is to these that we now turn.

3.2   STRATEGIC CONTROL SYSTEMS

The simplest approach to control in middle management examples is the basic feedback model which tracks performance against a standard and triggers action to correct variance. While this might be suitable for control at operational level, the special nature of strategic control exposes its limitations. Band and Scanlan (1995) summarise these as follows:

- The feedback model does not adequately deal with uncertainty, complexity, change and the lag between formulating strategy and obtaining evidence of its effect, thus reducing its value to organisations which wish to be nimble and innovative.

- The approach is vulnerable to poor specification of objectives, standards and measures, and to false or misleading information arising from inadequate information processing capabilities.

- The approach is vulnerable to errors in interpretation, evaluation, and prescription, since these depend on correct inferences about causality, accurate diagnosis of performance problems, knowledgeable selection of corrective actions, and assumptions about the probability of success in such actions.

- There is a temptation to reduce control to a single measure of performance, such as profitability, or rate of return.

(p. 108)

A strategic control system based solely on feedback mechanisms is therefore likely to be possible only in stable, predictable environments. Another approach to strategic control is based on the idea of 'feedforward' control, in which actions are taken in advance on the basis of prediction and judgement – as would be required in more turbulent environments. Under this approach, control needs to:

> ... subject strategic goals, assumptions, plans and revisions to continuous, searching critique... . To undertake this function effectively, strategic control needs to be pitched at a level which is sufficient to capture the full range of threats, opportunities and contingencies which might bear upon an organisation's strategic choices. It also needs to focus on the future rather than the past.

(Band and Scanlan, 1995, pp. 105–6)

Building on previous theoretical work, Band and Scanlan suggest four types of 'feedforward' control:

1 *Premise control* – Continuous monitoring of the environment to verify prior planning premises such as inflation or interest rate forecasts.

2 *Implementation control* – Identifying and evaluating critical factors and events not foreseen during strategy formulation.

3 *Strategic surveillance* – Monitoring the full range of emerging events which could threaten the course of strategic action.

4 *Special alert control* – Scanning for low-probability, high-impact events such as natural disasters or hostile take-overs.

A more comprehensive approach is advocated by Simons (1995), which uses both feedback and feedforward control and integrates corporate culture. Simons presents empirical evidence for the existence of 'levers' of control based on a study of 50 American corporations over a 10-year period:

1 *Beliefs systems* – These are the explicit values encapsulated in mission statements which inspire and guide the search for and discovery of entrepreneurial opportunities; and which provide a framework within which to take decisions.

2 *Boundary systems* – These indicate the boundaries of the 'acceptable domain of activity'. Codes of conduct and ethical principles (revisited

in Book 8) are common examples of 'business conduct boundaries', while planning documents, mandates and activities which define the scope of its activities are 'strategic boundary systems'.

3   *Diagnostic control systems* – These are the feedback control systems mentioned earlier, such as budgets and project monitoring systems, which should be focused on important dimensions of strategy, such as Key Success Factors.

4   *Interactive control systems* – These stimulate search and learning, permitting new strategies to develop throughout the organisation as individuals respond to perceived opportunities and threats. Here the focus is on strategic uncertainties, and challenging existing assumptions. Scenario planning techniques are a useful example of this type of control system.

In Simons' analysis these four levers of control are in dynamic tension, as shown in Figure 3.1.

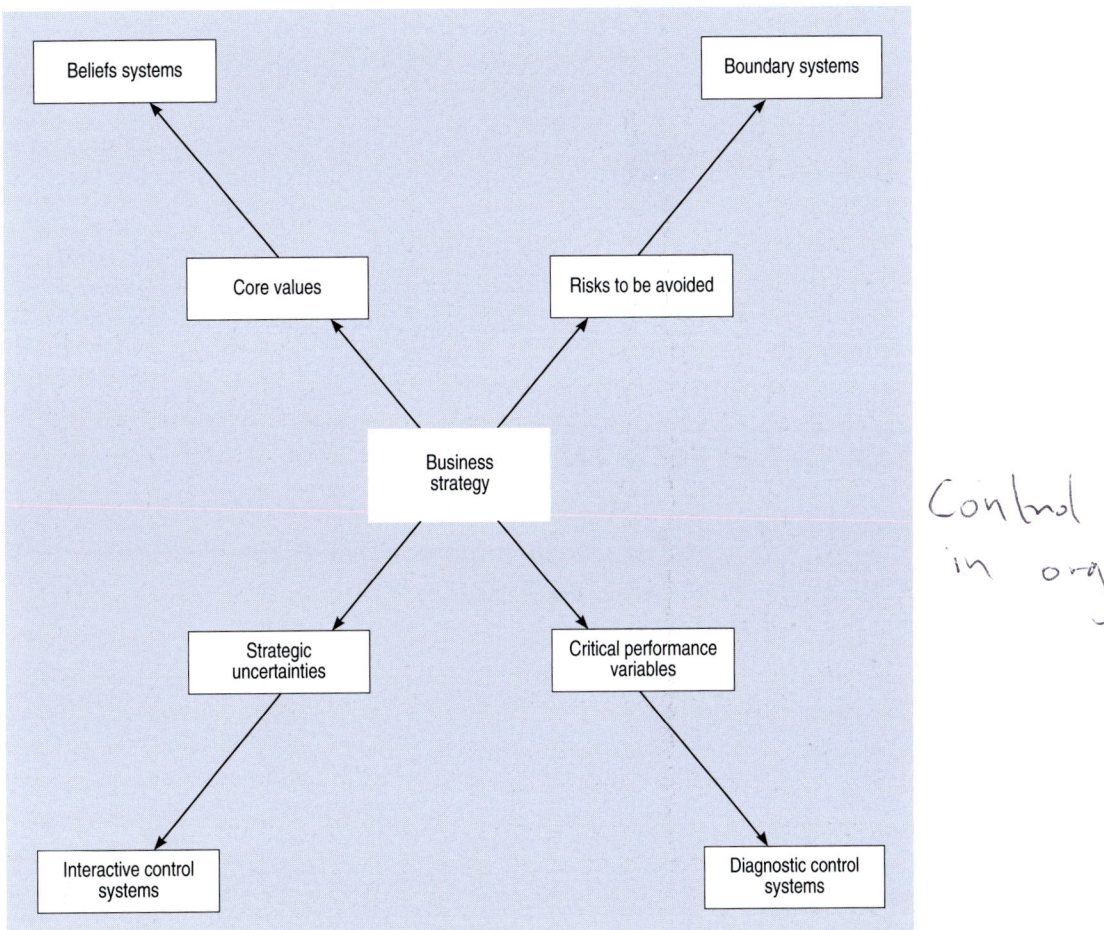

Control system in organisation

Figure 3.1   Basic control levers (Simons, 1995)

Using a simple life-cycle model, Simons shows which of these control systems are used over the life-cycle of the firm (Figure 3.2 overleaf).

There is, however, likely to be resistance to strategic control systems in operation. Lorange and Murphy (1984) concluded that there were three kinds of barriers to effective strategic control; one or more of these are likely to apply in the approaches to control outlined above, and can be summarised as follows:

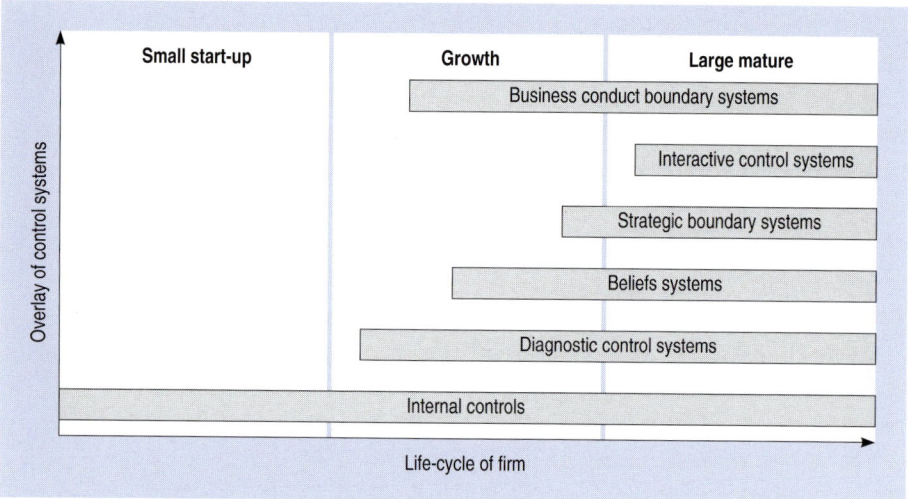

Figure 3.2   Evolution of control systems over firm's life-cycle (Simons, 1995)

- *Systemic barriers* – Arising from deficiencies in the design or management of the control system such as defining adequate performance measures, excessive complexity, reconciling a diversity of variables.

- *Behavioural barriers* – Conventional thinking, corporate culture, cognitive limits to managers' intellectual capacity; fear of being proved wrong.

- *Political barriers* – Difficulties in reaching agreement over direction and resource allocation; political acceptability to key stakeholder groups; unwillingness of managers to report unfavourable results upwards.

3.3   SYSTEMS IN ACTION

Activity 3.2

Read the article in Box 3.1 below.

BOX 3.1   GAINING A HARDER EDGE FROM THE 'SOFT' OPTION

Routinely monitoring 265 aspects of a company's performance might seem excessive. But according to John Hudson, chief executive of the diversified UK engineering business Wagon Industrial, this attention to detail will sort out the winners from the losers in today's manufacturing environment.

Wagon makes industrial goods that are sold to a range of businesses, including car manufacturing, retailing and general distribution and storage. All these industries are operating under highly competitive conditions – brought about by weak economic growth across Europe and a new emphasis on value for money by consumers and industrial customers alike.

'The technology of production machines has moved on as far as it is going to in the foreseeable future,' says Hudson. 'So the one way you are going to make the necessary improvements (in efficiency) is through better organisation.'

Hudson's company is among thousands of businesses addressing these mainly 'soft' management issues in an attempt to stay ahead of the game. At one Wagon subsidiary – its Link 51 UK storage products division which mainly makes warehouse racking – the company monitors 265 variables covering anything from the volume of goods in stock to the time it takes to answer the telephone. The data are used to focus on areas where changes are needed. They provide a direct link between how the company organises itself internally and how it operates in the external marketplace.

[...]

Hudson admits that [in the current economic climate], while the potential for increasing volumes in UK manufacturing is 'as good as I've ever known it', holding up margins 'is very tough'. All the more reason, he suggests, for the new emphasis on the workplace organisation in evidence at Link. This part of Wagon makes products which could hardly be more basic – bits of steel cut and welded into thousands of shapes and sizes which are fitted into position for customers, including warehouse companies, IKEA and B&Q retail outlets, and libraries. Wagon claims a quarter of the UK market for such racking systems – with its main competitor, US-owned Dexion, having a similar share.

According to Neil Hannah, Link's managing director, who is taking over the added responsibility for Wagon's racking activities in continental Europe, the detailed business monitoring at Link enables the company to pick up quickly on areas where it is not meeting customer needs.

With the average Link order value around £1,000, the company is dealing at any one time with perhaps 3,500 customers. It receives up to 1,200 new orders each week.

A close watch is kept on the speed at which customers get their racking. Five years ago, customers would have to wait up to six weeks for a standard product; now, the time is three to four weeks. 'We consider ourselves as much a service company as a manufacturer,' says Hannah. 'We can win business if we say we can deliver next week.'

On phone calls, according to the data, salespeople usually pick up the phone in three seconds while technical operatives take an average of five seconds.

In the factory, Wagon aims at efficient organisation of cutting up the steel pieces and uses computer-aided design to assemble them in the most cost-effective way for fitting in customers' premises. In a strong focus on training, the 670 employees are expected to spend up to 2 per cent of their time in this area.

'Our storage products are physically not fundamentally different from anyone else's,' says Hudson. 'But we can differentiate ourselves from our competitors by changing what happens in our workplace.'

(Source: Financial Times, *28 February 1996*)

Which of Simons' four levers of control are being used here?

Discussion

Primarily diagnostic control systems to track performance variables internally – stock levels, delivery times. Customer monitoring could also provide pointers on strategic uncertainties, providing interactive monitoring.

Note the emphasis in the article on better organisation as the basis for greater efficiency, and the systems of control being used to 'differentiate' Wagon from its competition. Wagon believes that its capabilities in using control systems can be a source of advantage.

Activity 3.3

Consider the strategic information and control systems of your organisation (or one with which you are familiar) and consider the following questions:

- What are the main systems?
- What evidence is there for each of Simons' four levers of control?
- Which of the three barriers to control are evident?
- How effective is strategic control overall?
- Is there any sense in which the organisation's systems capabilities can provide a source of competitive advantage?

4 STRATEGY, STRUCTURE AND SYSTEMS

4.1 STRUCTURE AND SYSTEMS AS ORGANISATIONAL CAPABILITIES

In the introduction to this book, we stated that the proposition of this book is that managers seek out structural forms and systems configurations which might give their organisations some form of competitive advantage. Formal and informal capabilities in structuring activities, which enable the flow of information, build value as knowledge is created or control or co-ordinate strategy implementation, may be a source of distinctiveness between competitors. The more highly developed these capabilities are, the more they may be potential sources of advantage.

This approach to the capabilities of organising is echoed in the work of Miyazaki, who included organisational skills as 'core competences' (akin to capabilities, as discussed in Book 4). In a study of technological innovation in the opto-electronics industry, Miyazaki noted that core competences:

> ... enable firms to survive over long periods. Thus strategy would require not only technological skills but *organisational* manufacturing and marketing skills.
>
> *(Miyazaki, 1995 – emphasis added)*

To understand this, we must explore the relationship between strategy, systems and structures. There is an extensive collection of academic writings which have considered the relationship between strategy and structure. There is less written explicitly about systems, but – as with Mintzberg in Section 2 – most authors adopt wide definitions of structure to embrace systems.

The most famous of these writings is that by Chandler (1962), referred to in the Set Book, who derived the dictum that 'structure follows strategy'. Chandler was a business historian who studied the particular experience of large US corporations in the period from the late nineteenth century. Indeed, a theme of this area of study is the evolution of structures over time, as strategies change.

4.2 STRUCTURAL PROGRESSION

In an early attempt to model the changing strategies and structural progression of organisations, Greiner (1972) developed the idea that organisations typically progressed in a determined way through five phases of 'evolution and revolution', which are summarised in Figure 4.1 overleaf.

Figure 4.1   The five phases of growth (Greiner)

Table 4.1:	Greiner's five phases (summarised from Greiner, 1972)				
Phase	**1 Creativity**	**2 Direction**	**3 Delegation**	**4 Co-ordination**	**5 Collaboration**
Strategy	Setting up, making and selling new product	Organic growth	Growth by acquisition	Top management seek to regain total control over whole company	Building flexible, responsive approach
Organisation structure	Embryonic	Direction by business manager; functional specialisation within hierarchy	Decentralised; top executives focus on acquisitions	Merging of decentralised units into product groups; large central staff units established; some functions, e.g. data processing, centralised	Teams combined across functions in task groups; reduced HQ staffs; matrix structures
Communication	Frequent, informal	Formal and impersonal, hierarchical	Infrequent between top and operating units	Communication between centre and product groups; procedures important	Frequent conferences held to focus on major problem issues
Control	By founder, based on market-place feedback	By business manager via accounting systems	Management by exception	Formal planning procedures established; many bureaucratic paper systems	Real-time information systems; formal systems simplified and combined into multi-purpose systems
Ensuing crisis	Leadership	Autonomy	Control	Red tape	Unknown

Activity 4.1 _____

What parallels do you see between Greiner's five phases and Mintzberg's six structural configurations identified in Section 2?

Discussion _____

The fit is by no means perfect. Phase 1 (Creativity) could be seen as a description of Mintzberg's simple structure. The Direction phase could be thought (through functional specialisation) to describe a machine bureaucracy. The Delegation phase in some respects looks like a divisionalised form which is then followed in the Co-ordination phase by machine bureaucracy. Greiner's Collaboration phase looks to fit well with adhocracy. There is no clear evidence for Mintzberg's professional bureaucracy or missionary organisation.

4.3   SYNTHESISING STRATEGY AND STRUCTURE

Miller (1986), in a pathbreaking article, produced a set of relationships between four of Mintzberg's structural types and types of generic strategies using the frameworks of Porter introduced in Book 5. The article does not provide an explanation of how these evolve, but it is interesting for the attempt to link structure and strategy in terms of 'fit' or configuration rather than strategy demanding a particular structure as argued by Chandler.

Miller sets out to show the close fit between strategy and structure:

> The theme we wish to pursue here is that there are ties that unite strategy and structure; that given a particular strategy there are only a limited number of suitable structures and vice versa.

Miller goes on to identify four dimensions of strategy – differentiation, cost leadership, focus and asset parsimony – which interact to produce five strategic configurations:

A1: niche marketers

A2: innovators

A3: marketers

B: cost leaders

C: conglomerates.

Both theoretical and empirical evidence for the emergence of these relatively stable strategic configurations is presented, and Miller argues that four of Mintzberg's structural configurations may be matched to each of the five strategies:

- simple structures matched to niche marketers (A1)
- adhocratic structures matched innovators (A2) and marketers (A3)
- machine bureaucracies matched to cost leaders (B)
- divisionalised forms matched to conglomerates (C).

Miller's argument does not suggest a one-way causal relationship between strategy and structure as did Chandler, but a more complex interrelationship between these two and other factors:

> ...the appropriateness of a strategy in general, as well as the relative effectiveness of its various elements, will be a function of much more

than structure. It will depend on economic, competitive and customer factors, as well as conditions in international markets.

(Miller, 1986 p. 248)

4.4 STRUCTURE AND THE PURSUIT OF COMPETITIVE ADVANTAGE

Alfred Chandler (1962) is probably best known for the three words 'structure follows strategy', but the insights in his study are much more extensive. He does, for example, identify many of the roles and tasks of the general manager in the development of the corporation – of which we will consider more in Book 9. He also believes that the market and technological changes of the period he studied in the USA drove all organisations towards the same structural responses eventually. The process of structural change, however, is one of organisational innovation, and there are very many responses which managers may choose to make to those market and technological pressures. Chandler (1977) identifies two types of response:

- An *adaptive response* results in structural changes which nevertheless remain within the broad range of existing practice.
- A *creative innovation* goes beyond current custom in structural arrangements.

Both types of response, if they develop an organisation's structuring capabilities, might enhance or create competitive advantage. It is probably in innovative restructuring, however, that the best evidence of structural capability as a source of advantage exists.

The first great structural innovation in the US noted by Chandler was the development of the administrative hierarchy to facilitate the creation of the multifunctional company. The geographical expansion of the US railway companies in the late nineteenth century resulted in the need for functional managers, controlled by an 'administrative command', monitoring, evaluating, co-ordinating and controlling the company's geographically dispersed activities.

Growth of large corporations continued into the early twentieth century, however, and Chandler also examined the multi-divisional innovation introduced by four large corporations – General Motors, Du Pont, Standard Oil of New Jersey (now Exxon), and Sears Roebuck – in response to the difficulties created by this growth.

The case of General Motors is also written up in the memoirs of its Chief Executive, Alfred P. Sloan (1963). General Motors had grown through strategies of brand acquisition (Oldsmobile, Buick, Cadillac, Chevrolet and Pontiac) and volume expansion, under its founder, William Durant. Its many operating units formed an extremely loose federation. The lack of overall control was exposed by a slump in demand in 1920; inventory had grown out of control, product lines proliferated, and there was little accounting or control information available. Over the next five years, Durant's successor, Sloan, created a multi-divisional structure based on the apparent paradox of 'co-ordinated decentralisation' (Sloan, 1963). The chief executives of General Motors' divisions were granted complete operational responsibility and authority, while the general office took responsibility for strategy, policy, resource allocation and overall co-ordination.

The importance of the multi-divisional structural innovation for General Motors' success can be conjectured from its victory over Ford in the battle to become the world's biggest car company. Its great rival had originated the principles of centralised mass production with the introduction of its 'Model T' in 1906. However, the strategic planning to replace the Model T in the 1920s was, to say the least, underdeveloped. In the meantime, Sloan's great structural innovation enabled General Motors to become the world's largest and most profitable automobile manufacturer despite the great complexity of its product lines.

Teece (1982) demonstrated that each of the four corporations in Chandler's study had, in fact, obtained advantage from moving first to the divisionalised form in their respective industries, examples of 'first-mover' advantage. Further studies (Chandler and Daems, 1980) demonstrated similar histories in Britain, Germany and France, where first-mover multi-divisional corporations obtained advantage.

As might be expected, however, the evident success of the multi-divisional innovation led to a period of imitation by other large diversified organisations. By the 1970s, the multidivisional structure had become the norm for diversified conglomerates and large multi-product organisations. With the adoption of the structure by most competitors, Armour and Teece (1986) noted that superior performance for multi-divisional firms had been eroded by the 1970s; this particular type of organisational capability was unlikely to remain a source of advantage.

4.5 INNOVATION IN STRUCTURES

The search for competitive advantage is at the heart of strategy, so we can only expect that the most competitive managers are constantly trying to find better ways to organise. Indeed, recent history suggests a period where managers have been experimenting, innovating and tentatively exploring new structural forms. In addition, the market and technological drivers identified by Chandler are still active. Some of the reasons why new structural innovations are sought include:

- The erosion, through imitation, of advantage from existing structural forms (such as the multi-divisional form above).

- The impact of new information and communication technologies in enabling the rapid flow of information and knowledge up and down, and *between*, hierarchies.

- The competitive need to offer flexible product and service offerings at low prices, combined with the harnessing of computing power to control flexible manufacturing systems.

- The more rapid pace of competitive innovation, which may indicate a preference for 'organismic' rather than 'mechanistic' structure (Burns and Stalker, 1961).

- The competitive focus on time (Stalk, 1988) as a source of advantage suggests a need for more flexible or adaptive responses to the problems of structuring.

- The growing importance of knowledge-based assets in competition, assets which seem less amenable (as yet) to being organised in formal hierarchical structures.

Greiner, in his work described above in Section 4.2, suggests a final phase of growth through collaboration, and an unpredicted further crisis.

He ends his analysis by asking what the next structural forms will be. Mintzberg (1989) predicted that, whereas he believed that machine bureaucracies had been the 'norm' for structuring in the past, adhocracies would fulfil that role in the future. Grant, in the Set Book, refers to the ideas of adhocracies, 'shamrocks' and 'honeycomb' organisations. While academics have the luxury of speculating over these developments, it is managers like Pierre Du Pont and Alfred Sloan who are constantly acting to innovate.

As we saw in the ABB mini-case which started this book, organisations grapple with developments of the adhocratic structure. Practice therefore extends the range of the vague term 'liaison devices', to identify task forces, standing committees, integrating managers and matrix structures.

Now read the mini-case below, on 'cell' working, which describes one way of designing flexible operational capabilities to support responsive strategy.

MINI-CASE: THE CELLING OUT OF AMERICA

Early this century, [...] the art of building motor cars to order was all but killed off by Henry Ford's moving assembly line. Until now, that is. After 80 years of me-too mass production, consumers are once again demanding infinite variety. To meet such demands, firms are adopting 'cell manufacturing' – a technique in which small teams of workers make entire products. Can a descendant of the (early industry) 'craft' production [...] really rival the economies of scale of mass production?

A study of manufacturing technology in 1,042 American factories, published by the National Association of Manufacturers on December 15th, shows that 56% of them are now trying it out to some extent. According to Paul Swamidass of Alabama's Auburn University, who wrote the report, the keenest users are big firms, rather than cottage industries. The survey found that three-quarters of factories with 100 or more employees use cells, compared with 40% of smaller plants. That would not surprise Japanese giants such as Mazda, Toyota and Sony, which have been toying with cells for years. But it is new in America.

In cell manufacturing, workers are divided into teams – usually of between two and 50 employees – grouped around the manufacturing equipment that each needs. A single cell makes, checks and even packages an entire product or component. Each worker performs several tasks, and every cell is responsible for the quality of its products. As such, cell manufacturing is the ultimate factory-floor refinement of other team-management techniques that western companies have embraced in recent years. But so far, team-based practices have usually focused on bringing together people from different departments, such as design, production, marketing and sales. Cell manufacturing is a narrower process, concentrated purely on the factory floor.

More important, it directly challenges mass production. Cellists – as they might wish to be known – concede that long assembly lines of semi-skilled workers make sense if you want to churn out large volumes of standardised goods. But introducing variety, or changing the product being made, means stopping the whole assembly line. Breakdowns and stoppages are costly for mass-producers, so they have to carry large stocks of parts and spares. And stocks of partly finished products also tend to be high: those that have undergone part of the production process sit idle, waiting for the next stage. Big warehouses and mass production go hand in hand.

By contrast, introducing variety in a cell-based factory is simple: each cell can make a different product. A breakdown or product-change will stop only the cell involved; a slow worker will hinder only his own cell, rather than the entire line. And because products are made in one burst, cells do away with stocks of partly finished goods. Mr Swamidass notes that, of all the technologies covered in his survey, cells produced the biggest benefits, the most notable of these being speed, productivity, flexibility and higher quality.

The Road King, one of the 1997 range of Harley-Davidson motorcycles. The introduction of cells to some of Harley-Davidson's production processes increased stock turnover by a factor of ten.

For example, before Harley-Davidson, a motorcycle maker, introduced cells at its engine-and-gearbox plant, components were machined and stored repeatedly by the firm's 900-strong workforce. The parts meandered along the assembly line, often corroding while they sat idle. A cylinder-head took a week to make. Now, manufactured by a two-man cell, the process takes less than three hours. That means that the firm no longer has to carry big stocks so as to be ready if demand suddenly jumps. The upshot, according to Gary Kirkham, a manufacturing manager at the plant, is that the floor space occupied by the factory has fallen by a third. It now turns over its stock 40 times a year, compared with just $4\frac{1}{2}$ times in 1981.

[...]

The effect of cells on productivity seems to be equally encouraging. Compaq, a big Texas-based personal-computer maker, has replaced three of its 16 Houston assembly lines with 21 cells; four more will be converted early next year. So far, says Brij Kathuria, manager of product integrity, productivity has risen by between 20% and 25%. The cost of converting to cells will, he says, 'pay back in six months'. Lexmark, a manufacturer of computer printers based in Greenwich, Connecticut, has also converted 80% of its 2,700-employee factory in Lexington, Kentucky, to cells – and productivity has soared by 25%.

Increased flexibility is another gain. Compaq's long-term goal is to build all its computers to the specifications laid down by customers or retailers. With its planned 100 or so cells in Houston, the company will be able to build a wide variety of different models – and to increase or decrease production of individual models in line with demand. With 16 production lines, such adaptability would not be cost-effective. Harley-Davidson's Mr Kirkham says that cell manufacturing has given the company 'huge flexibility' to adjust to short-term fluctuations in demand for its products.

Ask Mr Kathuria the secret of cells, and he will reply in two words: employee satisfaction. Stuck on an assembly line, each worker may spend just a few seconds on each product before it passes on. Few see the finished widget. Worse, notes Marshall Fisher of Wharton business school, on an assembly line 'the first worker never meets the 60th worker'. In cells employees see their product through from start to finish: in Mr Kathuria's words, 'they own the serial number'. Problems are tackled as they arise, rather than uncovered down the line.

As a result, cell manufacturing leads to big improvements in product quality. At Harley-Davidson's cell-based plants, the number of quality inspectors has been cut significantly. Bill Ramsey, head of operations at Compaq, believes that 'a very minimal quality audit' of cells will eventually be needed. Lexmark not only gets better quality, it gets it faster. With its old assembly lines, it used to take several months to raise quality to acceptable levels when a new product was introduced. Now, this process takes days – and is driven by workers, not managers. As a result, Lexmark's cell-based factories have raised the number of employees per manager from fewer than 20 to around 100.

Cells are not, however, without drawbacks. They work most effectively with products (such as PCs) that rely on a relatively labour-intensive use of flexible machinery for their manufacture, and which share some common 'building blocks'. Mr Kirkham notes that the heat-treatment of some motor-cycle components can at present be carried out only in large centralised ovens, making those parts unsuitable for cell manufacturing. The company is, however, thinking of investing in smaller, cheaper ovens that could be incorporated into each cell.

[...]

Such challenges seem not to deter those companies that believe in cells. All say they aim to scrap more assembly lines in favour of cell manufacturing; Compaq hopes eventually to use cells to make all of its products. And in an era where shrinking product life-cycles and widening product variety mean that traditional economies of scale are less easily exploited, more firms will follow suit. ...

(Source: The Economist, 17 December 1994)

The survey and examples cited in this article show how the need for overall flexibility can be translated into small cells which also deliver lower costs, shorter lead times and improved quality, as well as motivational benefits. Managerial spans of control can also be increased by as much as a factor of five. The rapid diffusion of the approach indicates the urgency of the search for advantage from it.

4.6   NEW ORGANISATIONAL FORMS

The ABB mini-case is a good example of an organisation restructuring to perform better. There was a vogue for 'corporate restructuring' in the US and Europe during the late 1980s and 1990s, extending into Japanese and Asian markets in the 1990s. The popular impression was often one of 'downsizing' and 'rightsizing' to save costs, and indeed the emphasis on internal structure rather than external opportunities may reflect a need to deliver corporate profits growth at a time when general economic growth had slowed. This book is more concerned, however, with reviewing restructuring activity to identify possible new structural forms.

Section 4.5 noted Mintzberg's view that the adhocracy may be the organisational structure of tomorrow. The adhocracies and flexible operational cells already considered do not necessarily spell the end, however, of the machine bureaucracy or functionally structured hierarchy. Galbraith and Lawler (1993) identified six new variants on the functionally based organisation (see Table 4.2), which they see as responses to:

> ...the strategic initiatives of total quality, total customer service, and time-based competition (which) expose the weaknesses of the functional organisation, since they require multi-functional responses...
>
> (p. 64)

Table 4.2: New functional structures (summarised from Galbraith and Lawler, 1993)		
Type	**Characteristics**	**Examples**
1 Modified functional unit	Still functionally structured but fewer levels and fewer functions for faster response	BMW – Fewer levels, combined routine engineering and maintenance with operations
2 Lateral unit	Cross-functional teams; flatter than hierarchies and organised around product sections, supported by information technology	Aircraft industry-design, manufacture by major aircraft sections
3 Superfunctions unit	Grouped around core processes (e.g. materials management, customer service)	Product generation process in Hewlett-Packard combines R&D, manufacturing and purchasing
4 Front-end/back-end hybrid	Hybrid structure with front end organised around customer/geography and back-end organised around products and technologies; requires effective lateral integration process (e.g. new product development) to tie both ends together	Digital Equipment Corporation, Visa International
5 Network organisation	Separate companies perform functions they do best; co-ordinated through network integrator	Nike, Reebok, Benetton
6 Functional specialist	Perform single function; contribute this to informal networks	Research 'boutiques'; product design houses

If the demands of competition lead to changes in the functionally based hierarchy, however, it seems apparent that it is the advances in information and communications technologies ('ICTs') and the development of sophisticated information systems which enable the development of the new structures Galbraith and Lawler identify. We shall consider this further in the next section.

4.7   ORGANISATIONS AS NETWORKS OF TRANSACTIONS

A theoretical approach to understanding the emergence of new structures such as those identified by Galbraith and Lawler, and the role of information systems in enabling them, can be gained by returning to the Transaction Costs Economics ('TCE') theory introduced in Book 4 (Williamson, 1975), which you may remember identified the strategic choice between 'making' or 'buying' services or products.

TCE may be considered to be a theory of the boundary of the firm. It views organisations as networks of exchange transactions, carried out by individuals acting as agents for organisations. It is very concerned with the issues of structure we have been discussing, but shifts the analysis away from the design parameters and dimensions of structure in Mintzberg's work. It analyses organisational structure according to the relative economic efficiency of alternative means of conducting transactions.

TCE has origins in the theory of contract law (Williamson is a qualified US lawyer), which we considered briefly in Book 2. It assumes that all individuals are prone to behaving opportunistically for their own benefit, especially where individual goals are not aligned fully with those of the organisation. It describes the risk of opportunistic behaviour as the 'moral hazard' of transactions. Such opportunistic behaviour is possible when there are discrepancies or differences between the information that each party to the transaction has. This *information asymmetry* (or 'impactedness' in Williamson's terms) can exist over the information needed by either party to define the terms of exchange or to implement a transaction. These transaction costs, therefore, are the costs of incomplete or missing information, or the cost of obtaining it, and are four-fold:

1   search costs

2   contracting or negotiation costs

3   transaction control, regulation and audit costs

4   maintenance costs to develop the contract or transaction between phases of implementation.

'Spot contracts' (recall Book 2) represent an extreme type of transaction, and are negotiated in the marketplace. All the information that both parties need to know about the transaction is freely available to all, and is built into the price. For example, a commodity such as West Texas Blend crude oil can be purchased on a market at the lowest price with little risk that the product will not conform to its understood specification. Other markets, however, are subject to imperfections concerned with the free flow of information and the equivalence of knowledge. Consider, for example, these observations from a study of a Moroccan bazaar:

> In the bazaar, information is poor, scarce, and maldistributed, inefficiently communicated, and intensely valued ... The level of ignorance about everything from product quality and going prices to market possibilities and production costs is very high, and a great deal of the way in which the bazaar is organized and functions can be interpreted as either an attempt to reduce such ignorance for someone, increase it for someone, or defend someone against it.

These ignorances mentioned above are known ignorances, not simply matters concerning which information is lacking. Bazaar participants realize how difficult it is to know if the cow is sound or its price is right, and they realize it is impossible to prosper without knowing.

[Therefore] the search for information – laborious, uncertain, complex, and irregular – is the central experience of the life of the bazaar. Every aspect of the bazaar economy reflects the fact that the primary problem facing its participants (that is, 'bazaaris') is not balancing options but finding out what they are.

(Geertz, 1978, pp.29–30)

Notice how Geertz states that, 'a great deal of the way in which the bazaar is *organized and functions* can be interpreted as either an attempt to reduce such ignorance for someone, increase it for someone, or defend someone against it'. The economics of imperfect knowledge and information therefore drives the structuring of the Moroccan bazaar. In the same way, according to Williamson, the functional hierarchy (the machine bureaucracy in Mintzberg's terms) evolved as a Western response to the problems of market transactions where information asymmetry and opportunism exist. By setting up a hierarchy based on legitimate authority, elaborate control mechanisms, and aligned employee and organisational goals, opportunism was curbed. By establishing functional specialisations within the hierarchy, information could be made more transparent and handled more efficiently. The 'hierarchy' evolved, therefore, specifically to overcome imperfections in otherwise efficient markets. Hence, the title of Williamson's book, *Markets and Hierarchies*.

According to Ciborra (1993), however, the relative economic efficiency of conducting transactions through markets or hierarchies has been changing because of changes in the information systems that underpin the exchanges. Ciborra describes these as the economic efficiencies of 'the matching of information technology and organisational structures'. The importance of innovative ICTs in determining efficient structures should not surprise us, given the many commentators who explain the extraordinarily prolonged growth in US competitiveness in the 1990s as the result of that country's particularly effective integration and creative use of ICTs in business. Ciborra's view is that ICTs have been responsible for the increased transparency of markets, increased agility (through flexibility and opportunity-creation) in some hierarchies, and the effectiveness of teams. The adapted functional structures of Galbraith and Lawler in Table 4.2 can be revisited in the light of the impact of ICTs as enablers.

- First, the *modified functional unit* can be considered as a relatively straightforward adaptation where the computational power, flexibility and speed of information systems can speed up information flows through the hierarchy, increase spans of control, and provide more transparent and accurate information within the hierarchy. The effectiveness and flexibility of the hierarchy are enhanced, and its relative costs (through 'delayering' and 'flattening' the structure) reduced.

- The *superfunctions unit* describes the type of structure most often associated with the 'Business Process Re-engineering' movement (see, for example, Hammer and Champy, 1993). This approach redesigns the organisation as if it were a 'green field' sight, ignoring the current structure and radically rethinking how processes can be handled most efficiently. Where successful, such design interventions have re-aligned structures with key processes (often identified by customer value measures) to achieve substantial improvements in speed, flexibility, quality or cost (Segal-Horn and Bowman, 1996). The requirement for successful re-alignment includes a need to ensure human resources and information systems are also re-aligned. In systems terms, for example, this will often mean the development of a credible activity-based or value-adding accounting system, and an appropriate incentive system (Eriksen and Amit, 1996). The approach may also reduce the number of controls on the grounds of their economic justification.

- More *perfect markets* (and the more perfect information these require) can also be an outcome of improved public-access information systems. For example: improved systems have enabled outsiders to cut their transactions costs when dealing in stocks and shares; the use of the internet or electronic markets, such as France Telecom's Minitel, as channels for selling goods and services allows buyers to access suppliers in other regions or countries, and to quickly compare prices and specifications; the growth in direct-selling telephone insurance allows customers to quickly obtain multiple quotes on car insurance; and the regulatory changes in the European Union that require more and more company contracts to be offered to competitive tendering opens up more supply arrangements to more suppliers. More and better information concerning market conditions, therefore, encourages buyers to *outsource* more of their transactions.

The above three ways to restructure transactions all show the impact of using ICTs to speed up the flow of information, to make it more transparent, to use computing power as a substitute for layers of hierarchical management, and to radically rethink the information needed to control and enable the underlying key business processes in an organisation. They still describe a choice between markets and hierarchies, however, albeit restructured and more efficient markets and hierarchies.

Ciborra argues, however, that 'network technologies' additionally create new ways for an organisation to structure itself, other than through a functional hierarchy. Ciborra identifies the role of technologies such as groupware (starting with Lotus Notes), electronic mail, relational databases, intranets and the internet, open architectures and open systems software (such as Java), shareware and electronic data interchange, and local and wide area networks, in enabling a new way for organisations to work cross-functionally or laterally. Ciborra states that these forms of cross-functional or lateral working have created new types of organisational structure, and a new way to organise transactions: transactions can now be conducted through *markets, hierarchies or teams*.

Returning to Galbraith and Lawler's typology of new functionally-based organisational forms, we can see the role of these network technologies in creating internal 'team' structures:

- The *lateral unit* is, as Galbraith and Lawler suggest, a cross-functional team-based organisation, where specialists interact in teams using technologies such as groupware, electronic mail and open data-bases to ensure free flow of information within the team. Project teams on large construction or product development projects, for example, will require technical and commercial specialists from across an organisation (and from outside it) to be able to interact effectively.

- The *front-end / back-end hybrid* requires an effective integrative network to enable two different structures with different information needs to deliver a seamless, effective and efficient service or product. For example, retail banks need to offer their customers an individual service. For this, customer service officers need to be able to access all the banks' data concerning the customer, to seek the benefits of scope from cross-selling products and services – all the different deposits, accounts, loans, equity investments and trust services provided. The bank's operations centre, however, needs the same information to be structured differently to obtain the economies of scale of processing the data – for example, all three-month deposits need to be identified in order for the bank's treasury department to re-lend that money in the most profitable way. The information system must be able to take the data which originates at one 'end' of the hybrid and reconfigure to the needs of the other end, while still ensuring the overall integrity of that data.

Finally, Galbraith and Lawler consider the related co-venturing types of organisation: the Network Organisation and the Functional Specialist. In this course, we will consider inter-firm alliances and networks in more detail in Book 9, and international aspects of managing these in Book 10. The difference between the two types of network identified by Galbraith and Lawler lies in the degree to which they are formally managed by 'integrator' companies.

- *Network organisations* rely on one organisation or lead partners to integrate the network. The case of Benetton, described in Book 4, comes to mind, as do the retail supply networks managed by large retail chains such as Sears, Carrefour, Makro, and Marks and Spencer. The 'New Way of Life' video which you studied depicted a network of supply companies contributing to the development of the Andrew oilfield, being integrated initially by BP, and then by the 'Andrew Alliance' of leading construction companies.

- The *functional specialist*, however, describes a supplier who relies on their ability to contribute specialist skills to any number of informal network partners. It is their very expertise that enables such specialists to survive. The biotechnology industry is an area where the specialist research skills of biotech 'boutiques' allow such companies to partner many different network partners. We will look at the biotechnology industry in Book 9 when considering alliances and networks in more detail.

Inter-firm networks generally demand flexibility and adaptive capabilities; they represent inter-firm 'teams', and are a challenge to some of the traditional conclusions of TCE as a theory of the boundary of the firm. The dichotomous emphasis on markets and hierarchies in Williamson's original ideas has been supplemented in the most recent thinking by a recognition of intra- and inter-firm 'teams'. Once again, it is the enabling power of new information communication technologies that has transformed the economics of structuring the flow of information and knowledge across markets and between organisations:

> This redesign of firms' boundaries requires higher connectivity between different information systems, the extension of networks and protocols to an inter-firm environment and underlies the importance of systems such EDI and groupware applications.
> *(Ciborra, 1996, p. 10)*

To conclude this section, consider the example in Box 4.1 which discusses the well-known shoe manufacturer Nike, and the networks it has established and manages. The article summarises the thinking on the difficulties of managing networks by Miles and Snow (1992):

BOX 4.1

Nike, an American sports-shoe and clothing firm, is a networker's dream. Instead of manufacturing the $3.4 billion-worth of shoes and clothes it now sells each year, Nike has created a vast but closely knit network of subcontractors in China, South Korea, Taiwan and Thailand. Each develops its own products. Nike, in turn, spends more on R&D than any of its rivals, and channels the results into its subcontractors' manufacturing processes. Nike is happy for its subcontractors to make products for other firms: that may help Nike's competitors, but Nike is gambling that what its subcontractors learn as a result will help it most of all.

Being a network organisation, reckons Nike, keeps it as fit as the people who wear its trainers wish they were. One of the firm's great competitive advantages is that it can respond to changes in fashion faster than its rivals: by rearranging what each supplier does on its network, Nike can change its product mix almost overnight. Its nimbleness has helped Nike gain a 32% (and rising) share of America' sports-shoe market. Philip Knight, Nike's founder and chairman, confidently expects his firm's sales to grow to $6 billion-a-year by 1996.

Nike is one of a small band of big companies – others include Harley-Davidson, Chaparral Steel, Lithonia Lighting, Benetton and parts of Motorola – which have pushed networking to the point where barriers between the firm, its customers and its suppliers have almost disappeared. All believe that networking makes them more competitive; Harley-Davidson and Chaparral might not have survived without it. But are networks immune to the sort of structural problems which beset old-style, vertically integrated conglomerates? Raymond Miles, a professor at the University of California's Haas School, and Charles Snow, a professor at Pennsylvania State University's Smeal College, suggest that, for all their virtues, networks also have faults.

Most network organisations, because they seek to build loose, long-term relationships with their customers, suppliers, subcontractors and distributors, rapidly become part of what the two American academics call a 'stable network'. But stability can lead to staleness. If a supplier or subcontractor becomes too dependent on the 'core' firm in the network (for example, if one of Nike's subcontractors supplies soles only to Nike), the price and quality of its products will no longer be tested in the wider market. If that happens to several firms in the network, the core company may fail to exploit innovation elsewhere in the subcontractors' industry. Nike prevents that happening by ensuring that its networks also work for firms outside the Nike network.

Messrs Miles and Snow reckon that the principal cause of over-dependence is 'customisation'. As it tries to get an edge over competition, a network's core company tends to encourage subcontractors to customise their production facilities to its needs. This strategy can be costly if taken too far.

As a subcontractor is drawn ever closer to the core company, it can become over-specialised and unable to compete in markets outside the network. Worse, it may lose the innovative edge it gained from working for several, equally demanding customers. With no innovations to contribute to the network, the subcontractor will eventually lose even the core firm's business. Examples of such failure are hard to pin down, but various subcontractors to Marks and Spencer, Benetton and Motorola are on what is a growing list of network victims.

Too much customisation can also threaten a network's core company. As it becomes more deeply involved in specifying subcontractors' operating processes – Motorola, for instance, insists that all its suppliers apply for the Baldrige quality award – the core firm can find itself, in effect, running and managing its subcontractors. This not only stretches the core company's managerial and technical resources; it also turns the network into something resembling an old-style vertically integrated firm.

IBM PCs being assembled. In recent years the company has been trying to transform its hierarchical structure into a cluster of self-managed businesses.

Big multinationals that are trying to turn themselves into 'internal networks' are especially prone to reverting to their old, vertically integrated ways. Consider IBM, which is trying to transform its rigid, centrally planned hierarchy into a cluster of self-managed businesses, free to buy and sell goods and services to each other and to outside clients. Such an ambitious plan will succeed only if IBM is able to throw off its 'top-down' corporate culture. Whereas companies as diverse as ABB, Control Data and Alcoa appear to have created successful internal networks, some people in the computer industry think IBM will have to split itself up, formally severing all its rigid vertical links.

Networks like Nike's work well if the core company transfers technological advances quickly enough from one subcontractor to another. There is a danger, however, that once a network is working, the core company will become blinkered, concentrating on tying up its suppliers in a maze of long-term contracts and ignoring better ideas from new subcontractors. The company's existing subcontractors have a direct interest in seeing that this happens. The network becomes less good at reallocating resources quickly. When Harley-Davidson found itself going that way, it stopped the rot by introducing a simple, flexible contract for its network of subcontractors, which gave both sides more opportunities to escape onerous obligations.

Networking headaches are easier to prevent than cure. The over-dependence of a supplier on a single customer can be avoided by explicitly setting a limit on the proportion of assets (say, 20–30%) a subcontractor or supplier should dedicate to the core firm. Contracts between a core company and its network of subcontractors should be flexible enough to leave both sides free to withdraw. Most important, networkers must shed their old, confrontational always. General Electric's 'workout' programme brings together not only its managers and subcontractors, but also subcontractors and General Electric's own customers, to help them work as a team. Would-be networkers should listen and learn.

(Source: The Economist, *10 October 1992)*

Activity 4.3

Having read Box 4.1, consider the following questions:

What are the features of network structures that you can note in the example?

In summary, what are the main opportunities and threats from structuring your activities through networks?

Discussion

The Nike example describes the network as a vehicle for learning, for the transfer of knowledge and information between and amongst the network integrator and its sub-contractors. Related to this is an acceptance that knowledge will leak out to competitors where sub-contractors also supply them, but that knowledge from competitors will also be gained; that is, that a complex network of competing networks allows for the exchange of information and knowledge in a way that mimics the exchanges of an efficient marketplace.

The article does not dwell on new ICTs in networks, as such, but note how a quality standard has been used by Motorola as a structuring system and integration device for its networks. Finally, the relationship between networks and the relational contract theory discussed in Book 2 is made explicit: most network organisations 'build loose long-term relationships'.

The article suggests that members of open networks must be prepared to have their quality standards benchmarked against the best in the marketplace. For the best network organisations, this develops their flexibility and capability to adapt quickly to changes in the marketplace.

The article dwells on the dangers of over-specialisation in 'stable' networks, however. Specialisation is a natural tendency of organisations involved in long-term relationships. Williamson describes this as the creation of 'asset specificity', and it is a natural outcome of long-term investment in a particular set of distinctive resources and capabilities. In supply arrangements, for example, organisations will be more likely to invest in a specialist piece of manufacturing machinery if the customer being served has been purchasing its goods for many years, and is likely to continue doing so.

The specialisation of Galbraith and Lawler's 'functional specialists' is in a specialist skill available to a number of informal networks. This investment seems a valid strategy as long as the skill is in demand across a broad range of customers. The danger for members of stable networks of specialisation, however, is of a risky over-investment in a specialised relationship which ties the supplier commercially.

These 'stable' networks are also seen as having dysfunctional outcomes inasmuch as: they might discourage openness to all sources of innovation, they can encourage the network integrators to 'micro-manage' suppliers, and they can simply extend poor resource allocation decisions across organisational boundaries.

5 SUMMARY AND CONCLUSION

Structure, strategy and systems are mutually interdependent. In this book we have examined structures and systems and their relationship to strategy. We have traced the growing interrelationship between them, from Chandler's dictum that 'structure follows strategy' to the realisation that structure, strategy and systems are iterative and mutually independent. Innovation in structure and/or systems can be a source of advantage. Beyond Greiner's fifth phase of collaboration we are into an uncertain world in which no predictive model of structure and its associated systems exists. Emerging structures at present are generally developments of adhocracy or networks.

Mintzberg's thinking has developed beyond earlier approaches in ways that help to make sense of this uncertainty (and you will recall that the empirical evidence he cited contained many 'hybrid' configurations). He recalls the Darwinian distinction between 'lumpers' and 'splitters':

> Lumpers categorise; they are the synthesisers prone to consistency. Once they have pigeonholed something into one box or another, they are done with it. To a lumper in management, strategies are generic, structures are types, managers have a style (X, Y, Z, 9-9 etc.). Splitters nuance; they are the analysers, prone to nuance. Since nothing can ever be categorised, things are never done with. To a splitter in management, strategies, structures, and styles all vary infinitely.
>
> *(Mintzberg, 1989, p. 254)*

Configurations in structure are very much the approach of the lumper, and the approach seems increasingly inadequate for strategic thinking as it attempts to create wholly new structures in response to recent trends. Mintzberg recognises the need to consider other ways to think about structure and the process of structuring. Once he was happy with his theory and his configurations:

> But then, a student of mine, Alain Noël, came along and asked a question that upset this nice lumping. He wanted to know whether I was intending to play 'jigsaw puzzle' or 'LEGO' with all the elements of structure and power that I described in those books. In other words did I mean all these elements of organization to fit together in set ways – to create known images – or were they to be used creatively to build new ones? I had to answer that I had been promoting jigsaw puzzle even if I was suggesting that the pieces could be combined into several images instead of the usual one. But I immediately began to think about playing 'organizational LEGO'. All of the anomalies I encountered – all those nasty, well-functioning organizations that refused to fit into one or another of my neat categories – suddenly became opportunities to think beyond configuration. I could become a splitter too.
>
> *(Mintzberg, 1989, p. 255)*

Reviewing the literature, Mintzberg summarises five views of organisational effectiveness:

- *Convergence* – The 'one best way'.
- *Congruence* – A portfolio of best ways in a portfolio of situations.
- *Configuration* – Categorising patterns of portfolios of best ways ('lumping').

- *Contradiction* – Types of configurations do not exist in practice, they combine or convert into new ones. Here, effectiveness equates with managing the tension of change and the contradictory forces between configurations.

- *Creation* – Beyond configuration and contradiction, playing 'organisational Lego'. From our observations of the high levels of organisational restructuring activity, this may be the closest to an explanation of what organisations are currently trying to do in their search for new advantage.

As a glimpse of the future, a recent set of predictions about future organisations emphasises a trend towards self-adaptation through organisation learning:

1   Organisational design will be understood to be a temporary configuration of components that will change as the organisation's strategy and environment change.

2   There will be greatly increased, ongoing application of resources to the development of skills and knowledge, throughout the organisation.

3   Organisations will be flatter and more capable of successive changes.

4   Organisations will become excellent at integrating a rich constellation of task teams, 'overlay' organisations, and intergroup networks that complement organisational capabilities and offset the focus of the core structures.

5   Organisations will be richly connected to a wide diversity of other organisations in the environment, with which they will learn and share earnings.

6   Organisations will foster diversity of practices and designs, in order to seed the learning process and enable various parts of the organisation to adapt to performance requirements.

7   The role of top management will be to formulate and communicate a clear vision of the organisation's strategy and vision and to continually challenge the organisation to achieve excellence in implementing the direction.

8   The psychological contract of employment will change irreversibly.
(Mohrman and Mohrman, 1993)

In the next book, we will consider some of the implications for organisational culture of these adaptations of structure and systems.

REFERENCES

Band, D.C. and Scanlan, G. (1995) 'Strategic control through core competencies', *Long Range Planning*, Vol. 23, No. 2.

Barnett, W. P. and Hansen, M. T. (1996), 'The Red Queen in organisational evolution', *Strategic Management Journal*, Vol. 17, pp. 139–57.

Burns, T. and Stalker, G.M. (1961) *The Management of Innovation*, Tavistock, London.

Chandler, A.D. (1962) *Strategy and Structure*, MIT Press, Cambridge, MA.

Chandler, A.D. (1977) *The Visible Hand: The Managerial Revolution in American Business*, Harvard University Press, Cambridge, MA.

Chandler, A.D. and Daems, H. (eds.) (1980) *Managerial Hierarchies: Comparative Perspectives on the Rise of the Modern Industrial Enterprise*, Harvard University Press, Cambridge, MA.

Ciborra, C.U. (1993) *Teams, Markets and Systems*, Cambridge University Press, Cambridge, UK.

Daft, R.L. and Macintosh, N.B. (1984) 'The nature and use of formal control systems', *Journal of Management*, Vol. 10, No. 1.

Eriksen, B. and Amit, R. (1996) 'Strategic implications of Business Process Re-engineering' in Foss, N.J. and Knudsen, C. (eds) *Towards a Competence Theory of the Firm*, Routledge, London.

Galbraith, J. and Lawler, E.E. (1993) *Organising for the Future*, Jossey-Bass.

Galbraith, J.R. and Nathanson, D.A. (1978) *Strategy Implementation: the role of structure and process*, West Publishing, St. Paul, MN.

Geertz, C. (1978) 'The bazaar economy: information and search in peasant marketing' in *American Economic Review*, 68(2): pp.28–32.

Greiner, L.E. (1972) 'Evolution and revolution as organisations grow', *Harvard Business Review*, July/August.

Hammer, M. and Champy, J. (1993) *Reengineering the Corporation: A Manifesto for Business Revolution*, Harper, New York.

Hastings, C. (1993) *The New Organisation*, McGraw-Hill.

Lorange, P. and Murphy, D.C. (1984) 'Systemic, behavioral and political considerations in strategic control: some empirical results', *Journal of Business Strategy*, Vol. 4, No. 4.

Miles, R. and Snow, C. (1992) 'Causes of failure in network organizations', *California Management Review*, Vol. 34, No. 4.

Miller, D. (1986), 'Configurations of strategy and structure: towards a synthesis', *Strategic Management Journal*, Vol. 7, pp. 233–49.

Mintzberg, H. (1979) *The Structuring of Organisations*, Prentice-Hall, Englewood Cliffs, NJ.

Mintzberg, H. (1980) *The Nature of Managerial Work*, Prentice-Hall, Englewood Cliffs, NJ.

Mintzberg, H. (1989) *Mintzberg on Management*, The Free Press, New York.

Miyazaki, K. (1995) *Building Competencies in the Firm: lessons from Japanese and European optoelectronics*, St Martin's Press, New York.

Mohrman, S.A. and Mohrman, S.M. (1993) 'Organisational change and learning', in Galbraith *et al. op. cit.*

Savage, C.M. (1990) *Fifth Generation Management*, Digital Press.

Segal-Horn, S. and Bowman, C. (1996) 'Strategic management and BPR' in Armistead, C. and Rowland, P. (eds) *Managing Business Processes: BPR and beyond*, Wiley, Chichester.

Simons, R. (1995) *Levers of Control*, Harvard Business School Press.

Sloan, A.P. (1963) *My Years at General Motors,* Sidgwick and Jackson, London.

Stalk, G. (1988) 'Time – the next source of competitive advantage', *Harvard Business Review,* July–August, pp. 41–51.

Teece, D.J. (1982), 'Towards an economic theory of the multiproduct firm', *Journal of Economic Behaviour and Organisation*, Vol. 3, pp. 39–63.

Zuboff, S. (1988) *In the Age of the Smart Machine*, Basic Books, New York.

ACKNOWLEDGEMENTS

Grateful acknowledgement is made to the following sources for permission to reproduce material in this book:

Text

Pages 7–8: Rodger, I. 1993, 'ABB managers strip for action', *Financial Times*, 25 August 1993; *Box 3.1:* Marsh, P. 1996, 'Gaining a harder edge from the "Soft" option', *Financial Times*, 28 February 1996; *Pages 30–32:* 'The celling out of America', *The Economist*, 17–23 December 1994, © The Economist, London; *Box 4.1:* 'Why networks may fail', *The Economist*, 10–16 December 1992, © The Economist, London.

Table

Tables 2.1 and 2.2: Mintzberg, H. 1979, *The Structure of Organizations*, Table 21-1, by permission of Prentice-Hall, Inc.

Figures

Figures 3.1 and 3.2: Reprinted by permission of Harvard Business School Press. Exhibits from *Levers of Control: How managers use innovative control systems to drive strategic renewal* by Robert Simons. Boston, MA. 1995, pp. 7 and 128. Copyright © 1995 by the President and Fellows of Harvard College; all rights reserved; *Figure 4.1:* Reprinted by permission of *Harvard Business Review*. An exhibit from 'Evolution and revolution as organisations grow' by Larry E. Greiner **50**(4), July–August1972, p. 41. Copyright © 1972 by the President and Fellows of Harvard College; all rights reserved.

Photographs

Page 31: Reproduced by permission of Harley Davidson, United Kingdom; *Page 39:* IBM United Kingdom Limited.

BOOK 8

ORGANISATIONAL CAPABILITIES: CULTURE AND POWER

Authors: Geoff Mallory, Susan Segal-Horn and Michael Lovitt

Book 1 & 2 — purpose
Vision
objectives
stakeholders.
key Success factors
Measures.

BK 3

External Environment — market places
Sunk cost. Compete for government money

Porters — Five forces

Internal environment — (Grants)

CONTENTS

1 INTRODUCTION

As we have consistently emphasised in this course, strategy is concerned with the question of how organisations of all types achieve and sustain superior performance. We have also emphasised the importance of the resources and capabilities that an organisation possesses, suggesting that opportunities emerge from an organisation's unique capabilities and the way these capabilities are utilised. As we discussed in Book 7, organisational features such as structures and systems, power configuration and culture may be considered to be capabilities in the strategic skill of organising. In certain circumstances, these organisational capabilities may be unique, and may provide sources of superior performance.

The conclusion to Book 6 also emphasised internal and external contexts as significant influences on strategic processes. In this book we will take this forward by examining two more contextual influences to add to the discussion of structures and systems in Book 7. We will look at organisational culture: its origins, some definitions and applications of the concept, and its impact on, and role in, strategy. We will also discuss power in organisations, and sources of power both within and external to the organisation. The discussion will include the nature of power structures and their impact on the strategy process, aspects of leadership, and ways of looking at the interrelationship between culture and power. We will emphasise the relationship between internal and external contexts of organisational culture and power structures and the practical application of these concepts to strategic thinking, strategy implementation and strategic change.

One useful way of looking at these contextual influences is to view them as parts of a 'cultural web': the network of internal structures and processes which both arises out of, and continuously reinforces, an organisation's view of itself (Johnson, 1988). According to Johnson this web shapes managers' and other organisational members' perspectives of themselves, their internal organisation and their external environment. It acts as a link between the two. While external forces and internal capabilities undoubtedly affect performance, according to Johnson (1992) they 'do not in themselves create organisational strategy: people create strategy'. Strategy is thus a product of social and political processes which are shaped by the beliefs and assumptions that people have about their world. These beliefs and assumptions embody 'an organisation's view of itself and its environment'. This he calls the organisational *paradigm*. The component parts of the cultural web, and hence the nature of the cultural web itself, will therefore be unique to each organisation. Figure 1.1 (overleaf) provides a simple model of Johnson's 'cultural web'.

The way in which the cultural web affects strategy will be examined more closely later. In this book we focus first on the three parts of the cultural web – the rituals and routines, the stories and myths and the symbols – which we will discuss as components of organisational culture. We will also place these elements of organisational culture in a broader context of differences in national and regional cultures, which in turn influence organisational strategy, structure, values and norms in different parts of the world. Then the other parts of the web (explored already in Books 6 and 7) will be revisited as we explore how power, structure and control are all

To study this book you need:
    Audio Cassette 1
    Audio Cassette 2
    Course Reader

Figure 1.1   The cultural web

influenced by, and in turn influence, organisational culture. We seek to show how organisational culture (as expressed and embodied in the paradigm), might create the capability for (or inhibit) the successful formulation and realisation of strategies.

1.1 LEARNING OBJECTIVES OF THIS BOOK

After reading this book, you should be able to:

- demonstrate the interdependence of national, corporate and organisational culture
- explain the implications of corporate and organisational cultures for strategic management
- explain what is meant by a paradigm and its importance within strategy, strategic change and strategic thinking
- show the importance of culture as a capability and the challenges this presents for managers
- explain the meaning of power in the context of strategic decision-making and leadership
- demonstrate understanding of the dynamics of selected approaches to culture change
- show the close interrelationship between culture, power, structure and strategy and recognise these features at work within your own organisation.

2 WHAT IS CULTURE?

An early definition by Deal and Kennedy (1982) suggests that organisational culture can be thought of as 'the way we do things around here'. It is difficult to know what to exclude from such an idea of culture. Everything within an organisation could be seen as being a component of, or a product of, culture. This definition is appealingly straightforward, but difficult to specify about your own or any other organisation.

2.1 SOME SPECIFIC ELEMENTS OF CULTURE

By returning to the cultural web (Figure 1.1), we may define some specific elements of culture more accurately. In previous books we have described and discussed the impact of some of the components of the web, such as structures and control systems, on strategy. Essentially, these are *formal* mechanisms for co-ordination and control within organisations. The other components of the web are *informal*. In cultural terms it is the meanings that they carry for participants which are significant.

Although it is difficult to define, culture is made 'visible' in the stories that people tell about the organisation, for story-telling is one way of making sense of events or actions. We hear the myths and legends that build up around particular events or people; that embed the present in the past. We can identify from these the negative and positive role models, the villains or deviants who do not fit with the organisation's way of doing things, and the heroes who do.

These myths and stories may or may not be strictly accurate, as their purpose is to convey a message showing who is valued, the reasons why they are valued and the behaviours or actions this represents. They also provide explanations for why things are done in the way that they are. For example, most senior managers at the UK engineering company GEC recount stories about the former Chairman Lord Weinstock and his unique approach to performance appraisal of the managers of GEC's business units, by means of annual one-to-one target-setting meetings. The essential criteria he applied, and the actions he would or would not take, differed in detail but gave a clear view of what was valued and what was not valued at GEC.

In the US computer company Hewlett-Packard, the story is told of the Saturday that Bill Hewlett (one of the two founders of the company) went into a plant and found the laboratory stock room door padlocked. He cut the padlock off and left a note saying 'Don't ever lock this door again. Thanks, Bill'. He wanted engineers to have unhindered access to components to stimulate the creativity that was part of 'the HP way'.

In addition to stories, we can observe, participate in, or experience rituals, ceremonies and routines. The GEC story is also an example of a ritual or ceremony in that it involves a regular event. Other such events could include budget-setting meetings or New Year or Christmas parties.

Retirement presentations are also good opportunities for management to emphasise the behaviour that made the retiring employees so valuable.

Routines can be thought of as the ways in which interactions between organisational members are expected to take place. In some organisations very formal means of interaction such as written memos are used. In other organisations interactions are expected to be informal and agreements may be reached by verbal discussion. E-mail has recently contributed in many organisations to more informal interactions, both between colleagues and between organisations.

2.2   HOW ARE CULTURES FORMED?

A symbol is something that represents another thing. So in one sense ceremonies, stories and myths are all symbols which represent the deeper values of an organisation. There are, however, other more physical symbols which tend to focus attention on a specific item. Corporate logos, for example, might seek to express some aspect of the mission or values of the organisation. A reward system based on sales targets achieved, or the location and size of offices, is also symbolic of what is valued. The intangible aspects of beliefs and values become visible through these artefacts. A richer definition of culture can now be suggested:

> ... the basic values, ideologies and assumptions which guide and fashion individual and business behaviour. These values are evident in more tangible factors such as stories, ritual, language, and jargon, office decoration and layout and prevailing modes of dress among the staff.
>
> (Wilson and Rosenfeld, 1990, p. 229)

We have suggested that culture is bound up with values and beliefs and we see the effects in symbols and behaviour. As B820 is a management course, we will concentrate on organisational and corporate cultures. National and societal cultures will be discussed only in so far as they impact directly on the components of the 'cultural web' and the effectiveness of strategies.

Activity 2.1

Using Wilson and Rosenfeld's definition, can you suggest several sources of experience that may have impacted on your basic values, ideologies and assumptions?

Discussion

We suggest that your list might include:

- *your past experience, perhaps from childhood, the impact of your schooling and parents, your previous work experience or professional training*

- *your non-work environment, friends, families, clubs and organisations to which you belong; the urban or rural setting in which you live*

- *the policies and practices, the structures and systems, tasks and technology of your immediate work environment; the norms of behaviour, both formal and informal, that are required and are specific to your role and function.*

2.3 CORPORATE AND ORGANISATIONAL CULTURES

We can now come to a working definition of the differences between organisational and corporate culture and this difference is very important when considering the implementation of strategy. The best way to clarify this distinction is to ask two apparently trivial questions:

1   Who owns culture?

2   Is culture something that an organisation *is*, or something that an organisation *has*?

Taking the second question first, this was posed by Linda Smircich (1983). If culture is something an organisation has, then it can be treated as another variable, another contingency which impacts on structures and processes. As such it can be seen to be owned by the management of the organisation and is capable of being manipulated or changed in some way to improve efficiency or effectiveness. If, however, culture is something that an organisation is, then it is the product of negotiated and shared meanings that emerge from social and personal interactions. In this case culture is created and re-created by its participants in a process that is continuous and is not imposed.

So corporate culture refers to and reflects managers' values, interpretations and preferred way of doing things. Organisational culture is a much broader concept. It may embrace many sub-cultures and is almost impossible to define in concrete terms. The problem for managers is that they frequently assume that their understanding of the corporate culture is fully reflected in the organisational culture, whereas in effect it is only part of it. They also confuse compliance with corporate culture with the existence of a homogeneous organisational culture.

Activity 2.2

Anita Roddick is the founder and chief executive of a UK-based multinational which makes and sells cosmetics and personal care products. Body Shop is a global, multi-billion dollar business. It is a high-profile company – largely as a result of the policies and activities of Mrs Roddick herself, especially its environmentally friendly philosophy and the campaigning approach the company has taken to banning any animal testing in the development of its products. This was path-breaking in the worldwide cosmetics industry and created a new, and now very large, niche in the world cosmetics market.

Listen to the Anita Roddick interview (Audio Cassette AC2), paying particular attention to her views on the culture of the organisation.

What, if any, alignment is there between the corporate culture and the organisational culture at Body Shop in Mrs Roddick's view?

Would you say that this is a company with a strong culture? If so, or if not, why?

What impact might the culture have on the organisational structure?

Is this much the same as it would be in other similarly large organisations?

Discussion

Amongst other statements, Anita Roddick says:

' ... everything is embryonic ... people pop in or come from outside ... incredibly internalised ... openness ... running around by the seat of the pants – it's a fact they don't have a department to shore them up ... tea ladies have a big say ... very informal ... you see people in shorts ... language of irreverence ... a culture that is like a military organisation ... to try to break that from within ... being a Trojan horse ... the development of the human spirit ...'

In the view of Anita Roddick, Body Shop is a 'strong' culture embodying a great deal of commitment. The structure is informal and deliberately non-hierarchical. Certainly she believes that the organisational culture and corporate culture are identical. However, her view would have to be validated by testing whether it is widely shared amongst the staff of Body Shop.

How might you set about testing this?

One possibility might be to enquire about rituals and symbols, to ascertain the meanings that staff ascribe to particular symbols (of which Mrs Roddick herself is likely to be one) and events, to surface similarities and differences. Only a few similarities may be sufficient for a culture to be strong and pervasive.

Clearly the senior management of Body Shop deliberately set out to create an extremely informal structure with few conventional trappings of office and a commitment to 'openness' both internally and externally. Equally clearly, this is not a typical approach to the management of a multinational and this perceived informality of Body Shop's management structure has at times created a somewhat strained relationship between its senior management and the financial markets and business community.

2.4   CULTURE AS CAPABILITY OR RESOURCE

It will be obvious from the preceding discussion that how managers see culture is of crucial importance in the whole strategy process. It would seem to be appropriate to see culture as a capability, as something which can integrate a cluster of resources. We have already indicated that it can be seen as something that holds an organisation together, a form of glue which binds the organisation into its network of relationships.

We can debate the proposition that organisations with strong, cohesive and homogeneous cultures (such as Body Shop) have less need of formal systems and procedures, as the way things get done is known and shared by all. However, the notion of homogeneous cultures is often of doubtful validity in minds other than those of senior managers. We may now remind you of the material from Mintzberg and McHugh (1985) quoted in Book 6, in particular one of their main propositions: that strategies grow initially like weeds in a garden, and are not cultivated like tomatoes in a hot-house. Further, senior managers must beware of groupthink (recall the interview with Anne Huff). Groupthink, combined with a limited view of corporate, rather than organisational, culture can lead to strategic drift and unrealistically narrow horizons for decision-making. Alternatively, where an organisation does have a strong culture, it acts as a resource from which spring other capabilities such as rapid, decentralised decision-making or commitment to a strategic intent over the long term.

Ghemawat (1991) defined 'commitment' as 'the tendency of strategies to persist over time' (p. 14). He argues that 'initial choice constrains subsequent behaviour', and so 'it is difficult to flip-flop from strategy A to strategy B or vice versa. ... I define commitment as the degree of difficulty of flip-flops. More precisely, a strategy embodies commitment to the extent that, if adopted, it is likely to persist' (p. 15). For factors to wield such historic influence they must have a quality of 'stickiness' which Ghemawat characterises as durable, specialised (i.e. not easily imitated) and non-tradable. These characteristics are precisely those which define distinctive capabilities, as we discussed in Book 4. In this sense organisational culture is a capability which acts as a 'sticky' factor which can lock the organisation into particular commitments of resource and strategic trajectories and lock out others. To quote Ghemawat again:

> Organisational inertia is often modelled in terms of a particular sort of durable, specialised, untraded factor that the organisation is supposed to be stuck with, *its culture* ... there is less agreement about whether culture should be treated as a constraint or as a candidate for modification in line with the commitments the organisation is contemplating ...
>
> *(p. 25)*

How managers see culture and how they engage in developing, reinforcing or attempting to change culture, reveal culture as a powerful source of either advantage or inertia. The following brief case about the Japanese motor company Honda will illustrate some of these points.

MINI-CASE: HONDA

Two Honda executives (the designated president of American Honda Motor Co., Kihachiro Kawashima, and his assistant) arrived in the USA in late 1958. Their itinerary: San Francisco, Los Angeles, Dallas, New York, and Columbus. Mr Kawashima recounts his impressions.

My first reaction after travelling across the United States was: How could we have been so stupid as to start a war with such a vast and wealthy country! My second reaction was discomfort. I spoke poor English. We dropped in on motorcycle dealers who treated us discourteously and in addition, gave the general impression of being motorcycle enthusiasts who, secondarily, were in business. There were only 3,000 motorcycle dealers in the United States at the time and only 1,000 of them were open five days a week. The remainder were open on nights and weekends. Inventory was poor, manufacturers sold motorcycles to dealers on consignment, the retailers provided consumer financing; after-sales service was poor. It was discouraging.

My other impression was that everyone in the United States drove an automobile – making it doubtful that motorcycles could ever do very well in the market. However, with 450,000 motorcycle registrations in the US and 60,000 motorcycles imported from Europe each year it didn't seem unreasonable to shoot for 10% of the import market. I returned to Japan with that report.

In truth, we had no strategy other than the idea of seeing if we could sell something in the United States. It was a new frontier, a new challenge, and it fit the 'success against all odds' culture that Mr Honda had cultivated. I reported my impressions to Fujisawa – including the seat-of-the-pants target of trying, over several years, to attain a 10% share of the US imports. He didn't probe that target quantitatively. We did not discuss profits or deadlines for breakeven. Fujisawa told me if anyone could succeed, I could, and authorised $1 million for the venture.

The next hurdle was to obtain a currency allocation from the Ministry of Finance. They were extraordinarily sceptical. Toyota had launched the Toyopet in the US in 1958 and had failed miserably. 'How could Honda succeed?' they asked. Months went by. We put the project on hold. Suddenly, five months after our application, we were given the go-ahead, but at only a fraction of our expected level of commitment. 'You can invest $250,000 in the US market', they said, 'but only $110,000 in cash.' The remainder of our assets had to be in parts and motorcycle inventory.

We moved into frantic activity as the government, hoping we would give up on the idea, continued to hold us to the July 1959 start-up timetable. Our focus, as mentioned earlier, was to compete with the European exports. We knew our products at the time were good but not far superior. Mr Honda was especially confident of the 250cc and 350cc machines. The shape of the handlebar on these larger machines looked like the eyebrow of Buddha, which he felt was a strong selling point. Thus, after some discussion and with no compelling criteria for selection, we configured our start-up inventory with 25% of each of our four products in the 50cc Supercub and the 125cc, 250cc, and 350cc machines. In dollar value terms, of course, the inventory was heavily weighted toward the larger bikes.

The stringent monetary controls of the Japanese government together with the unfriendly reception we had received during our 1958 visit caused us to start small. We chose Los Angeles where there was a large second and third generation Japanese community, a climate suitable for motorcycle use, and a growing population. We were so strapped for cash that the three of us shared a furnished apartment that rented for $80 per month. Two of us slept on the floor. We obtained a warehouse in a run-down section of the city and waited for the ship to arrive. Not daring to spare our funds for equipment, the three of us stacked the motorcycle crates three high – by hand, swept the floors, and built and maintained the parts bin.

We were entirely in the dark the first year. We were not aware that the motorcycle business in the United States occurs during a seasonable April-to-August window – and our timing coincided with the closing of the 1959 season. Our hard-learned experiences with distributorships in Japan convinced us to try to go to the retailers direct. We ran ads in the motorcycle trade magazine for dealers. A few responded. By spring of 1960, we had forty dealers and some of our inventory in their stores – mostly larger bikes. A few of the 250cc and 350cc bikes began to sell. Then disaster struck.

By the first week of April 1960, reports were coming in that our machines were leaking oil and encountering clutch failure. This was our lowest moment. Honda's fragile reputation was being destroyed before it could be established. As it turned out, motorcycles in the United States are driven much farther and much faster than in Japan. We dug deeply into our precious cash reserves to air freight our motorcycles to the Honda testing lab in Japan. Throughout the dark month of April, Pan Am was the only enterprise in the US that was nice to us. Our testing lab worked twenty-four-hour days bench-testing the bikes to try to replicate the failure. Within a month, a redesigned head gasket and clutch spring solved the problem. But in the meantime, events had taken a surprising turn.

Throughout our first eight months, following Mr Honda's and our own instincts, we had not attempted to move the 50cc Supercubs. While they were a smash success in Japan (and manufacturing couldn't keep up with demand there), they seemed wholly unsuitable for the US market where everything was bigger and more luxurious. As a clincher, we had our sights on the import market – and the Europeans, like the American manufacturers, emphasised the larger machines.

We used the Honda 50's ourselves to ride around Los Angeles on errands. They attracted a lot of attention. One day we had a call from a Sears buyer. While persisting in our refusal to sell through an intermediary, we took note of Sears's interest. But we still hesitated to push the 50cc bikes out of fear they might harm our image in a heavily macho market. But when the larger bikes started breaking, we had no choice. We let the 50cc bikes move. And surprisingly, the retailers who wanted to sell them weren't motorcycle dealers, they were sporting goods stores.

The excitement created by the Honda Supercub began to gain momentum. Under restrictions from the Japanese government, we were still on a cash basis. Working with our initial cash and inventory, we sold machines, reinvested in inventory, and sank the profits into additional inventory and advertising. Our advertising tried to straddle the market. While retailers continued to inform us that our Supercub customers were normal everyday Americans, we hesitated to target toward this segment out of fear of alienating the high margin end of our business, sold through the traditional motorcycle dealers to a more traditional 'black leather jacket' customer.

(Source: abridged from Honda case study: Harvard Business School case 9-384-050)

Activity 2.3

Identify what you see as the key elements of Honda's culture.

Discussion

The strategy process of Honda's US subsidiary whereby it was decided to push the Honda Supercub, contrary to Honda's views that the larger machines would be more attractive, shows that Honda's strong culture supported the capability to change strategic direction. This illustrates a risk-taking culture within a hierarchical structure. You should also note the suggested lack of close scrutiny of the 'seat-of-the-pants' 10% US target market objectives proposed in Mr Kawashima's initial business plan. Agreement supporting the unresearched target of 10% of US market share is further indication of the 'loose–tight' nature of the 'strong' culture.

Imagine the importance internally for Honda as such a powerful success story permeates the whole company. It becomes part of the myths and legends in the cultural web, reinforcing the Honda cultural paradigm of 'success against all odds' encouraged by Mr Honda, the founder. Honda's mould-breaking strategic initiative also highlights concepts discussed earlier in the course such as emergent strategy, the breaking of industry recipes and the (potentially negative as well as positive) power of both organisational and national cultural preconceptions and assumptions.

A further brief section from the same source will lead you into Activity 2.4.

'The success of Honda, Suzuki and Yamaha in the States has been jolly good for us,' Eric Turner, Chairman of the Board of BSA Ltd., told Advertising Age. 'People here start out by buying one of the low-priced Japanese jobs. They get to enjoy the fun and exhilaration of the open road and frequently end up buying one of our more powerful and expensive machines.' The British insist that they're not really in competition with the Japanese ('they're on the lighter end'). The Japanese have other ideas. Just two months ago Honda introduced a 444cc model to compete, at a lower price, with the Triumph 500cc.

(Advertising Age, 27 December 1965)

'Basically we do not believe in the lightweight market', says William H. Davidson, son of one of the founders and currently President of Harley-Davidson. 'We believe that motorcycles are sports vehicles, not transportation vehicles. Even if a man says he bought a motorcycle for transportation, it's generally for leisure time use. The lightweight motorcycle is only supplemental. Back around World War 1, a number of companies came out with lightweight bikes. We came out with one ourselves. We came out with another one in 1947 and it just did not go anywhere. We have seen what happens to these small sizes.'

(Forbes, 15 September 1966)

Activity 2.4 _____

Where in these press reports can you find examples of:

(i)   groupthink?

(ii)   a paradigm?

To what extent do either of these enable or inhibit action?

Discussion _____

Groupthink – *Triumph, Harley Davidson and US managers, as well as Honda itself, initially thought that the US market was not interested in small bikes.*

Paradigm – *The reaction of Honda's rivals shows how cognitive dissonance was coped with by conservation of their existing paradigm. Honda, however, as we have seen, modified its paradigm and in so doing broke the industry recipe.*

Reflection _____

The Honda mini-case is an interesting one on many levels. In addition to the points already discussed, you may find it useful to consider the role played by national culture, as well as the different (contrasting) organisational and corporate cultures of Honda and its main UK and US competitors in the motorcycle industry.

This role of culture as a capability, as a very rich resource, operates across all sectors. A common aim in the public sector nowadays includes the promotion of a culture that is more responsive to citizens as customers. This of course is problematic since citizens often have roles both as clients and as taxpayers, and such dual demands may be hard to reconcile. Many new managers in the public sector are endeavouring to develop a corporate culture which gives greater emphasis to value for money possibly at the cost of deeply held beliefs about 'public service', encompassing values such as equity, fairness and consistency. These new managers have many problems in building on the existing culture and the beliefs and values in terms of commitment and experience and yet at the same time trying to respond to demands from the state on the one hand and from citizens and customers on the other.

Activity 2.5

Box 2.1 contains extracts taken from the 1996 corporate strategy statement of the London Metropolitan Police in the UK: 'The London Beat: The Metropolitan Police Service into the 21st Century'.

(i)   Consider the Met's strategy statements and list the main issues it is addressing.

(ii)   What organisational culture problems may face managers in endeavouring to implement this corporate strategy?

(iii)   What is the intended paradigm for the Met that this document is attempting to create?

BOX 2.1   THE LONDON BEAT
The Metropolitan Police Service into the 21st Century

Statement of our common purpose and values

'The purpose of the Metropolitan Police Service is to uphold the law fairly and firmly; to prevent crime; to pursue and bring to justice those who break the law; to keep The Queen's Peace; to protect, help and reassure people in London; and to be seen to do all this with integrity, common sense and sound judgement.

We must be compassionate, courteous and patient, acting without fear or favour or prejudice to the rights of others. We need to be professional, calm and restrained in the face of violence and apply only that force which is necessary to accomplish our lawful duty.

We must strive to reduce the fears of the public and, so far as we can, to reflect their priorities in the action we take. We must respond to well-founded criticism with a willingness to change.'

Foreword

Over the past 167 years the Metropolitan Police Service has built a reputation for providing a world-class service to our capital city. [...]

As Commissioner I am keenly aware of a sense of stewardship of the Met. Our predecessors have, over the years, built us a reputation as a world leader in terms of service, standards, integrity and performance. This is a highly valuable legacy that we take into the next millennium. [...]

We need to ensure that we stay closely in touch with the public. We know that they want us to:

• tackle crime effectively

• provide patrolling officers to reassure and improve their quality of life

• respond well to emergency calls.

The core of our work is delivering these services in a way which is fair and professional and shows we provide value for money. Almost everything else we do is in support of this.

Policing the capital brings with it particular challenges as well as additional and unique responsibilities. We are not just the largest police service in the country. We deal with serious crime and events which are unique to the capital city. [...]

Also, we must continue to ensure the security of ceremonial occasions in London. Our responsibilities to protect the Royal Family, Parliament and the diplomatic community are duties we will continue to honour with pride and courage.

Despite the demands on us and the violence sometimes encountered, I am still committed to Met officers primarily remaining unarmed. The majority of officers support this view and do not wish to carry guns. However, I am determined that my officers should have the very best protection. They deserve no less.

The public expect us to make efficient use of all the money we spend. Providing value for money is not just good business, it is vital if we are to retain public support. [...]

These are enormously exciting times to be policing London. Although the demands are great, the challenges are stimulating and rewarding. London's population is becoming increasingly diverse, demands on our resources are rising and the public have high expectations of us. Success in the future will depend on our having the right people, doing the right things, in the right way.

[...] The Met's managers have a tough job. There are now fewer of them and I will expect them to play an increasingly important role in formulating strategy and in giving clear leadership. [...]

We have shown that crime can be tackled successfully with the support of the public. We rely on effective partnerships in all aspects of policing; whether in the criminal justice system, with car manufacturers in the prevention of car crime, or with voluntary groups in the care of victims.

This document identifies where we will focus effort to ensure that Londoners receive the highest possible quality of service. The proposals provide direction for the next five years but clearly our ability to deliver these will be affected by the funding we receive.

I am proud of the progress the Met has made in recent years and I look forward to leading the Service through some challenging times ahead. I am confident the proposals in this document will get us into even better shape for policing London into the 21st Century.

Sir Paul Condon, Commissioner

[...]

The right people

[...]

The Met needs people with integrity, who are thoroughly competent at their jobs, and able to give a lead to their colleagues and those they serve.

[...]

Leading and managing

[...] Our people have set extraordinary standards in the way they have acted as leaders, supporting and serving the people of London in their times of need.

We need to lead by:

- giving direction of purpose with unmistakable clarity
- building a team environment within which individuals can develop
- allowing each person to achieve fulfilment and acknowledging the value of their contribution
- telling people what is expected and holding them to account for their performance.

[...]

Choosing and developing our people

The dedication and ability of the Met's staff are the envy of many other organisations.

We need to ensure that we are recruiting and selecting the right people for the needs of the future, and fully developing the talents of the people we already have.

[...]

Communicating our values

The public have more confidence in the police than in almost any other profession. The Met has a world-class reputation for the quality and professionalism of its people and service.

We must demonstrate these qualities in all we do. We must be open and explain police action in ways which gain us understanding and support.

[...]

Doing the right things

The Met is a large, complex organisation that provides a wide range of services to the people of London. However, most of our effort is concentrated in three key areas: tackling crime, patrolling and responding to calls from the public.

We must ensure that we are doing the right things effectively and efficiently.

Tackling crime

Over the last few years the Met's performance against crime has greatly improved. Crime levels have fallen more than at any time in the last 30 years, and the clear-up rate for all crime has risen from 16 per cent to 24 per cent.

We intend to continue to improve our performance. Crime affects the quality of life in London and the level of public confidence. [...]

Our aim is to reduce crime using intelligence and proactive operations to target prolific criminals and locations which are prone to crime. We will support all victims, especially those who are repeatedly victimised. To sustain the momentum of crime reduction, we will need help from the wider community.

[...]

Patrolling effectively

The London 'bobby' is a powerful image throughout the world. Surveys show that the public are more satisfied with the level of foot patrol in London than anywhere else in the country. We deploy over 14,000 officers on patrol and, for many, they are symbolic of a well-ordered society. Our patrolling officers are accountable to local people and provide a service which is not dependent on people's ability to pay.

We believe that high visibility patrol strengthens public confidence and trust and, when carefully targeted, makes people feel safe and keeps crime levels down.

[...]

In the right way

Our Statement of Common Purpose and Values appears at the front of this strategy and clearly lays out the standards we aspire to. We first published it in 1989, building on the 'primary objects of policing' laid down by our first commissioners in 1829.

[...] All our people must be honest, fair, sensitive and deserving of public trust. We will not compromise our integrity. We will deal firmly and swiftly with breaches of these standards.

We will become world leaders in ethics and fairness, as well as serving the public by making our organisation truly responsive and effective.

[...]

Pursuing ethics and fairness

We have long prided ourselves on our integrity and commitment to public service. Our values are apparent every day in the actions of our people. We set ourselves high standards but accept that our actions do not always meet our ideals. [...]

We will ensure that ethical standards are at the heart of all our systems and procedures, as well as our actions.

[...]

Upholding integrity

The vast majority of Met staff act with professionalism and integrity. We owe it to each other to deal effectively with those of our colleagues who let us and the public down.

[...]

While genuine error can be understood and often forgiven, there is no place for deliberately unethical behaviour, dishonesty or corruption. We will deal with these speedily and without compromise, to inspire public confidence in our investigation of complaints.

[...]

Policing diversity

[...]

It is vital to have the active confidence of all people living within the diverse communities of London. We must maintain and improve this confidence by working in partnership with agencies and associations in those communities. All members of the Met must be caring and compassionate to victims and witnesses, professional with suspects, and courteous in their dealings with all other members of the public, irrespective of their ethnic background or social position.

We will provide a service to all that is fair and seen to be so. We will ensure that all members of the public, whoever they are and wherever they live or work, consistently enjoy the same high quality of service.

[...]

Shaping the organisation

We are accountable for the way in which we use public money. Everything we do should support the core activity of policing. [...]

As a result of service restructuring we have a more effective and streamlined structure to meet modern demands. [...]

We must retain resilience and flexibility to deal with emergencies, and expertise to meet our national commitments. We must ensure that our divisions meet their corporate responsibilities to keep The Queen's Peace and are able to work effectively with other agencies.

[...]

Using information for action

Accountability for results should drive managers' decision-making. [...]

We are devolving decision-making to local managers. They in turn will hold their staff accountable for high standards of performance, while supporting them in the difficult job they do.

[...]

Discussion

(i)   *Issues are likely to include:*

- *clarifying strategic objectives for a high-profile public-sector/ public-service organisation with an extensive and sensitive list of stakeholders with very varied and frequently contradictory priorities*

- *identifying priorities in resource allocation, especially in balancing conspicuous needs (such as protection of important personages) against more mundane and pervasive demands for secure communities*

- *stakeholder management, including internal and external perceptions of fairness*

- *determining acceptable and meaningful performance measures*

- *the centrality of human resource management, especially recruitment (broadening representativeness and changing the skill-base), selection and all aspects of training and development.*

(ii)   *Organisational culture problems may include:*

- *continuity of historical core values and heritage into a new criminal security and policing context*

- *existence of organisational subcultures, as well as general problems of internal representativeness of the population at large*

- *tensions between law enforcement and perceptions of fairness and social justice*

- *concerns as to whether the corporate strategy document represented the corporate culture or the organisational culture*
- *identifying possible gaps between the intended and the realised strategy.*

(iii)   The paradigm which the strategy document espouses might include:

- *effective crime prevention*
- *effective law enforcement*
- *'fair policing'*
- *acting to reduce the fears and reflect the priorities of the public*
- *organisational and public integrity.*

2.4.1   Corporate culture, national culture and institutional culture

Implicit in the structures and systems which shape our experience are value statements about what is important, not only within organisations but also concerning what is important in a society. These are largely the product of the re-creation of both past and present models of those who are dominant and powerful within organisations and societies – parents, managers or significant peers. This leads some writers to take the view that it is the values of the dominant which are important rather than the aggregated values of individuals within organisations. This finds immediate expression in a distinction between corporate culture (what the dominant members value) and organisational culture (what the other members value) that we returned to in our discussion of Box 2.1.

It is also important to recognise that not all values are shaped by work-related experiences. Other influences are apparent and important, such as experiences within the wider society. The effects of the wider institutional environment, such as government systems and education, are formative experiences for us. Thus, national or societal values are carried with us as we participate in, and work for, organisations. This institutional environment is easily visible in the professional or occupational training we might receive – such as for doctors and lawyers – which is intended to impact on our belief systems as professional ethics.

If we differ in the values that we hold, the experiences that shape our values and beliefs, and in the ways in which we as individuals act, how then can we talk of collective cultures? Is there something more fundamental underpinning this? Hosmer (1994) suggests that there are indeed some fundamental ethical principles that do transcend cultures, time and economic conditions. These are the basic rules or principles that have been proposed to ensure 'good' society. Whether or not this proposition is tenable, ethical values are an important part of the formal policies (and therefore the culture) of many organisations. In the next sub-sections we will explore the issues that this raises.

2.5   CULTURE AND ETHICS

As we discussed in Section 2.4, many of our more deeply held values are shaped in our early life and subsequent socialisation, such as moral principles which govern our behaviour and expectation as to what is right and what is wrong. They set standards as to what is good or bad in conduct and decision-making. These can be seen to be different from the rule of law, as this is based on a set of codified principles that delineate how we are to act. They often reflect some combination of moral values but not all of these are codified into laws. Ethical standards mostly apply to behaviour not covered by the law, and some law covers behaviour but not necessarily ethical values. The morality of trying to save a drowning person is not covered by the law and parking a car in a prohibited area does not have a moral basis; for behaviour such as theft, however, legal and moral standards do largely overlap.

2.5.1   Culture, ethics and advantage

Do organisations which act ethically achieve some additional advantage? Hosmer (1994) encapsulates this position when he points out in discussing ethics and strategy:

> I do not claim that all equitable acts lead to strategic and financial success. I do not claim that all inequitable acts lead to strategic and financial disaster. I do, however, claim that a pattern of equitable acts over time does indeed lead to trust and that trust to commitment, and that a committed effort which is both co-operative and innovative on the part of everyone does eventually lead to success.

Activity 2.6 _____

Recall the tape where Anita Roddick is discussing Body Shop's social audit. Is this a good example of a happy marriage of business and ethics?

You may need to clarify which main stakeholders are involved and where the power lies among them. To help you in your evaluation, Body Shop's mission statement is reproduced for you below.

Body Shop's Mission Statement

Our reason for being

To dedicate our business to the pursuit of social and environmental change.

To creatively balance the financial and human needs of our stakeholders: employees, franchisees, customers, suppliers and shareholders.

To courageously ensure that our business is ecologically sustainable: meeting the needs of the present without compromising the future.

To meaningfully contribute to local, national and international communities in which we trade, by adopting a code of conduct which ensures care, honesty, fairness and respect.

To passionately campaign for the protection of the environment, human and civil rights, and against animal testing within the cosmetics and toiletries industry.

To tirelessly work to narrow the gap between principle and practice, whilst making fun, passion and care part of our daily lives.

Boxes 2.2 and 2.3 illustrate the changing balance of power between wider groups of internal and external stakeholders which influences perceptions of ethics and advantage for organisations.

BOX 2.2   THE FUN OF BEING MULTINATIONAL

It is Myanmar (previously known as Burma) that happens to be in the news right now. Protesters have recently demonstrated at Unocal petrol stations across America to complain about the oil firm's involvement (with France's Total) in an off-shore gas field – a project, say the protesters, that helps to prop up an unlovely regime. Last week, two European brewers, Carlsberg and Heineken, pulled out of investments in Myanmar.

But Myanmar is only one place where controversial investments are once again causing grief to big multinationals, especially to oil and mining companies:

- RTZ-CRA, which is Britain's (and the world's) biggest mining group, and Freeport-McMoRan, an American firm, are under attack from environmentalists for a copper and gold mine in Irian Jaya, Indonesia. RTZ-CRA last year made pre-tax profits of $2.46 billion, up 42% on the year before. But when the firm held its annual meeting in London in May, journalists preferred to write about the tribespeople who turned up to protest about the company, and about the environmental activist who tried to storm the podium.

- Royal Dutch/Shell has similar woes. Despite being in the throes of a far-reaching reorganisation, the oil giant has seen all the public's attention focus instead first on its aborted plans to dump the Brent Spar, an oil platform, at sea and then on its relations with the military regime in Nigeria. These provoked an international outcry last year when Nigeria executed nine dissidents.

It hurts

The average oil baron or mining boss might once have shrugged off such events as little local difficulties. Some even relished a brawl. Nowadays, they recognise that the stakes are higher. It is not only the prospect of consumer boycotts that worries them. In addition, staff morale can suffer (many Shell employees opposed the sinking of the Brent Spar), political contacts can be upset (Nelson Mandela denounced Shell's behaviour in Nigeria), and – worst of all – sanctions can be imposed (the state of Massachusetts recently banned contracts with firms doing business in Myanmar).

To some extent, multinationals have themselves to blame. Many have been in the forefront of campaigning for higher ethical standards. They have drawn up ethics statements, appointed ethics officers and signed international agreements such as the International Chamber of Commerce's Business Charter for Sustainable Development. This do-goodery also brings them commercial advantage. Foisting complex regulations on local competitors in the third world can help multinationals; and it is often easier for them to operate under one set of standards everywhere than to tailor standards for individual countries.

This 'ethical' strategy has paid dividends. Multinationals have shaken off their old sinister image. The United Nations, which used to try to control them, now regards them as agents of modernisation and good practice. The developing world, having once feared them, now competes to attract their factories. But they are also now being judged against the high ethical standards which they themselves have helped to promulgate.

[...]

At the same time, the multinationals' professional critics – environmental and human-rights lobbyists – have become more organised. Greenpeace is no longer an amateurish affair of beards and T-shirts but a professional, global organisation which has offices in 33 countries, including Latin America and Eastern Europe, and which – like the multinationals it shadows – is keen to expand in Asia. Robert Weissman, editor of *Multinational Monitor*, a campaigning magazine based in Washington DC, says that green campaigners based in the rich world are increasingly travelling to remote trouble-spots, or whisking the 'victims' of multinationals to the West.

In South-East Asia, groups representing local people co-ordinate their campaigns using e-mail. In Asia and Latin America tribes have put old enmities to one side and joined forces to exert pressure on multinationals and governments. Various Amazonian tribes, for example, have united under the Confederation of Indigenous Nationalities of Ecuador, and in the Philippines the Cordillera Peoples' Alliance has lobbied against mining and forestry companies. In both countries such groups have found eager allies among the rich world's green campaigners.

Campaigners are also using new tactics. One is to take multinationals to court in rich countries for their behaviour in poor ones. Freeport-McMoRan, accused among other things of environmental violations (which it denies) in Irian Jaya, is being sued in New Orleans. Another tactic is to lobby shareholders. Friends of the Earth has complained to RTZ-CRA's institutional shareholders about a proposed new mining project in Madagascar.

Moral maze

All this has had an impact. One oil manager admits that after Shell's troubles his firm would have to think 'very carefully' before investing in Nigeria. 'Companies check out the situation much more carefully than in the past,' says Mark Collins, director of the World Conservation Monitoring Centre, which advises firms on the ecological sensitivity of remote regions of the world.

The difficulty for companies intent on avoiding trouble is that they may forfeit the best opportunities of growth. It just so happens that much of the world's mineral and oil wealth is located in countries with fragile politics and environments. Many mining and oil firms have therefore chosen to press ahead, but to work harder to accommodate the worries of campaigners. Senior Shell managers have recently held meetings with Greenpeace and Amnesty International. 'We have to listen a damn sight harder,' says one oil boss. Chevron, an American oil firm, is giving the World-wide Fund for Nature money to preserve forests in Papua New Guinea.

Multinationals are also paying more attention to indigenous groups. Before signing a deal in May to develop a gas field in Peru, Shell met local tribespeople. Keen to avoid repeating the mistakes it made in Nigeria, it also discussed the deal with more than 60 government and pressure groups around the world. In Indonesia, in the wake of riots near its mine in Irian Jaya, Freeport-McMoRan has been trying to soothe local feelings. Freeport Indonesia, the firm's local branch, has promised to spend 1% of its revenues every year on local people. Much of the money will go into health care and education.

This is not mere public relations. One hardened observer, Robin Bidwell, chairman of ERM, a British environmental consultancy, thinks many multinationals have crossed an intellectual Rubicon. They once saw local political or environmental problems as the concern of governments. Now they see them as their responsibility too. In the words of Sarah Tyack, campaigner for Friends of the Earth, 'people are realising that these multinationals have a soft underbelly.'

Source: The Economist, 20 July 1996

This article raises fundamental issues about moral dilemmas. It particularly emphasises the rising concern of consumers in the richer developed economies with where and how their goods and services are produced. Some voices question whether it is possible to run a business ethically, thus posing a very simplistic view which sees a basic contradiction between the search for profit and ethical conduct. However, there has been a consistent historic tradition in all cultures of many companies managed on the basis of clear underlying principles. Furthermore, it is inadequate for managers to look no further than this simple statement since these moral dilemmas are also about commercial necessities which are complex and have serious unintended, as well as intended, consequences.

Box 2.2 shows that ethical behaviour does not mean simply following the law; managers do have to be sensitive to emerging norms and values in society and in the worldwide community that impact on the way that they conduct operations. It also shows a complex mix of outcomes. Daft (1992) gives some examples:

- The executive in charge of a parts distribution facility told employees to tell phone customers that inventory was in stock even if it was not. Replenishing the item only took one to two days, no one was hurt by the delay, and the business was kept from competitors.

- A North American manufacturer operating abroad was asked to make cash payments (a bribe) to government officials and was told it was consistent with local customs, despite being illegal in North America.

As you will see, these may present the manager with a dilemma in that each choice is in some way undesirable. However, such choices can be guided by the values and culture within an organisation. Thus ethical values are in part shaped *by* culture and are part *of* culture. In some cases our individual values might clash with those of the organisations we work for – so that our interests as employees or managers may not be congruent with our preferences as consumers, parents, voters, tourists or environmentally concerned individuals.

2.6   NATIONAL CULTURES AND ORGANISATIONAL CULTURES

In the 1980s, commentators attempted to explain the decline of Western industrial competitiveness and the simultaneous rise of Japanese economic competitiveness by contrasting Japanese and Western cultures and their respective impact on management practice. These included such writers as Ouchi (1981), Peters and Waterman (1982) and Deal and Kennedy (1982). The obvious differences in the way that Japanese and Western firms were run, especially in terms of the relations among employees and managers, led to the conclusion that national values, as expressed in organisational practice, were the key to Japan's economic philosophy and its business.

Peters and Waterman (1982) cautioned against the rush to adopt Japanese management culture practices wholesale. Instead they emphasised 'simultaneous loose–tight coupling'. Briefly, this argument suggests that organisations which emphasise strong conformity to 'tight' core values, may use 'looser' control systems for day-to-day operational decision-making. As Mintzberg points out in the Course Reader article for Book 7, when an organisation socialises its members to believe in a strong ideology (corporate culture), it can then allow them considerable freedom to act in accordance with the prevailing norms. The result can be genuine decentralisation ('empowerment'): a 'democratisation' of structure and shared decision-making within a clear hierarchy of power and seniority. Organisations may thus be formally defined, yet have flexibility in procedures and routines.

It is hard to overestimate the impact that this line of thinking has had on managerial thought and practice. It appealed strongly for two reasons. First, it gave an explanation for Japan's meteoric rise in the world economy in the 1970s and early 1980s. Second, it suggested an alternative managerial model. If different competitive performance could be explained in terms of national culture as manifested through managerial styles within organisations, then the culture of any organisation could and should be made closer to the 'Japanese management model'. The possibility that such organisational and managerial differences might be more deeply rooted in mixtures of political, socio-economic and cultural factors was not seriously considered in the early enthusiasm. Managers and policy makers ignored those of Japan's advantages that were rooted in its financial structure, its industrial policy, its long-term investment in new plant and processes while focusing on an important but partial explanation of Japanese success. Since Japan is one of the most ethnically homogeneous nations in the world, and is also a culture which places a high emphasis on conformity, the case for a direct connection between national culture and organisational culture and practice seemed proven. But for precisely the same reasons it rendered the wholesale transfer of such approaches unlikely and inappropriate.

It should also be stated at this point that the Japanese economic 'miracle' of the 1960s, '70s and early '80s, gave way in the late '80s and early '90s to problems of over-rigidity and the collapse of its interconnected property and banking sectors – a direct outcome of some of the factors so much praised earlier.

The ways in which values and behaviour differ between societies, and their impact on organisations, have been the subject of Hofstede's pathbreaking work (1980). We will give a brief outline of his work here. The sheer scale of his source data from 116,000 IBM employees in 40 countries is impressive. The respondents were all sales and service employees of IBM. This research design enabled a number of factors to be controlled. All respondents were doing the same task (selling and servicing IBM products) within the same general overall framework for the same company. Thus the technology, job content and some formal procedures were the same. Only their nationalities differed. The differences in attitudes and values could therefore be said to be related to cultural differences rather than organisational ones. Factor analysis of the responses to 32 questions revealed four underlying dimensions of culture:

- Power Distance (PDI): an indication of the extent to which a society accepts the unequal distribution of power in organisations.
- Uncertainty Avoidance (UAI): an indication of the degree to which the members of a culture/society tolerate uncertainty or ambiguity.
- Individualism (IDV): an indication of the degree to which the culture/society emphasises personal initiative and achievement rather than collective group-centred concerns.
- Masculinity (MAS): an indication of the extent to which the dominant values in a society reflect the so-called 'masculine' tendencies of assertiveness, the acquisition of money and property and not caring for others.

He went on to relate PDI and UAI to the structure of organisations. He suggests that in cultures where PDI is high, 'power is the leading principle which keeps the organisation together and which protects it against uncertainty'. In cultures where PDI is low, there are two possibilities. If people have an inner need for living up to rules (high UAI), the leading principle which keeps the organisation together can be formal rules. If people do not have an inner need for living up to rules (low UAI), the organisation has to be kept together by more *ad hoc* negotiation, a situation which calls for a larger tolerance for uncertainty from everyone' (Hofstede, 1980, p. 319). The dimensions of PDI and UAI can thus be related to organisation structure: power distance (PDI) with concentration of authority (centralisation) and uncertainty avoidance (UAI) with the degree to which activities are structured.

Hofstede's main and unequivocal finding is that organisations are indeed culture-bound and that this 'applies not only to the behaviour of people within organisations and to the functioning of the organisation as a whole; even the theories developed to explain behaviour in organisations reflect the national culture of their author, and so do the methods and techniques that are suggested for the management of organisations' (p. 372). Table 2.1 gives a flavour of some of the insights generated by his work.

Table 2.1   53 countries and regions according to their level of uncertainty avoidance

Uncertainty avoidance		
Weak	**Medium**	**Strong**
Australia	Austria	Argentina
Canada	Brazil	Belgium
Denmark	Colombia	Chile
Great Britain	Equador	Costa Rica
Hong Kong	Finland	France
India	West Germany	Greece
Indonesia	Iran	Guatemala
Ireland	Israel	Japan
Jamaica	Italy	South Korea
Malaysia	Mexico	Panama
New Zealand	Netherlands	Peru
Norway	Pakistan	Portugal
Philippines	Switzerland	Salvador
Singapore	Taiwan	Spain
South Africa	Thailand	Turkey
Sweden	Venezuela	Uruguay
USA	Arab countries	Yugoslavia
	East African countries	
	West African countries	

Source: Hofstede, 1989, p. 393

While it is difficult to map Hofstede's value dimensions exactly on to organisational behaviour and functioning, his work does throw light on the problems of developing strong homogeneous cultures in international organisations and whether homogeneous national cultures could, or should, be translatable into homogeneous corporate cultures. The broader implications of these issues for corporate and international strategy will be discussed further in Books 9 and 10.

2.7   CULTURE AND THE PARADIGM

It is germane at this point to revisit the linkage between culture and paradigm. Johnson (1987, 1988, 1992) makes no mention of values in his definition of paradigm. For him, the paradigm represents persistent sets of beliefs about how to compete that have been built up over time and reinforced through the activity of managing. Core values refer to beliefs about how the world should be and how we should behave within it. Such beliefs guide our actions. Beliefs which are repeatedly validated become taken-for-granted assumptions of how the world is. The same holds true within organisations and is the basis for the relevance of the paradigm to strategy-making, strategy formulation and strategy implementation. In this sense paradigms are empirically driven. They are built on experiences rather than driven by a model of how we believe we should behave.

If we view the paradigm as a map of the organisation, how do managers use these maps and how do these forces shape strategy? The use of the cognitive perspective in strategy was introduced in Books 1 and 6. A distinction was made between two ways that managers process information in making strategy. These were top-down and bottom-up processing. Bottom-up processing is essentially data-driven, in that the manager makes few inferences about the data. Top-down involves the manager in being selective as to which data to pay attention to. Past experiences of similar circumstances are used to guide current thinking. This provides the basis for selecting which information is most appropriate.

Top-down processing implies that concrete reality (in the form of phenomena which have an independent existence from the strategist, for example car plants, banks, NGOs and so on) is created by the patterns and linkages between the events, objects and situations that appear meaningful to the manager as strategist. It defines the environment as a social construct. The environment is constructed in much the same fashion as organisations are created, by the patterns that people draw. Thus we create the environment by the use of maps, models or frameworks which are the product of our experiences or cultural forces.

Since strategy-making is a collective activity (as we saw in Book 6), it must involve sharing our constructions, of both organisation and environment, with others and arriving at a collective course of action. This involves the interplay of the sense-making system with the political system and explains once again the non-linear, non-rational side to strategic thinking and why strategy must in part be understood as a social and cultural construct. Box 2.3 provides an illustration of this.

BOX 2.3

Johnson (1987) made a detailed study of the strategy-making process in a UK menswear retailing group. His 10-year study has contributed to the development of a cognitive perspective in strategy.

He found that the managers were aware of environmental changes, in particular the changing strategies of other retailers, and that they did implement changes in strategy in response to these perceived changes. The problem was that, with hindsight, the strategic changes were inadequate and inappropriate. How did this happen?

As we have argued, managers use cognitive devices to help them make sense of the complexity and diversity facing them. Johnson proposes that relevant environmental change will be defined in terms of consonance, or dissonance, with the existing paradigm held by management. This means that:

1   Some environmental signals will simply not be perceived as being relevant in terms of the paradigm and will be ignored. For example, competitors' activity may be interpreted as not impinging on the company because they are perceived to be operating in a different market sector.

2   Other signals might be seen as 'consonant' with the paradigm in that they can be interpreted and acted on within the bounds of that paradigm.

3   Some signals are seen as 'dissonant' with the paradigm, in which case the responses seem to follow this pattern:

  (a)   dissonance is coped with symbolically through the mechanisms within which the paradigm is embedded

  (b)   since the threat may challenge those most associated with the core constructs of the paradigm, such threats may well take on a political complexion and be strongly resisted by the current power-holders.

  (c)   the dissonance will be 'resolved' by adapting the organisation within the bounds of the paradigm.

The paradigm then effectively defines environmental 'reality' and responses to environmental change, and its cultural and political context means that it is likely to stifle tensions and threats resulting from dissonance between the paradigm and the environment.

So, while strategic change is typically adaptive and incremental, it is also the case that, periodically, organisations experience fundamental strategic change. Such a realignment is likely to occur when strategic drift has become so marked that a significant grouping of managers recognises that performance decline cannot be overcome by a typical adaptive change. Rather, what occurs is a break with the constraints of the paradigm, which leads to a more fundamental realignment of strategy. These three stages of adaptation, from coping with the existing paradigm to eventual shift to paradigm change, are expressed in Figure 2.1.

Figure 2.1   The steps from paradigm reinforcement to paradigm change

In order for fundamental change to take place, the paradigm must be challenged, discredited and devalued, a process which will clearly be painful. This will be examined in Section 3.

We thus see the paradigm not only as a powerful tool for coping with complex situations but also as a liability under changed conditions causing strategic drift.

Activity 2.7 _____

Think of two or three examples in your department or section (or in an organisation with which you are familiar) where the paradigm has proved a liability or constraint.

Remember that the paradigm can be very active at all levels in an organisation: at the top, at business level and at the operational level.

Discussion _____

As Johnson points out, paradigms can constrain actions by colouring managers' perceptions of their world. This can cause them to discount competitor activity; to miss the emergence of new sorts of competitors; to persist in producing outmoded products; to discount market research evidence and so on. We will cover these issues more fully in a later section. Table 2.2 gives three of Johnson's examples of paradigm constraint on strategic change.

In each of the three cases the paradigm constrained action and contributed greatly to blocking change, especially blocking the perception that fundamental strategy change might be needed. For Case A – the menswear retailer – attempts to shift the strategy towards a more fashionable offering to rescue sales were blocked by the old paradigm of 'gentleman's outfitter'. For Case B – the management consultancy partnership – avoidance of risk and preservation of the privileges of partners were dominant. For Case C – the regional newspaper – the suggestions of younger staff that the paper was actually an advertising medium and needed to focus on that to protect market share and revenues was blocked by the dominant paradigm about being a newspaper which must allocate its resources primarily to news-gathering.

Table 2.2 How managers define the cultural web – three cases

A	B	C
A menswear clothing retailer	**A consultancy partnership**	**A regional newspaper**
Paradigm	**Paradigm**	**Paradigm**
We sell to 'the working lad's market'.	We are the biggest, the best, certainly the safest.	We are in the newspaper business.
Retailing skills (as they define them) centrally important.	Client satisfaction at all costs.	Our paid-for daily will always be there.
Retailing is about buying: 'we sell what we buy'.	Any job is worth doing – and we can do it.	Readers will pay for news.
Volume is vital.	Professionalism is important.	Advertisers need newspapers.
Staff experience and loyalty important.	Avoid risks.	
Low cost operations (e.g. distribution channels) important.	(The implication is that this consultancy is concerned to provide a very wide range of services, but is unlikely to provide services which are contentious or risky.)	
(Note what is not here: retailing is not about shop ambience, service etc.)		
Power	**Power**	**Power**
The Chairman regarded as all-powerful – 'but nicely'.	Diffuse and unclear power base in a partnership structure.	The parent company – a newspaper group.
Divisions of power significant: the major menswear business vs ('peripheral') businesses: head office operations vs field retail operations.	An external power base in the parent audit firm clearly important.	The autocratic CEO.
Insiders with experience traditionally powerful: outsiders without company experience not powerful and do not last long.		Departmental rivalry between production, commercial and editorial departments.
Organisation	**Organisation**	**Organisation**
Highly compartmentalised operations with vertical reporting relationships (e.g. buying distinct from stores).	Regional partnership structure giving a flat if complex matrix.	Vertical, hierarchical system with little lateral communication and much vertical referral.
Every department with a Director, leading to a heavy superstructure.	Decision making through a networking system loose and flexible but based on 'who you know'.	Autocratic management style.
Top-down decision making with board involvement in operational decisions.		
Paternalistic.		
Control systems	**Control systems**	**Control systems**
Margin control.	Emphasis on time control and utilisation of consultants.	Emphasis on targeting and budgeting.
Long established 'proven' rigid and complex systems.		To achieve a low cost operation.
Paper-based control systems.		

Rituals and routines

Long established merchandise sourcing in the Far East.

Induction into the company way of doing things through attrition and training: 'outsiders serve an apprenticeship until they conform'.

Emphasis on pragmatic rather than analytic decisions.

Lack of questioning or forcing: 'you can challenge provided I feel comfortable'.

Heavy emphasis on grading systems.

Promotions only within functions.

Rituals and routines

Writing and re-writing of reports – 'the product of the firm'.

Partners' signatures on anything that goes to clients.

Gentlemanly behaviour – particularly with clients and partners.

Rituals and routines

Deadlines for publication.

'Product' developed in hours and minutes, not days and months.

Long working hours common.

Ritualised executive meetings.

Stories

Big buying deals of the past.

Paternalistic leaders (usually chairman) of the past.

More recent 'villainous' leaders who helped cause problems.

Stories

Big fee assignments.

Big disasters and failures.

The dominance of the audit practice.

Mavericks who would not follow the systems.

Stories

Macho personalities and behaviour.

Scoops and coverage of major events.

Major errors in print.

The defeat of labour unions.

Symbols

The separate Executive Directors' corridor.

Use of initials to designate Senior Executives and 'Sir' for the Chairman.

The dining room for Directors and 'selected' Senior Executives.

Named and numbered car parking spaces rigidly adhered to.

Source: Johnson, 1992, p. 32

Symbols

The partnership structure itself.

The symbols of partnership – the tea service, office size, partners' secretaries, partners' dining rooms.

One regional partnership that had always refused to integrate with other partnerships.

Symbols

Symbols of hierarchy: the MD's Jaguar, portable phones, car parking spaces etc.

The 'press'.

Technical production jargon.

The street vendors.

2.8 THE KNOWLEDGE-CREATING COMPANY

What kinds of cultural values and power structures lend themselves to creative activities rather than blocking activities? Recent work by Japanese academics (Nonaka, 1991; Nonaka and Takeuchi, 1995) has suggested some useful answers. In particular they highlight the re-evaluation of the contribution made by middle-level managers.

BOX 2.4   MIDDLE-UP-DOWN MANAGEMENT PROCESS FOR KNOWLEDGE CREATION

We start [...] by examining two dominant models of the management process, the top-down model and the bottom-up model, both of which fall short of fostering the dynamic interaction necessary to create organisational knowledge. We propose a new model, which we call middle-up-down, and explain why it is superior for knowledge-creation management than the more traditional models. The new model puts the middle manager at the very center of knowledge management and redefines the role of top management as well as of front-line employees. We will draw on the product development case of the Mini-Copier at Canon to describe the expected roles of the key players in the middle-up-down model.

Top-down and bottom-up

Sooner or later, any organisation ends up creating new knowledge. But in most organisations this process is haphazard, serendipitous, and therefore impossible to predict. What distinguishes the knowledge-creating company is that it systematically manages the knowledge-creation process. And the experience of the Japanese companies we have been studying suggests that the management process best suited to creating organisational knowledge is substantially different from the traditional managerial models with which most executives are familiar, namely the top-down and bottom-up management models.

Top-down management is basically the classical hierarchical model. [...] Simple and selected information is passed up the pyramid to top executives, who then use it to create plans and orders, which are eventually passed down the hierarchy. Information is processed using division of labour, with top management creating the basic concepts so that lower members can implement them. Top-management concepts become the operational conditions for middle managers, who will decide on the means to realise them. The middle managers' decisions, in turn, constitute the operational conditions for front-line employees, who will implement the decisions. At the front-line level, execution becomes largely routine. [...]

A top-down organisation is shaped like a pyramid, if we visualise the dyadic relations between top vs. middle managers and middle vs. front-line employees. An implicit assumption behind this traditional model of organisation is that only top managers are able and allowed to create knowledge. Moreover, knowledge created by top managers exists only to be processed or implemented. [...] As such, the concepts are strictly functional and pragmatic. It is this deductive transformation that enables workers with limited information-processing capacity to deal with a mass of information.

Bottom-up management is basically a mirror image of top-down management. [...] Instead of hierarchy and division of labour, there is autonomy. Instead of knowledge being created at and controlled from the top, it is created at and, to a large extent, controlled by the bottom.

A bottom-up organisation has a flat and horizontal shape. With hierarchy and division of labour eliminated, the organisation might have only three or four layers of management between the top and the front line. Few orders and instructions are given by the top managers, who serve as sponsors of entrepreneurially minded front-line employees. Knowledge is created by these employees, who operate as independent and separate actors, preferring to work on their own. There is little direct dialogue with other members of the organisation, either vertically or horizontally. Autonomy, not interaction, is the key operating principle. Certain individuals, not a group of individuals interacting with each other, create knowledge.

These two traditional models may seem like alternatives to each other, but neither is adequate as a process for managing knowledge creation. The top-down model is suited for dealing with explicit knowledge. But in controlling knowledge creation from the top, it neglects the development of tacit knowledge that can take place on the front line of an organisation. Bottom-up, on the other hand, is good at dealing with tacit knowledge. But its very emphasis on autonomy means that such knowledge is extremely difficult to disseminate and share within the organisation.

Put another way, both managerial processes are not very good at knowledge conversion. The top-down model provides only partial conversion focused on combination (explicit to explicit) and internalisation (explicit to tacit). Similarly, the bottom-up model carries out only partial conversion focused on socialisation (tacit to tacit) and externalisation (tacit to explicit).

[...]

The core process for creating organisational knowledge takes place intensively at the group level. Successive rounds of direct and meaningful dialogue within the group, for example, trigger externalisation. Through these dialogues, team members articulate their own thinking, sometimes through the use of metaphors or analogies, revealing hidden tacit knowledge that is otherwise hard to communicate. This kind of intense interaction hardly takes place in the military-like hierarchy of the top-down model or among the autonomy-driven individuals of the bottom-up model. Furthermore, notions such as noise, fluctuation, and chaos are fundamentally not permitted in the top-down model and are incarnated only within individuals in the bottom-up model.

The fact that knowledge is formed primarily in the minds of individuals and not amplified or refined through interaction creates another potential problem. In the case of the top-down model, there is a danger of the alignment of the fate of a few top managers with the fate of the firm. In the case of the bottom-up model, the pre-eminence and autonomy given to an individual make knowledge creation much more time-consuming, since the pace with which creation takes place is dependent on the patience and talent of the particular individual.

Another obvious, but major, limitation of the two models is the lack of recognition and relevance given to middle managers. They seem almost to have been neglected by the two models. In top-down management, the knowledge creator is top management. Middle managers process a lot of information in a typical top-down organisation, but play at most a minimal role in creating knowledge. In a hierarchy, middle managers are often responsible for submitting reports to top managers, analysing business problems and opportunities, or transmitting commands and orders from above to those below them, but nothing more relevant. In bottom-up management, the knowledge creator is the entrepreneur-like individual lower in the organisation. Given the small headquarters, a flat organisational structure, the propensity for top managers to serve as direct sponsors, and the autonomy provided to individuals, middle managers do not even seem to have a place within a typical bottom-up model.

Middle-up-down management

The Japanese companies we have been studying suggest a third way to manage knowledge creation. It is neither top-down nor bottom-up, but 'middle-up-down'. As strange as this term may sound, it best communicates the continuous iterative process by which knowledge is created. Simply put, knowledge is created by middle managers, who are often leaders of a team or task force, through a spiral conversion process involving both the top and the front-line employees (i.e. bottom). The process puts middle managers at the very center of knowledge management, positioning them at the intersection of the vertical and horizontal flows of information within the company.

The fact that middle-up-down management emphasises the dynamic role of the middle manager sharply distinguishes our theory from the conventional managerial wisdom. In the West, where companies are laying off middle managers by the thousands, the very term 'middle manager' has become almost a term for contempt, synonymous with 'backwardness,' 'stagnation,' and 'resistance to change'. Yet we are arguing that middle managers are the key to continuous innovation.

Middle managers usually have been portrayed in recent literature as frustrated, disillusioned, stuck in the middle of a hierarchy ... with little hope of career progression, and increasingly subject to being replaced by technological advancements. ... Doomsayers argue ... that the traditional role of middle managers as strategy implementers is disappearing as a result of new management philosophies and notions such as total employee involvement, the self-designing organisation, and socio-technical systems and autonomous work teams. [...]

We see middle managers playing a key role in facilitating the process of organisational knowledge creation. They serve as the strategic 'knot' that binds top management with front-line managers. They work as a 'bridge' between the visionary ideals of the top and the often chaotic realities of business confronted by front-line workers. As we shall see later, they are the true 'knowledge engineers' of the knowledge-creating company.

[...] People don't just receive new knowledge passively; they interpret it actively to fit their own situation and perspectives. Thus what makes sense in one context can change or even lose its meaning when communicated to people in a different context. The main job of middle managers in middle-up-down management is to orient this chaotic situation toward purposeful knowledge creation. Middle managers do this by providing their subordinates with a conceptual framework that helps them make sense of their own experience.

But the conceptual framework that middle management develops is quite distinct from that of top management, which provides a sense of direction regarding where the company should be headed. In the middle-up-down model, top management creates a vision or a dream, while middle management develops more concrete concepts that front-line employees can understand and implement. Middle managers try to solve the contradiction between what top management hopes to create and what actually exists in the real world. In other words, top management's role is to create a grand theory, while middle management tries to create a mid-range theory that it can test empirically within the company with the help of front-line employees (see Figure 2.2).

In Honda City, top management dreamed of creating 'something different from the existing concept' and began the City project with the slogan, 'Let's gamble'. Hiroo Watanabe, a middle manager who was 35 years old at the time, developed more concrete concepts – 'Automobile Evolution', 'man-maximum, machine-minimum', and 'Tall Boy' – that front-line employees could understand and implement. One of these front-line employees recalled, 'I feel, however illogical it may sound, that the success of this project owes a lot to the very wide gap between the ideal and the actual. A revolutionary reformulation was necessary, and, in order to achieve this, new technologies and concepts were generated one after another.'

Figure 2.2   Middle-up-down knowledge-creation process

Table 2.3 compares and contrasts the relevant features of the three models discussed above.

[...] The middle-up-down management model is by far the most comprehensive in terms of *who* gets involved; the most all-inclusive in terms of *what* kind of knowledge is created; the broadest in terms of *where* knowledge is stored; and the most flexible in terms of *how* knowledge is created.

[...]

(Nonaka and Takeuchi, 1995, pp. 124–30)

Table 2.3   Comparison of the three management models regarding knowledge creation

		Top-down	Bottom-up	Middle-up-down
Who	Agent of knowledge creation	Top management	Entrepreneurial individual	Team
	Top management role	Commander	Sponsor/mentor	Catalyst
	Middle management role	Information processor	Autonomous intrapreneur	Team leader and knowledge engineers
What	Accumulated knowledge	Explicit	Tacit	Explicit and tacit
	Knowledge conversion	Partial conversion focused on combination/ internalisation	Partial conversion focused on socialisation/ externalisation	Spiral conversion of internalisation/ externalisation/ combination/ socialisation
Where	Knowledge storage	Computerised database/ manuals	Incarnated in individuals	Organisational knowledge base

How	Organisation	Hierarchy	Project team and informal network	Hierarchy and task force (hypertext)
	Communication	Orders/ instructions	Self-organising principle	Dialogue and use of metaphor/ analogy
	Tolerance for ambiguity	Chaos/ fluctuation not allowed	Chaos/fluctuation premised	Create and amplify chaos/ fluctuation
	Weakness	High dependency on top management	Time consuming. Cost of co-ordination.	Human exhaustion. Redundancy.

Reflection

Think back to the interview with Anita Roddick, the Honda mini-case and the Metropolitan Police Service statement of aims. Which, if any, of the models of knowledge creation in Table 2.3 do they each fit?

2.9   SUMMARY

In this section we have introduced the notion of culture and explored some of its various manifestations and implications for strategy-making, strategic change programmes and the management of meaning within organisations.

- We should recognise that individuals have deeply rooted values which are products of wider societal influences and are relatively impervious to change, alongside other norms which are more instrumental and are responsive to modification.

- Most organisational cultures are heterogeneous. Sub-cultures cluster around different functions, roles, skills or levels. These are useful in that they create a sense of identity, but can be counter-productive if they limit co-operation, exacerbate conflict or reinforce entrenched views and positions. This explains many difficulties arising from culture change programmes or attempts to create homogeneous corporate cultures.

- Culture is just one of the interrelated components of an organisation. Evolutionary change may stem from change in any component part, such as organisation structure, power structure, technology, knowledge, environment or strategy. However, culture may enhance or frustrate the role of any of these other elements.

- Finally, Johnson (1992) argues that to achieve paradigm and culture change it is not the more obvious 'hard' elements of the cultural web (structure, systems, control) which must change, but the 'soft' elements (stories, rituals, symbols).

3 CULTURE, POWER AND CHANGE

In this section we will look more closely at the dynamics of change, and at how power and culture interact in this process.

3.1 MANAGEMENT OF STRATEGIC CHANGE

Organisational culture and internal paradigms represent that which is 'taken for granted' and which finds expression in various symbols, myths, ceremonies etc. We have argued that in these ways meaning is created and shared throughout an organisation. Shifts in these 'meanings' may be imperceptible and are often evolutionary rather than revolutionary, or deliberately engineered, shifts.

3.2 THE INTERSECTION OF POWER AND CULTURE CHANGE: THE CASE OF PARADIGM CHANGE

In Section 1 we located the organisational 'paradigm' firmly at the centre of the cultural web of an organisation and outlined some of the problems for strategy-making which result from it remaining highly resistant to change. Indeed, since the paradigm is itself the *outcome* of the constituent elements of the web, cultural change is unlikely to result from attacking the paradigm head-on, or from a simple attack on existing power structures. Power structures are only *one* element of a cultural web.

Activity 3.1

Check back to Section 1 and note down the problems that Johnson identified.

How can paradigms be changed?

Discussion

Johnson argues that for fundamental change to occur the paradigm must be challenged, discredited and devalued. Any such process will be painful. There are several mechanisms for doing this:

1 By use of the outsider: someone with little or no commitment to the existing paradigm. The outsider brings a questioning attitude and is unlikely to feel constrained to seek solutions from within the existing paradigm. He/she does not solve problems by seeking solutions close to the existing state of affairs, something that Cyert and March (1963) call 'simple-minded search'.

2 By exposing the paradigm: using formal mechanisms to expose the divergent views within an organisation. Setting up a conference to discuss declining performance can act as a symbol of the need for change. This alone is unlikely to have much impact as managers are likely to feel constrained by the existing power structure and unable to openly express 'deviant' opinions. To be effective such meetings must be able to encourage the 'zone of uncomfortable debate' (i.e. that which looks outside the prevailing orthodoxy of 'how we do things around here').

This may require three further mechanisms:

3 Power reconfiguration: taking deliberate steps to disrupt 'conservative' power groups. They may, for example, be excluded from decision-making committees. Simultaneously, the perceived status of individuals not associated with the paradigm could be raised. The question for us would be who would, or could, do the 'disrupting'. This role often requires the appointment of an outsider.

4 Advocating and legitimising dissent: giving encouragement and probably protection to managers, particularly those at middle or junior levels, to voice their criticisms of the existing paradigm.

5 Powerful advocacy: the leadership could show commitment to change by supporting those who challenge the paradigm and by engaging in symbolic acts that indicate that all is in fact not well with the existing state of affairs.

While these mechanisms do provide a way for the existing paradigm to be challenged, they do not in themselves reformulate strategy and create a new paradigm.

Such an unfreezing process creates anxiety since the old map of the manager's world no longer provides a base for action. The map has to be reformulated (Weick, 1995) and a new strategy, based on the new map, created. For this process leadership is required. Stories and other manifestations of success of new strategies play a powerful symbolic role in shifting the beliefs that the organisation holds about itself from the old to the new paradigm. New stories are needed.

Activity 3.2

Now read the article by Senge in the Course Reader.

To whom does he ascribe the role of managing meaning?

To what extent do you see this in practice within organisations known to you?

Discussion

Senge gives pride of place to leaders, but as designers, teachers and stewards. He supports Schein's views that leadership is intertwined with culture formation, and that leadership's unique and essential function is to build an organisation's culture and shape its evolution. So within the learning organisation leaders manage meaning and build the organisation's ability to learn – internally and from outside. Senge is particularly helpful in his suggestions for how to 'build vision' and 'shape culture' – concepts which are frequently stated as self-evident public benefits, with little practical detail as to how they are to be accomplished in practice.

Suggestions such as recognising and defusing defensive routines, focusing on areas of high leverage and sympathetic explanations of negative short-term management practices ('dilemmas') such as the 'tragedy of the commons', give imaginative guidance to effective leadership whilst avoiding 'motherhood' statements empty of content.

3.3 STRATEGIC CHANGE: MANAGING MEANING AND THE ROLE OF THE LEADER

The events and managerial practice described in the Honda mini-case reflect many of the ideas and precepts of leadership espoused by Senge. The leader is thus crucially important in changing culture. In the words of Peters and Waterman she can 'transform' rather than 'transact'. Senge sees leadership as culture-formation through building shared vision. The leader's definition of reality must feed the evolution of organisations where people are continually expanding their capabilities. It is in this role that the intersection of power and culture is most visible. Remember the Honda mini-case, where autonomy was given to the US trio to take risks and to 'try'.

Activity 3.3

In 1995, Asda was one of the six largest supermarket groups in the UK. Asda had been trying to derive a source of competitive advantage to maintain its position against two dominant competitors, Tesco and Sainsbury.

Read the following mini-case on Asda carefully and evaluate it using the seven parts of the cultural web.

MINI-CASE: ASDA

[...] 'For five years, Asda had been trying to become like Sainsbury and Tesco,' comments Cox [Asda's finance director]. This was theoretically a good idea, since Sainsbury and Tesco had been encroaching on Asda's traditional territory in the north, but it had proved disastrous in practice. The move upmarket – a wider range, own-label products, the designer hand of Rodney Fitch ... in the stores, new layers of management to support new activities, and so on – had pushed up costs, which had to be recouped by higher prices. This, however, had meant that many Asda customers in the second half of the 1980s had simply walked away, to find cheaper goods elsewhere. 'Our customers absolutely demand value for money,' Cox points out, explaining that three-quarters of Asda stores are in catchment areas whose population comes home with only average and below-average UK earnings. 'If we're not the cheapest, we lose customers.' In what the group now calls the 'Doom Loop', prices had to be pushed up further to maintain turnover, and so on.

The new trading strategy, termed the 'Virtuous Circle', was to restore the traditional Asda price differential of 5–7% below its competitors, thereby selling bigger volumes; to increase traffic-sensitive purchases; to reduce fixed costs as a proportion of sales; to benefit from the higher sales volumes through being able to strike better deals with suppliers; to push up store productivity and push on a newly focused product range; and so to keep prices down. 'Our attitude to gross margins is that they should come down each year, so we can provide better value; and at the same time, we should grow profits by selling more,' says [Archie] Norman [Asda's CEO].

Financially, the new strategy can also be simply described. The previous management had paid out £700 million for the Gateway chain in 1989, choosing to borrow rather than to place a rights issue for the purpose. This [...] had led to a gaping £1 billion debt. [...] Says Cox, who joined Norman in

January 1992: 'Our initial reaction was: "We knew it was bad, but not that bad." We were about to breach our banking convenant.' The new financial strategy aimed, quite simply, at restoring financial stability to the business. This was achieved by selling off what were now seen as 'peripheral' rather than 'related' businesses; selling some property, and some large stores to the competition. [...] Within six months, the team had announced its renewal programme. Within a year it was under way, debt had been reduced, [...] – allowing the renewal programme to proceed on a sound financial footing.

The other changes Norman outlines – in the way people work together and communicate with each other – are more complex. The company's goal is to become a genuine leader in fresh foods and clothing [...] and also to create an 'organisation which is the preferred place to work', offering customer service 'with a personality derived from the heart of the company'. One change has, accordingly, been in the approach to recruitment, which now aims to seek out people for the stores who really do want to serve the customers and who genuinely like selling.

There is no point, he remarks, in employing people who won't like the 'Asda Way of Working'. This is the name given to the new approach, intended to transform the old culture, which had grown autocratic and slow-moving, to one where all members of Asda feel involved in improving the business – the equivalent, within the context of a corporation, of market-stallholders, who run their own show, and who engage actively with their customers.

This new culture is being nurtured in a host of ways. Since July there have been the much publicised share options, available to all members of staff on the same terms as to the top executives – and now taken up by 36,000 out of a total of 68,000 employees. There have been changes in organisational structure, not only in eliminating layers of management, 'getting rid of the treacle', as trading director Tony Campbell puts it, and thus shortening the line between head office and the stores, but also in the way departments are now organised. Thus, for example, each in-store bakery or fishmonger's department is a team effort with its own profit and loss account. At head office, meanwhile, Campbell's own trading department is divided into business units (for meat, drink, clothing, gifts, and the like), each of which in turn is split into categories: spirits, wines, soft drinks and beer, for example. In each category the head of marketing and buyers work with the category managers, to develop their category business and to 'deliver the Asda proposition in their particular way'. In this fast-moving superstore business, comments Campbell, 'you've got to move quickly to invent the next thing': the team-based approach is one way of speeding things up.

Table 3.1					
	1995 (£m)	1994 (£m)	1993 (£m)	1992 (£m)	1991 (£m)
Turnover	5,285.3	4,822.2	4,613.8	4,529.1	4,468.1
Operating profit	253.8	198.0	191.2	182.1	258.3
Net interest	(7.6)	(15.0)	(50.8)	(95.3)	(90.0)
Exceptional items	(11.0)	(308.9)	65.2	(451.6)	–
Profit (loss) before tax	257.2	(125.9)	187.4	(364.8)	168.3
Dividend per share (p)	2.20	1.76	1.60	2.10	4.80
Net assets	1,493.2	1,376.4	1,567.7	1,107.3	1,136.9

More generally, he explains, 'We aspire to an "inform and involve" culture, rather than one of "command and control" as in the old days.' This takes a variety of forms. There are listening groups on current issues, and 'We're listening' surveys that collect opinions on areas such as working conditions and pay. Backstage at the stores, communication boards record achievements in cutting down on waste. Instead of the old-style weekly managers' meetings, there are now twice-daily 'huddles' between managers and their working teams in the stores, to plan ahead for the practicalities of the day's and evening's trading. There is the 'Tell Archie' suggestion scheme, which has attracted 14,000 suggestions in the first 18 months: the ideas have won their originators anything from a 'Tell Archie' pen to a weekend in Paris. There are also monthly 'Colleague Circles', to stimulate the flow of ideas.

The style of senior management now combines a high degree of approachability (symbolised by rolled-up shirt sleeves) with the readiness to take decisions. Colleagues are expected to challenge management decisions, and to take decisions of their own: although the term 'empowerment' is happily used sparingly at Asda, the concept is embodied in the new ways of working. Thus, all managers in the stores have now been on management information systems courses: 'We know how to get into the computer, and how to use it'. They have also, for example, been trained in the art of appearing on television, and are actively encouraged to act as company spokespeople to the media. They are also encouraged to move between functions – between training and administration, for example, or customer services and provisions so as to gain an understanding of the wider business as a whole.

If all this sounds like an abstract from the management textbooks, look again at the open-plan head office, which could serve as one emblem of the new Asda approach. Communication is encouraged in all sorts of ways – by an abundance of news-sheets, charts of prices, how Asda Price matches up to the competition, and printouts of customer compliments displayed on the walls; by little gestures like the notice which invites comments on the drinks machine on trial, or on women's experience at work; by the ample number of inviting meeting rooms, which make discussion congenial. High-tech research companies have long known that a pleasing working environment, with plenty of opportunity for informal meeting, stimulates creativity and sparks off ideas; the same applies here. Ideas leap across boundaries and narrow functions: it was the PR department, for example, which thought up the notion of 24-hour trading in the run-up to Christmas, and whose members helped to serve at the check-outs, when the idea was adopted.

Outside, the only reserved parking space is for the company Jaguar, which does not belong to the chairman or chief executive or any other such VIP, but, for a month, to the winner of the VPI – volume-producing items – scheme, whose efforts have brought about an outstanding increase in sales. Inside, there are no executive suites or corporate status symbols, in what aims to be a single-status company. The culture change is not complete, of course, given the huge number of employees, but the new approach is palpable. So, too, are the results of the change in strategy and culture, with Asda back in the black (see Table 3.1) – and an increase in customers of 30% since Norman arrived. 'Two million people have voted with their feet,' he says decisively. Like-for-like sales rose by 8.4% over the last financial year, outperforming all the company's competitors.

Source: Management Today, December 1995, pp. 50–4

Discussion

Some initial notes about Asda might contain the following points:

- Paradigm – *'inform and involve' culture; value-for-money; 'Virtuous Circle'; 'preferred place to work'; 'ASDA way of working'; store staff as 'market-stallholders'.*

- Organisational structure – *'getting rid of the treacle'; delayering; in-store profit centres; category management responsibilities; single-status company; decentralised; team-based approach.*

- Control systems – *tight financial targets and controls; management of margins; management information systems and training; company share options; recruitment.*

- Power structures – *power of Archie Norman (CEO); informality, approachability; 'empowerment'.*

- Symbols – *'tell Archie' pens; meeting rooms; news-sheets; customer compliments; company Jaguar car for VPI winner only; no corporate status symbols; senior management's 'rolled-up shirt sleeves'; open plan Head Office.*

- Stories and myths – *PR staff serving at checkouts in Christmas rush; store managers as media spokespersons.*

- Rituals and routines – *listening groups; 'We're Listening' surveys; monthly 'Colleague Circles'; twice-daily 'huddles'.*

The senior management of Asda made changes in all areas of the cultural web, thus creating a new paradigm. It illustrates the dynamic interdependency of all the elements of the web and the mutual influence of culture and power in bringing about change.

Reflection

To what extent do you think that the changes described in the Asda mini-case reflect Nonaka and Takeuchi's ideas on 'middle-up-down' management processes described in Box 2.4?

3.4 STRATEGIC CHANGE: RECOVERY STRATEGIES AND TURNAROUNDS

In a period of crisis, top management has to take decisive action to rescue and turn a failing enterprise around, as happened when Asda implemented its recovery strategy. The way in which managers implement recovery strategies has lessons for managers in more stable strategic contexts.

Activity 3.4

Before reading further, spend a few minutes considering what actions you would take if appointed as a 'turnaround' manager for an ailing business.

What would be your priorities?

What would you do on the first day of your appointment?

What would you do during the first week?

Slatter (1984, p. 78) identified ten key actions that were often implemented as part of a recovery strategy:

- change of management
- strong central financial control
- organisational change and decentralisation
- product-market re-orientation
- improved marketing
- growth via acquisitions
- asset reduction
- cost reduction
- investment
- debt restructuring and other financial strategies.

Gaining immediate control over the organisation's cash flow is usually the major initial priority. Once the current cash position is established, routine cash flow information on a weekly basis will normally be required over a period of many months. In some cases this reporting frequency may be retained, as an element within the overall control system, on a permanent basis. A cash flow forecast must be developed, and all the underlying assumptions checked for reasonableness. If no cash flow forecast is available, a rough and ready forecast should be prepared at once, to be followed later by a more detailed budget. It is essential in these early stages to know what the cash flow position will look like over the next few weeks and months if the existing operations continue unchanged. The aim of these early forecasts is to establish a realistic picture of the cash situation from which the severity of the required recovery strategy can be assessed.

Where subsidiary companies or autonomous divisions are involved, central control of cash has proved to be an important factor in recovery situations. In such cases, group headquarters will have one central account into which all receipts are put and from which all payments are made. All cash balances of operating units are credited to headquarters on a daily basis and any negative balances are similarly debited. Operating managers are then held responsible only for the working capital they employ in their units. Thus they become responsible for how capital is employed but not for how it is financed.

Control over capital and revenue expenditure is imperative and typical controls in a turnaround situation might include the need for all capital expenditure to be approved by the chief executive, for all contracts due for renewal to be approved by the chief executive, and for pay increases and recruitment to be temporarily suspended. Similar firm control over stock and debtors is also necessary. Remember the importance of the financial strategy in Asda's turnaround.

This firm action on expenditure, apart from its obvious importance in controlling cash flow, also has a symbolic importance. It brings home to staff at all levels the values and standards of the recovery manager and his/her determination to establish firm control from which to build recovery.

If the recovery strategy is to succeed, credibility must be established with key stakeholders so that their contribution to the recovery can be obtained. A new chief executive's credibility will be derived from a combination of personality, negotiating and influencing skills, a demonstrated understanding of the organisation's problems and how they can be resolved, and his/her previous track record. Credibility may be hindered if those associated with the organisation's recent decline and present problems remain in key positions. For this reason, among others, not only may the managers involved need to be replaced, but also the professional advisers such as auditors and accountants if a new and credible image is to be created.

The organisation's bank will normally have been among the first outsiders to know of difficulties. The relationship with the organisation's bank will have been a priority of the recovery manager from the time of his/her appointment. Some information concerning the organisation's difficulties, both fact and fiction, will also probably have circulated among employees, customers and suppliers. All of these groups will need to be reassured about their position *vis-à-vis* the company, and to be convinced about the outcome of the recovery strategy. The success of that strategy will depend on the continuing support of these stakeholder groups. Consequently, effective communication with them is essential. The recovery manager needs to persuade them that they have more to gain from continuing their association with the organisation than from withdrawing. He/she may well have to persuade them to accept reduced 'terms and conditions' in the short term, in order to ensure the benefits of full recovery in the longer term. The force and logic of the recovery strategy and the skill with which it is communicated to those involved will be of critical importance if the recovery is to be successful.

These immediate actions may be followed by a more detailed evaluation of the business. To begin with, an evaluation based on the Pareto principle can provide a rapid overall assessment. On this basis it is assumed that some 20 per cent of the factors involved will have 80 per cent of the impact on the situation concerned. Hence, identifying and focusing on these relatively few, but critical, factors will channel management attention where it will have most effect. At the operational level, however, more detailed attention must be given to, for example, sales analysis by major product lines and customers. Profit and contribution analysis for major lines using several different methods of allocating overheads will be important. Important also in a recovery situation will be analyses of back orders, customer complaints, capacity utilisation and efficiency, and staffing levels.

Although we have already discussed the importance of personal leadership during strategy implementation, in recovery situations this is, if anything, even more important. In his/her day-to-day contacts with staff at all levels the recovery manager will be observed with interest. From his/her actions and behaviour, rather than words, people will form views about the new leader's values and expectations.

Slatter (1984) and Grinyer *et al.* (1988) provide striking examples of how the management of strategic change is a combination of the human, procedural and technical resources of the organisation. It is also an illustration of the influence of all the various parts of the cultural web on strategic change, whether gradual or in the crisis situation of a turnaround.

Reflection

We will return to the managerial issues in turnarounds when we discuss corporate strategy in Book 9. Meanwhile, think back once again to the Asda mini-case and consider how many of Slatter's turnaround strategies were used by Archie Norman and his team.

4 POWER

Child (1972) argued that managers have scope for choice. We have supported that view of strategic choice within this course. The influence of stakeholders on strategy formulation and choice was discussed in Book 2. The impact of power and influence on strategy processes was considered in Book 6. These issues were illustrated in the Asda mini-case. In this book so far we have mentioned power structures as part of the cultural web of an organisation and briefly looked at the impact that different forms of power have on the paradigm that managers voluntarily and involuntarily use to guide organisational actions (see Table 2.2). It is now appropriate to consider both structures and sources of power in more depth. Before doing this, however, we should clarify what we mean by power.

4.1 WHAT IS POWER?

When two American researchers carried out a study on the impact of power their sample of managers had absolutely no problems in discussing their use of this notion without ever having it defined! However, we do need a definition and we offer one used by Henry Mintzberg (1983).

Power is the capacity to effect (or affect) organisational outcomes.

This definition immediately sets a context for our discussion, as we are not concerned with power in societies or between individuals, although you may find some of the ideas useful for looking at power in these situations. It is important to stress that power in our view is a property of a relationship. On the other hand a propensity to use power to influence events might be an individual characteristic.

To reiterate: power is a property of a relationship between two (or usually more) entities, be they individuals, groups, departments, divisions, organisations or countries. Early definitions of power which have become subsumed in others, such as the one above, focused on the relationship and (usually) the ability of A to get B to do something they would otherwise not have done.

4.2 POWER STRUCTURES

In organisations, the basis of interrelationships is determined by the way in which the task is structured. Very simply, the structure of an organisation sets up the relationships between sub-units and essentially the task sets up the relationships between the organisation and the environmental context of operations. For example, a university has faculties or departments (sub-units) all designed to educate (the task). The environment consists of would-be students, parents, government, funding bodies, employers, academic and support staff, etc. This pattern of relationships leads to the creation of what Thomson (1967) has called 'interdependencies', in that, to complete the overall task, department A depends on department B for material supplies and on department C for scheduling information. So we can push our thinking on power a little further and say that power is about *degrees* of independence or dependence on others for resources which enable your organisation to function and fulfil its objectives. So department B has power over A to the extent that A is dependent on B for resources to complete its task. But B may in fact only receive its resources from the organisation because it services A.

Activity 4.1 _____

In Books 2 and 6 we introduced Morgan's (1986) ideas on power bases within organisations. Look back at these in terms of the resource dependence framework we have just discussed.

Think of an example where one section of your organisation appears to be dependent on another. What is the resource it depends upon?

Discussion _____

- *The bases from Morgan that fit most closely are formal authority and control of scarce resources, since we depend on others for decisions about resource allocation. (Remember, for example, the influence of changing public opinion on the priorities of the UK Metropolitan Police.)*

- *Organisational structure and procedures set the pattern of interdependences, since they determine how each task fits together. Remember the changes made at Asda in structure and procedures.*

- *Control of decision processes is also a function of structure, but structure as an integrative device for managing relationships between units rather than as a differentiating device for breaking down the task (as in the 'Tell Archie' scheme or daily 'huddles').*

- *Control of knowledge and information is an important power base since information is a key resource. Even getting departments (or individuals) within the same organisation to share knowledge is extremely difficult since they rightly identify control of knowledge as a scarce power resource.*

- *Gender power may be an organisational issue where control of a resource or resources lies exclusively with one gender group or another and the organisation is less effective as a result. This is certainly an issue in most police forces and armed services, with an additional effect on recruitment and how those organisations are perceived.*

- *Countervailing power is a tactic whereby groups may shift the balance of a dependence relationship by co-ordinating the exertion of influence. (Anita Roddick uses her personal mission to provide countervailing power against the influence of financial institutions, as also does Greenpeace against multinational enterprises.)*

- *Boundary and alliance and network management can be seen as managing a relationship or series of relationships with other external organisations whose role or resource as supplier, customer, channel, etc. is critical.*

- *The management of meaning is linked to the organisational paradigm since the paradigm is a way of reducing and filtering the signals received and thereby coping with the uncertainties that the organisation faces. Johnson (1988) suggests that the paradigm represents a belief set about reducing uncertainty: those who operate within the dominant paradigm are likely to have power within that organisation but may be less able or willing to manage uncertainty and cope with requirements for change, whether internally or externally induced (Hickson et al., 1971; Pfeffer and Salancik, 1978).*

At the heart of understanding power, both within and between organisations, lies the issue of coping with uncertainty. Control of resources is a way of coping with uncertainty and it provides the basis for the power that one unit or one organisation has over another. The question of how dependent a unit or organisation is can be determined by examining three conditions:

1 [*The importance of the resource.*] This is a combination of the amount of that resource used and how critical it is to operations. This may be revealed by looking at how severe the consequences of its withdrawal might be and how soon the unit would be unable to operate without it. A school may conceivably function without computers or even books, but could not function without teachers.

2 [*How much discretion those who control resources (or cope with uncertainty) have over their allocation and use.*] If a unit has complete freedom and can limit access, then any organisation or unit which needs that resource can be put in a very dependent position.

3 [*To what extent the resource is substitutable.*] If the supply is a virtual monopoly then dependence is high.

Organisations usually have options about using less of any given resource, substituting an alternative or doing without altogether. This includes finance, people, buildings and so on.

Activity 4.2 _____

Can you think of a non-substitutable function within an organisation that is familiar to you?

What factors made you decide it is not substitutable?

Discussion _____

Expertise may be non-substitutable, whether it is detailed knowledge of a particular client and their business; the workings of the organisation's computer system; how to carry out a kidney transplant. Contacts (informal networks) may be non-substitutable: these may be professional, political, geographic, etc.

These may also be understood as rare inimitable resources, as discussed in Book 4.

It is possible to suggest that effectiveness can be defined as the way in which organisations or units manage their dependence relationships, rather than by more commonly used measures. Altering dependence relationships, to reduce the power of other organisations or departments, may have important strategic consequences. Indeed, this is at the heart of 'business process re-engineering' – thinking of organisations as processes rather than structures and redesigning them accordingly (Hammer, 1990). Organisations become networks of inter-unit and inter-organisational relationships which have differential power due to their ability to manage the uncertainties of other linked units. Obvious examples might be the greater (external) bargaining power of a large organisation and its ability to secure its sources of supply, compared with a small organisation, whose custom may be less critical to its supplier; or a production unit coping (internally) with a surge in demand resulting from an advertising campaign by the organisation's marketing department.

4.3   POWER OVER WHAT?

We should remember Mintzberg's definition of power – the capacity to effect (or affect) organisational outcomes. Power is a means of exerting influence to control decisions and actions, particularly in times of uncertainty. This view of power is broader than MacMillan's (1978) distinction between power and influence explored in Book 6. We would argue that power and influence cannot be easily distinguished in practice. Power sometimes may show itself as influence, for example to modify (influence) an outcome. It is apparent that some interests can have a significant impact on both decision-making processes and outcomes (Book 6), that the power to speed up or block decisions, to close off options, to construct meaning, suggests that while there may be many stakeholders, they differ in their power and their ability to influence outcomes. Organisations are thus surrounded by a web of expectations concerning not only what they should be doing (that is, their formal goals which were discussed in Book 2) but how they should do it.

Activity 4.3

 Please listen to the interview with Sir Anthony Cleaver on Audio Cassette AC1, Side 2.

At the beginning of the interview Sir Anthony Cleaver talks about five relationships always present in anything that you recognise as a company. Examine your organisation in terms of the relative power of relationships. This is not just another stakeholder analysis: you should consider these relationships in relation to the cultural web. Try to identify the impact the other elements of the cultural web of your organisation have on the relative power of the different relationships. What are your views on the sixth stakeholder indicated in the discussion and in particular on its relative importance compared to the other five relationships?

Discussion

According to Cleaver, the five relationships always present are:
- *with shareholders/financial investors*
- *with employees*
- *with customers*
- *with suppliers*
- *with the community in which the organisation operates.*

The sixth relationship is the one mentioned by Anita Roddick in her interview:
- *with the planet/environment.*

You should have identified aspects of each of these respective relationships for your own organisation or department. What is the connection between these relationships and the cultural web?

In order to fully develop your response to this Activity, you should have attempted at least a rough analysis of your own organisation (or your own department within your organisation) in terms of its cultural web.

The relative significance and nature of all six 'relationships' will be influenced by the organisational paradigm and the particular elements of the cultural web of your organisation. With respect to the sixth relationship – with the planet/environment – Sir Anthony Cleaver's comment is that he saw that as part of, and influencing, the other five, rather than as something separate, as did Anita Roddick. The complexity of the issues behind these contrasting views has already been discussed in Section 2.5.

Winstanley *et al.* (1995) adopt a simpler approach by using the term 'criteria power': the power to define goals, aims or purpose. They identify a second dimension: operational power, which reflects the power of stakeholders to determine how the service (their paper is about public service) is provided through the allocation of resources, be they money, knowledge or skill. These two dimensions (or facets) can be combined into a stakeholder power matrix, represented by Figure 4.1, which enables managers to plot out the power of stakeholders and to track shifts in power through time.

Figure 4.1   The stakeholder power matrix

Perhaps not surprisingly, these two dimensions create four quadrants which do not really describe distinct areas of reality, as each dimension is continuous and not an 'either/or' dichotomy.

In quadrant A stakeholders have little power in detailed decisions but have significant *arm's length* power to drive the organisation from outside. This implies that they have power over the rules of the game. The stakeholders thus constrain or determine action rather than act themselves. This is in contrast to the situation in quadrant B, where stakeholders have *comprehensive* power, a situation reminiscent of planned economies or wholly owned and managed subsidiaries.

As an example of quadrant A 'arm's length' power, consider the photographs of simultaneous protests held in London (UK) and Berlin (Germany) on World Food Day to campaign against genetically altered food. These stakeholders are members of the public organised into pressure groups such as the Greenpeace environmental movement. They seek to exert influence both on governments (to introduce regulation) and on companies (to change research programmes or develop alternative types of products).

In quadrant C, stakeholders are empowered to influence operational decisions but do so on the basis of rules decided elsewhere. As Winstanley *et al.* suggest, this is the case for organisations which may be subject to strong market forces – where the rules of the market and the power of stakeholders in quadrant A dictate the criteria; or alternatively where government exerts significant criteria control. This is *operational* power.

In the final quadrant D, stakeholders have low power on both dimensions: they are effectively *disempowered*. These might be customers or groups of staff who have little or no opportunity to secure alternative sources of supply or markets for their product or skill.

Activity 4.4

Use the Winstanley *et al.* framework to characterise the stakeholders of your own organisation.

Does your use of this framework echo your analysis of Activity 4.3, or are there differences in the insights gained?

Discussion

This simple model can be a useful way of capturing the magnitude of change, though not the nature of that change over time. It focuses attention on the power of stakeholders and encourages managers to think through the implications of the strategy process in which they are engaged.

4.4 MANAGING STRATEGY AND POWER

In this section we looked at the nature of power in organisations and went on to explore the relationship between power and structure. This leads us into considering the implications of our analysis for managing strategy.

- The most obvious point to make is that *power is present in all forms of organisation*. This recognises that there are varying interests (or interest groups) who have different expectations and stakes in an organisation, in whatever sector or country. This means that not everyone is going to think as you do, or as the members of your interest group do, or value what you value. Interests may cluster around an issue in ways that do not make sense to us, although this clustering may itself be transitory. Recognising this is an important skill for the manager who thinks strategically.

- Effective managers use power in a variety of its many manifestations (position power, expert power, etc.) to get things done, to implement strategies, to achieve objectives. Therefore *it is important to understand power structures and how to manage within them*.

- Examples of how to manage dependence relationships include organisational restructuring, mergers or diversification, all of which *alter existing dependence relationships and the internal control of critical resources*.

- Increasingly, organisations are coping with uncertain situations by forming joint ventures and alliances and by *entering into long-term external networks of relationships across their range of activities*. Such networks, if successful, may establish a shared base of knowledge between the participants. This docs depend crucially on the nature of the shared expectations each party brings to the alliance and the trust or reliability each of the other parties feels able to place in the other over the longer term. External networks of this type rest on different power relationships from internal networks, with their own risks and problems (which will be discussed further in Books 9 and 10).

- Finally, managers often seek to influence, or are influenced by, political and economic policies. Externally they may lobby, for example, for favourable taxation and tariffs for their industry, while sometimes simultaneously charging others with unfair trade practices. We may question the legitimacy and the ethical basis of some of these activities as they may be deliberate tactics to reduce the influence of other stakeholders. In a democratic system, however, *creating countervailing power by the exercise of influence by legitimate means* is open to all parties. The problem may be more suitably considered to be one of an acceptable balance of power and resources *between* different stakeholders.

There is a well-known quotation taken from a letter written by Lord Acton (a British diplomat) in 1887:

> Power tends to corrupt and absolute power corrupts absolutely.

What we have tried to show in this section is that in an organisational context there is no such thing as 'absolute power'. There are only power relationships and ways of managing them.

5 SUMMARY AND CONCLUSION

Culture and power have a major impact on all aspects of strategy-making. They influence not only implementation but also analysis and choice of strategy. The impact of culture on strategy is best seen by considering how the paradigm guides the way that managers make sense of their environment, how they construct 'a reality' for their organisations with other organisation members. Power is an important shaper of this construction of each 'reality'.

Power may also hinder, or be used to challenge, the dominant view. Power structures reinforce and are reinforced by stories of heroes and mavericks in each organisation. Honda's low-key heroic assault against the (then) mighty US motorcycle manufacturers is the stuff of legend, as, in different ways are 'Tell Archie' of ASDA, Anita Roddick's 'language of irreverence', the London 'bobby' and Hewlett-Packard's open doors.

Recovery strategies
change management
Strong financial control
Organisational change and decentralisation

REFERENCES

Brown, A. D. (1994) 'Politics, symbolic action and myth making in pursuit of legitimacy', *Organisation Studies*, Vol. 15, No. 6 pp. 861–878.

Child, J. (1972) 'Organisational structure, environment, and performance: the role of strategic choice', *Sociology* , Vol. 26, No. 1, pp. 1–22.

Cyert, R.M. and March, J.G. (1963) *A Behavioural Theory of the Firm*, New York, Prentice-Hall.

Deal, T.E. and Kennedy, A.A. (1982) *Corporate Cultures: The Rites and Rituals of Corporate Life*, Harmondsworth, Penguin Books.

Ghemawat, P. (1991) *Commitment: The Dynamic of Strategy*, New York, The Free Press.

Grinyer, P.H., Mayer, D.G., and McKiernan, P. (1988) *Sharpbenders*, Basil Blackwell, Oxford.

Hammer, M. (1990) 'Re-engineering work: don't automate, obliterate', *Harvard Business Review*, July/August.

Hickson, D.J., Hinings, C.R., Lee, C.A., Schneck, R.E. and Pennings, J.M. (1971) 'A strategic contingencies theory of intraorganisational power', *Administrative Science Quarterly*, Vol. 6, No. 2, pp. 216–29.

Hofstede, G. (1980) *Culture's Consequences: International Differences in Work-Related Values*, Beverly Hills, CA, Sage Publications.

Hofstede, G. (1989) 'Organising for cultural diversity', *European Management Journal* , Vol. 7 No. 4, pp. 390–7.

Hosmer, L.T. (1994) 'Strategic planning as if ethics mattered', *Strategic Management Journal*, Vol. 15, pp. 17–34.

Johnson, G. (1987) *Strategic Change and the Management Process*, Oxford, Blackwell.

Johnson, G. (1988) 'Rethinking incrementalism', *Strategic Management Journal*, Vol. 9, pp. 75–91.

Johnson, G. (1992) 'Managing strategic change – strategy, culture and action', *Long Range Planning*, Vol. 25, No.1, pp. 28–36.

MacMillan, I.C. (1978) *Strategy Formulation: Political Concepts*, St Paul, MN, West Publishing.

Mintzberg, H. (1983) *Power In and Around Organisations*, Englewood Cliffs, NJ, Prentice-Hall.

Mintzberg, H. and McHugh, M. (1985) 'Strategy formulation in an adhocracy', *Administrative Science Quarterly*, Vol. 21, pp. 246–75.

Morgan, G. (1986) *Images of Organisation*, Beverly Hills, CA, Sage Publications.

Nonaka, I. (1991) 'The knowledge-creating company', *Harvard Business Review*, November/December, pp. 96–104.

Nonaka, I. and Takeuchi, H. (1995) *The Knowledge-Creating Company: How Japanese Companies Create the Dynamics of Innovation*, Oxford, Oxford University Press.

Ouchi, W.G. (1981) *Theory Z: How American Business Can Meet the Japanese Challenge*, Reading, MA, Addison-Wesley.

Peters, T.J. and Waterman, R.H. (1982) *In Search of Excellence: Lessons from America's Best-Run Companies*, New York, Harper & Row.

Pfeffer, J. and Salancik, G.R. (1978) *The External Control of Organisations: A Resource Dependence Perspective*, New York, Harper & Row.

Senge, P. (1990), *The Fifth Discipline*, New York, Doubleday (chapter in Course Reader).

Smircich, L. (1983) 'Concepts of culture and organisational analysis', *Administrative Science Quarterly*, September, pp. 339–59.

Slatter, S. (1984) *Corporate Recovery*, Harmondsworth, Penguin Books.

Thomson, J.D. (1967) *Organisations in Action*, New York, McGraw-Hill.

Weick, K.E. (1995) *Sensemaking in Organisations*, Thousand Oaks, CA, Sage Publications.

Wilson, D.C. and Rosenfeld, R.H. (1990) *Managing Organisations: Text, Readings and Cases*, Maidenhead, McGraw-Hill.

Winstanley, D.D., Sorabji S. and Dawson, S. (1995) 'When the pieces don't fit: a stakeholder power matrix to analyse public sector restructuring', *Public Money and Management*, April–June, pp. 19–26.

ACKNOWLEDGEMENTS

Grateful acknowledgement is made to the following sources for permission to reproduce material in this book:

Text

Pages 11–13: Reprinted by permission of Harvard Business School. An excerpt from *Honda (B): A Case Study* by Pascale, R. T., Copyright © 1983, by the President and Fellows of Harvard College; all rights reserved; *Pages 40–2:* 'Asda's open plan', reproduced from an article by Anita Van de Vliet in the December 1995 issue of *Management Today*, with the kind permission of the copyright owner, Management Publications Ltd; *Box 2.1: The London Beat: The Metropolitan Police Service into the 21st Century*, Metropolitan Police Service; *Box 2.2:* 'The fun of being a multinational', *The Economist*, 20 July 1996, © The Economist, London; *Box 2.4:* Nonaka, I. and Takeuchi, H. 1995, *The Knowledge-Creating Company*, pp. 124–30, Oxford University Press, by permission of Oxford University Press.

Tables

Table 2.1: Reprinted from *European Management Journal*, **12**(1), March 1994, Hofstede, G., 'Organising for cultural diversity', p. 393, Copyright © 1994, with kind permission from Elsevier Science Ltd, The Boulevard, Langford Lane, Kidlington, OX5 1GB, UK; *Table 2.2:* Reprinted from *Long Range Planning*, **25**, February 1992, Johnson, G. 1992, 'How managers define the cultural web – three cases', p. 32, Copyright 1992, with kind permission from Elsevier Science Ltd, The Boulevard, Langford Lane, Kidlington, OX5 1GB, UK; *Table 2.3:* Nonaka, I. and Takeuchi, H. 1995, *The Knowledge-Creating Company*, table 5.1, Oxford University Press, by permission of Oxford University Press.

Figures

Figure 1.1: Johnson, G. and Scholes, K. 1989, *Exploring Corporate Strategy: text and cases*, Third edition, Prentice-Hall; *Figure 2.2:* Nonaka, I. and Takeuchi, H. 1995, *The Knowledge-Creating Company*, figure 5.1, Oxford University Press, by permission of Oxford University Press; *Figure 4.1:* Winstanley, D., Sorabji, D. and Dawson, S. 1995, 'When the pieces don't fit: A stakeholder power matrix to analyse public sector restructuring', *Public Money and Management*, **15**(2), April–June, figure 2, Blackwell Publishers Limited.

Photographs

Page 51: (left) *The Independent*/ Araminta de Clermont; (right) Associated Press/Jockel Fink.